HOPE

IN THE FACE OF

CONFLICT

Making Peace with Others
the Way
God Makes Peace with Us

Introducing the
Judeo-Christian Model of Peacemaking

Dr. Kenneth C. Newberger

Hope in the Face of Conflict
Making Peace with Others the Way God Makes Peace with Us
by Kenneth C. Newberger, Ph.D., Th.M.

Printed in the United States of America

Three Sons Publishing, SDM

ISBN 978-0-615-32741-9

For free downloadable small group discussion guides and other helpful
information go to:
www.HopeintheFaceofConflict.com

Wilmer,

May God bless you
with great fruit
in your service to
Him.

Ken Newberger

This book is dedicated to my wife, Mary. Your unyielding love and support in so many ways has made the publication of this work possible. This book is also dedicated to our three sons, Samuel, David, and Michael. May the significance of this study enrich not only your lives but the lives of your children and their children after them.

Table of Contents

Abbreviations

BDAG	Bauer, Danker, Arndt, Gingrich (A Greek-English Lexicon of the New Testament and Other Early Christian Literature, 3rd Edition)	NIV	New International Version
		NKJV	New King James Version
		NLT	New Living Translation
		NT	New Testament
cf.	compare or consult	OT	Old Testament
ESV	English Standard Version	p., pp.	page, pages
e.g.	for example	para.	paragraph(s)
ff.	and following	sec.	section
i.e.	in other words		
NASB	New American Standard Bible		

Brief Glossary of Terms

Judeo-Christian

Judeo-Christian means "being historically related to both Judaism and Christianity."[1] The New Testament could not have been written as it is apart from the existence of the Old Testament. Christianity could have not come into being apart from the existence of the Jewish nation of Israel. Although there are differences between Judaism and Christianity, the term *Judeo-Christian* positively speaks of the shared understanding that the God of the universe and the God of Abraham, Isaac, and Jacob are one and the same. This mutual understanding is based on the shared foundational belief that the Old Testament is the divinely inspired Word of God.[2]

Steps Versus Stages

For purposes of this book, steps are understood as sequential actions, one following the other. Step 2, for example, doesn't begin until Step 1 is completed. Stages, by contrast, may be sequential or overlapping actions. In the Judeo-Christian model of peacemaking, multiple stages may be in operation at any given time.

Preface

Why This Book?

Nothing Else Like It Exists

When I examined numerous Christian and secular books and articles that dealt with conflict in general and church conflict in particular, I was astonished to learn that the Christian books shared a characteristic with secular ones. Neither addressed or investigated two related questions: How does God make peace with us, and what would that model look like if we adopted it for peacemaking between people?

This is not to say that references to Scripture were not made in the Christian-authored books. Scripture was cited to varying degrees depending upon the writer, but none saw the forest for the trees! What I found was a potpourri of ideas about conflict that were connected to randomly selected Scriptures. Jesus's words on church discipline in Matthew 18 were cited for guidance, but that guidance was meant to be applied to very specific and limited circumstances. None of the books provided a roadmap on how to make peace with others the way God makes peace with us. This book fills that void and provides real hope in the face of conflict.

My Personal Experience

I once received an e-mail from a senior pastor who was inquiring about my conflict resolution and reconciliation services. He decided not to turn to his own denomination for help, even though the cost was nominal. He wrote, "Our denomination has a state staff which is available for mediation and conflict resolution. But my honest opinion is that they know just enough to be dangerous. I've not worked with them because every church I know of where they've 'helped' has ended up worse than before they intervened."

I quote this pastor because I identify with his perspective. After serving for more than five years as a senior pastor in my second church, conflict emerged. Without going into the details, suffice it to say that when the matter was over I said to myself, "There has to be a better way to resolve conflict than this." The trajectory of my career took an unexpected turn as I sought to find that better way.

My investigation uncovered, among other things, that church conflict is all too common. Research has revealed that in a given year about one in four churches experiences serious conflict with lasting impact.[3] Given the hundreds of people I have interacted with over the years relating to this subject, it is crystal clear to me that churches do not handle conflict very well. Upon reflection, this is not surprising. As noted above, they have not relied upon an all-inclusive approach to conflict resolution to guide them. That's the bad news. Here's the good news. When I started down this new path, I assumed that there had to be a better way. Today, I can confidently say, "There is!"

The Purpose of This Book

The purpose of this book is to set forth an all-inclusive peace-making process that can constructively and gracefully guide those in conflict toward reconciliation. This work is written for those who want to better understand what can and should be done in the midst of a conflict. It is written for church leaders who want their congregation to become "conflict competent" so that love remains the distinguishing mark of their fellowship. Jesus said, "by this all people will know that you are my disciples, if you have love for one another" (John 13:35). It also is written for peacemakers (whether budding peacemakers or seasoned practitioners) who want to roll up their sleeves and be part of the solution.

Best Wishes on Your Journey

To all I wish a captivating journey. Numerous illustrations from all over the globe and from all kinds of situations are cited throughout the book. These are presented not only to help maintain your interest, but also to bring clarity and depth to your under-standing. While true "shalomic peace" will not be fully realized on planet Earth until Jesus returns to set up God's kingdom,* we can create pockets of peace in the spaces we ourselves occupy. Toward that end, this book is offered.

---

* "At that time Jerusalem shall be called the throne of the Lord, and all nations shall gather to it, to the presence of the Lord in Jerusalem, and they shall no more stubbornly follow their own evil heart" (Jeremiah 3:17).

Part 1

Foundations

Chapter 1

The Key That Unlocks the Door to the Judeo-Christian Model of Peacemaking

Blessed are the peacemakers,
for they shall be called sons of God.
Matthew 5:9

Like Father, Like Son

The first half of Matthew 5:9, "Blessed are the peacemakers," is well known far beyond religious circles. It is referenced in books on conflict management for organizations,[4] in documents published by the United Nations,[5] and in secular magazine articles[6] and has even been inscribed on a gift from one world leader to another.[7] The significance of the second half of the verse, "they shall be called the sons of God," however, is regularly overlooked. Yet, it is the second half of the verse that unlocks the door to a distinctive model of peacemaking.

Jesus said that peacemakers "shall be called the sons of God." This description indicated close identification with God.[8] The phrase, "sons of God" was an expression that meant, "having the characteristics of" or "doing the work of" God.[9] In Jewish thought, the terms *son* and *daughter* often were used to convey the idea that they shared in the essence or nature of the one to whom they are said to be related.[10] The phrase "like father, like son" succinctly captures the meaning of Jesus's words.[11]

Relevance

Jesus's words in Matthew 5:9 indicate that God is the ultimate peacemaker. They also indicate that to the degree Jesus's followers emulate God in this respect is the degree to which they identify themselves as God's children. If we really want to become "chips off the old block" in making peace with others, the critical question that needs to be answered is, "How does God make peace with us?" If we can identify the pattern God uses in making peace with mankind, then we can extract a definitive model peacemakers can use when attempting to make peace between people. Happily, such a pattern can be found in the Scriptures. Matthew 5:9 is the key that unlocks the door to the model. The model is built on the concept, "like father, like son."* I have named this model "the Judeo-Christian model of peacemaking."

---

* There are numerous texts in the Old and New Testaments that explicitly direct people to take on the characteristics of God. These include, "You shall therefore be holy, for I am holy" (Lev. 11:44, 1 Pet. 1:16); "You therefore must be perfect, as your heavenly Father is perfect" (Matt. 5:48); "Be merciful, even as your Father is merciful" (Luke 6:36).

Chapter 2

The Three Major Characteristics of the Judeo-Christian Model of Peacemaking

---

Love, Not Justice, Is the First Foundation

Judeo-Christian Perspective
Relevance for Peacemaking

Reconciliation Is the Goal

Judeo-Christian Perspective
Relevance for Peacemaking

Mediation Is the Means

Judeo-Christian Perspective
Overview
New Testament
Old Testament Backdrop
Relevance for Peacemaking

Summary

There are three major characteristics of the Judeo-Christian model of peacemaking: (1) love, not justice, is the model's first foundation, (2) reconciliation is the goal, and (3) mediation is the means.

Love, Not Justice, Is the First Foundation

Judeo-Christian Perspective

The Judeo-Christian model of peacemaking differs from other models because the foundation of the entire process is not justice (as indispensable as justice is to peace), but love. This differs from what is commonly taught. For example, one scholar stated, "The only steady ground under peace is justice."[12] The charter of the United Nations[13] advances the same idea, not only by what it says but also by what it doesn't say. That is, the words *peace* and *justice* together are used dozens of times. However, the concept of love is not found at all.[14] Justice, however, is the second foundation of peace in the Judeo-Christian model. Undergirding justice is the orientation to love.

As evidenced below, God's love and willingness to embrace hostile humanity is the foundation that makes peace with God possible. In the Old Testament, God's love is vividly seen in his relationship to the people of Israel (cf. Deut. 4:37; 7:6-8). What is most striking about this is that God's love was constant despite the nation's history of rebellion and sin against him. It was a love that transcended the people's immoral behavior, even over long periods of its history when the Israelites forsook the God of their fathers altogether (See, e.g., Deut. 9:6-8, 26-27; Jer. 31:35-37; Rom. 11). In the New Testament, the expression of God's unconditional love reaches its highest pinnacle through the life and ministry of Israel's Messiah, Jesus of Nazareth. In the New Testament, we again see that God's love is expressed to all, despite people's rebellion against him.

John 3:16-17

16 For God so **loved** the world, that he gave his only Son, that whoever believes in him should not perish but have eternal life. 17 For God did not send his Son into the world to condemn the world, but in order that the world might be saved through him.*

Romans 5:6-8

6 For while we were still weak, at the right time Christ died for the ungodly. 7 For one will scarcely die for a righteous person—though perhaps for a good person one would dare even to die— 8 but God shows his **love** for us in that while we were still sinners, Christ died for us.

Titus 3:3-5

3 For we ourselves were once foolish, disobedient, led astray, slaves to various passions and pleasures, passing our days in malice and envy, hated by others and hating one another. 4 But when the goodness and **loving kindness** of God our Savior appeared, 5 he saved us, not because of works done by us in righteousness, but according to his own mercy.[15]

The question that may arise is: How can God's love for sinners be so relentless? The answer is found in his very essence. In addition to being holy (see chapter 3), the Scriptures also reveal that God is all-loving. On two occasions we read, "God is love" (1 John 4:8, 16). What God is, He is in whole, not in part.[16] "God is infinite in His essence, and love is the essence of God. Therefore, God is infinite love."[17] God's love "continually extends to the undeserving

---

* One scholar observed, "A study of the word 'world'—especially in John, where it is used 78 times—shows that the world is God-hating, Christ-rejecting, and Satan dominated. Yet that is the world for which Christ died" (Elwell, 1984, p. 99). Another scholar similarly remarked, "In John's vocabulary, *world* is primarily the moral order in willful and culpable rebellion against God. In John 3:16 God's love in sending the Lord Jesus is to be admired not because it is extended to so big a thing as the world, but to so bad a thing; not to so many people, as to such wicked people" (Carson, 2000a, p. 17).

and unloving,"[18] without discrimination (cf. Luke 6:32-36; Matt. 5:43-48), in order to bring those with whom he is in conflict into a right relationship with him.[19]

Relevance for Peacemaking

What does God's love mean for us when it comes to our making peace with each other? It means that even before the process of peacemaking begins, despite the hurt and pain, each offended party must have the will to find peace with the other side based on their ability to love. As with God, so with us. Civil rights leader Martin Luther King, no stranger to conflict, said in no uncertain terms that the reason you love your enemies, even if they are the worst persons you have ever encountered, is because that is what God does.[20] Christian theologian, Miroslav Volf, from war-torn Yugoslavia and well known for his writings on conflict resolution, stated, "The will to embrace precedes any 'truth' about others and any reading of their action with respect to justice…. It transcends the moral mapping of the social world into 'good' and 'evil.'"[21] When it comes to making peace, the will to express love is foundational.

Such an orientation is not something that has to be artificially generated. Because we are made in the image of God, we are by nature predisposed to love. To demonstrate this assertion, see Appendix 1, entitled, "When Love Fails." It examines how basic love is to our well-being. It drives home the indisputable point that the capacity to love and be loved is intrinsic to human beings in the same way that God's love is an intrinsic part of his essence.

That said, I hasten to add that the capacity to love in no way mitigates the reality of injustice and its need to be addressed. Nevertheless, as John Paul Lederach, a world-renowned peacemaker stated, constructive social changes in the midst of destructive conflict cannot occur without love.[22] Justice, though a condition for peace, is insufficient in and of itself to produce peace. Justice ensures that people are accountable for the wrongs they commit, but being held accountable does not build relations. "Some form of communion—some form of positive relationship—needs to be established if the victim and perpetrator are to be fully healed."[23] It is toward this end that this book is dedicated. Its entire thrust is to unpack the concrete and practical stages of transforming enemies into friends.

The starting point for God in his plan to make peace with humanity began with his nature to love regardless of the sins people committed against him. Being made in the image of God, we have the capacity to do the same. Love, therefore, is the first foundation of the Judeo-Christian model of peacemaking. Only love has the power to reconcile.

Only love has the power to reconcile.

Reconciliation Is the Goal

Judeo-Christian Perspective

Reconciliation is viewed in the Scriptures as the apex of God's desire for a world that has ignored, rebelled against, and turned away from him. Despite all this, "God was in Christ reconciling the world to himself" (2 Cor. 5:19 NASB). Jesus's ultimate role as Israel's Messiah was to bring God and human beings into harmony with each other.* Indeed, reconciliation has been considered "the central concept of Christianity."[24] Given that the original meaning of the word in Greek was to "change" or "exchange," when the New Testament states that people are reconciled to God, it means they exchanged a relationship of hostility for one of friendship.[25]

---

* "It could be said that the whole work of Christ has to do with reconciliation" (Guthrie, 1981, p. 486).

Relevance for Peacemaking

Though the concept of reconciliation is quite old, in the field of conflict resolution it is, surprisingly, relatively new. Talking about peace studies on college campuses in 2001, one practitioner observed, "On the far cutting edge of those programs courses are now offered in reconciliation.... The study, practice, and theory of reconciliation are barely in the stage of conception."[26]

In the conflict resolution field, reconciliation often is not the goal.[27] Certainly, on a global level and with matters of war, reconciliation has rarely been the goal. Historically, peacemaking efforts have been directed toward stopping the fighting and establishing nonviolent coexistence. One scholar captured the state of affairs in 2004 this way: "If you ask most political scientists and international relations scholars what role reconciliation should have in peace, you are apt to receive a dazed look and perhaps an uneasy silence as well."[28] What this means is that "although the concept of reconciliation has long been familiar to researchers and practitioners, only in the last decade has it emerged as a specific area of interest in peace studies."[29] Various reconciliation models of peacemaking are just beginning to emerge.[30]

The Judeo-Christian approach to peacemaking represents a distinct reconciliation model. In some respects, I feel like an explorer who has come upon pristine lands that have always been around but are being overlooked by the majority of travelers. I am of the opinion that the Judeo-Christian model of peacemaking is the gold standard. It is applicable in our homes, our congregations, our communities, and our world. I look forward to being your guide into the old, which has become new again.

Mediation Is the Means

Judeo-Christian Perspective

Some years ago, there was a discussion between a university faculty member and a graduate student. The teacher, who had been raised in a Protestant home, indicated that of late she had been attending a Jewish synagogue. When it came to approaching and making peace with God, the professor's attitude was, "none of this middleman stuff." What makes this statement so startling is that the professor taught in the department of conflict resolution. Mediation ("middleman stuff") is central to this area of work. Yet this professor failed to value this pattern of peacemaking when it came to establishing peace with God.[31]

Overview

The concept of a mediator between God and mankind begins in the Old Testament and continues into the New Testament, culminating in the person of Jesus Christ. The three Old Testament offices of king, prophet, and priest, all mediatorial in nature, were eventually fulfilled by Jesus.[32] Edwards summarized, "Our inquiry will have shown how central and prominent is the idea of mediation throughout the Scriptures. We might even say it supplies the key to the unity of the Bible. In the OT the principle is given 'at many times and in many ways'[33] but in the NT it converges in the doctrine of the person and work of the One final Mediator, the Son of God."[34] God established a mediatorial model to make peace with mankind. Consider the biblical data.

New Testament

Central to the work of Jesus was that of peacemaking mediator between God and human beings. (What made him uniquely qualified to fulfill this role will be discussed in Stage 2.) Though there are many passages that speak to this, the text that most explicitly refers to Jesus's mediatorial role is 1 Timothy 2:5. This verse, in context, reads,

> 1 Timothy 2:3-6
> 3 This is good, and it is pleasing in the sight of God our Savior, 4 who desires all people to be saved and to come to the knowledge of the truth. 5 For there is one God, and there is one mediator between God and men, the man Christ Jesus, 6 who gave himself as a ransom for all.

The word for "mediator" in 1 Timothy 2:5 is derived from a Greek word that means "middle" or "in the middle."[35] This word is used in John 19:18, where we read in the New International Version, "Here they crucified him, and with him two others—one on each side and Jesus in the middle."

Studying the use of this word prior to the New Testament,[36] a mediator referred to a person who was situated between two parties.[37] This person did not take sides but remained neutral as one whom both sides could trust.[38] The mediator helped others establish a relationship that would otherwise not be formed.[39] These meanings continued into the New Testament. A mediator was known as one "who mediates between two parties to remove a disagreement or reach a common goal."[40]   The primary goal was reconciliation.[41] As between God and man, the mediator "is the One who represents God to men and men to God, and brings them together."[42] This is clearly the case in 1 Timothy 2:5, where Jesus is situated between God and humanity for the purpose of bringing peace.

In addition to 1 Timothy 2:5, other New Testament passages, while they do not explicitly contain the word *mediator*, make clear that there is no other way to make peace with God apart from the mediatorial structure and process.[43]

John 14:6
Jesus said to him, "I am the way, and the truth, and the life. No one comes to the Father except through me."

Ephesians 2:17-18
17 And he [Jesus] came and preached peace to you who were far off and peace to those who were near. 18 For through him we both have access in one Spirit to the Father.

Hebrews 9:24
For Christ has entered, not into holy places made with hands, which are copies of the true things, but into heaven itself, now to appear in the presence of God on our behalf.

1 John 4:9
In this the love of God was made manifest among us, that God sent his only Son into the world, so that we might live through him.

It has been said that the apostle Paul "never preached a religion without mediation."[44] This can be said of the New Testament as a whole. "The gospel presents Christ as the mediator between God and men, who has been ordained by God to bring erring humanity back to Himself."[45]

Old Testament Backdrop

The concept of a mediator between God and mankind has roots deeply embedded in the Old Testament. Moses assumed the role of mediator between God and the newly birthed nation of Israel. Notice what occurred just after Moses led the Israelites out of Egypt to Mount Sinai. Not only did God speak to the people through Moses, but the people also expressly desired that Moses should speak to God for them. God said to Moses, "These are the words that you shall speak to the people of Israel" (Exod. 19:6). Conversely, the people made a similar request. "You

25

speak to us, and we will listen; but do not let God speak to us, lest we die" (Exod. 20:19). This was the first of many occasions when Moses served as a mediator between the people of Israel and the God of Israel.[46]

This mediatorial pattern continued throughout Israel's history by way of its prophets, priests, and kings. The prophets stood in the place of God to reveal his word and will, not only to the Israelites (Deut. 18:15-22),[47] but also to surrounding Gentile nations (Jon. 1:1-2; 3:1ff.). The priests stood between God and the Israelites in activities that dealt with cleansing from sin (e.g., Lev. 6:1-7; 16:1-34). The kings were charged with serving as God's viceroys, administrating justice and righteousness according to the laws God gave to Moses (Deut. 17:18-20; 1 Sam. 12:13-15, 24-25; 2 Kings 23:2-3; cf. Judg. 8:22-23, Isa. 11:1-11; 1 Kings 11:9).[48] These three offices, priest, prophet, and king, all mediatorial in nature, were established by God to maintain the nation's unique relationship with him. One Old Testament scholar well summarized, "Though the word is not used, mediatorship is at the heart of OT religion."[49]

Relevance for Peacemaking

The practice of mediation in the conflict resolution field ranges from "banging heads" in order to get results to exerting no influence upon the parties or the outcome. An example of the first approach comes from a Texas conference on mediation. A panel of attorneys spoke to the question, "What do lawyers want from mediators?" The unanimous answer was (paraphrased), "We want someone to bang heads, to knock some sense into our clients and get them to settle."[50] Similarly, a respected mediator in Australia asked, "What's wrong with head-banging and pressure? The parties come to me because they want to be out of there with a settlement by 6 PM. I give it to them. And if it takes a little arm-twisting, so be it."[51]

On the other end of the spectrum, a practitioner in an article entitled, "Confessions of a Public Dispute Mediator," revealed, "I admit it: I have tried to nudge participants in mediation towards agreement." He then sheepishly added, "I know we are supposed to be indifferent to whether or not agreement is reached."[52] This attitude represents the approach to mediation that says the mediator should do nothing to influence the outcome. "We must detach ourselves from the goal of settlement."[53] Getting the parties to respectfully communicate to each other is goal enough regardless of the outcome.[54]

In the Scriptures, the mediator is described as one who neither bangs heads nor is indifferent. We need go no further than understanding the meaning of the word *peacemaker* to understand the role the mediator should play. As in English, so in the Greek, the word was created by joining two separate words, "to make" and "peace." By itself, the word "to make" means, "to undertake or do something that brings about an event, state, or condition, *do, cause, bring about, accomplish, prepare,* etc."[55] Hence, the peacemaker will "endeavor to reconcile persons who have disagreements, making peace."[56] Free will, not coercion, underscores this approach.

Jesus was such a peacemaking mediator.[57] His work is described in these terms on two occasions. The first is found in Ephesians 2:15, where Jesus is shown to "make peace"[58] both between God and mankind and between Jews and Gentiles. A similar picture of Jesus reconciling God and his creation is found in Colossians 1:20.[59] When the Bible talks about Jesus's role as mediator in 1 Timothy 2:5, he is viewed as the causative agent of peace on the grandest of scales.

Peacemakers who follow the Judeo-Christian model will adopt Jesus's approach. The idea that the mediator is to be indifferent with regard to the outcome of the peace process is foreign to this model. Once the parties have given their freewill consent to the process, the peacemaker has the freedom to address past issues in any ethical manner he or she deems best in order to help the parties find new ways to resolve outstanding issues in the present and to forge a path toward reconciliation for the future. The Scriptures hold this work in high regard. Indeed, peacemakers are called blessed (Matt. 5:9). One biblical commentator aptly summarized by saying that peace-makers are "the active heroic promoters of peace in a world full of alienation, party passion, and strife."[60]

Summary

According to the Scriptures, God's decision to make peace with mankind is rooted in his love. The goal of the peacemaking process God established is to reconcile us to himself. The means by which he has chosen to accomplish this is through mediation. These then become the three major characteristics of the Judeo-Christian model of peacemaking ("like father, like son"; see chapter 1). Part 3 of this book will describe the stages of peacemaking that emerge within this overall framework, but first let's consider the conflict between God and mankind that requires a peacemaker.

Part 2

The Conflict

Chapter 3

The Conflict Between God and Mankind

Life on Planet Earth from a Secular Perspective

Humanist of the Year
Humanist Manifestos I and II
The Humanist Magazine
Reality Trumps Idealism

Life on Planet Earth from a Judeo-Christian Perspective

In One Corner, God: Holy and Righteous
In the Other Corner, Mankind: Free and Fallen
The Fall
The Result of the Fall
No Exceptions

The Conflict Between God and Mankind

All Evil Behavior Is First and Foremost Sin Against God
God Is Angry OveSins Committed Against Him

Overall Summary

Life on Planet Earth from a Secular Perspective

Humanist of the Year

Billionaire Ted Turner gave an acceptance speech when he won the Humanist of the Year Award from the American Humanist Association in 1990. In his address he made a number of negative references to Christianity. He said, among other things, "I mean, it starts out with this notion that we're all horrible. We're all born in sin."[61] He wondered out loud what problem there could be with simply believing that people are basically good.

Given his optimistic attitude regarding human nature, I was perplexed by what else he had to say. Turner noted that since the emergence of the industrial revolution in the eighteenth century, "civilized" human beings have displayed a propensity to hurt the planet and everything living on it. Turner railed, "We've wrecked it, we've exterminated species–and oddly enough, as a percentage, we've actually killed more of our own kind than we have of most anything else."[62] The question that immediately comes to mind is, how do basically good people commit such evil deeds?

Humanist Manifestos I and II

Such an inconsistency was recognized by the American Humanist Association itself in 1973 when it examined and rewrote its overly idealistic 1933 Manifesto.[63] The 1933 Manifesto suggested that man was at the dawn of a new age and had the ability to finally achieve the world he had always dreamed about. Of course, what soon appeared on the horizon was Nazism and totalitarianism, both of which inflicted massive death and misery on large segments of humanity. Cognizant of these and other atrocious realities, the 1973 Manifesto acknowledged that the tenor of the first manifesto was "far too optimistic."[64] Taken together, both manifestos reflected the same kind of contradictory thoughts about human nature expressed by Ted Turner.

The Humanist Magazine

Despite modifications to the first Humanist Manifesto, the 1973 Manifesto continued to reject the existence of God and remained optimistic about the "possibilities of human progress."[65] You can imagine my shock then when I read Nicholas Baldoni's 1999 article, "Kosovo: The Status of Human Brutality—Ethnic Slaughter and Human Rights Abuse," published in the Humanist magazine. Baldoni's analysis and description of the human condition, based on the ethnic slaughter of human beings in Kosovo was nothing less than stunning. He pointed out that crimes against humanity have not lessened over time. In fact, they may have increased, but why? One could draw the conclusion that church-sponsored massacres of Jews and others during the Middle Ages were the result of unenlightened men expressing archaic and erroneous theology. The same, however, cannot be said for modern times.

At the close of the twentieth century, concepts such as human rights, democratic rule, and fair and equal treatment for all were widely disseminated and understood. If there were ever a time when death, persecution, and human viciousness would begin to recede from the human experience, it would be now. But as mankind entered the twenty-first century, nothing could be farther from the truth. The unavoidable explanation, according to Baldoni, is that mankind has a "dark side," a dark side that is not touched by reason or education. Baldoni concluded, "Ultimately, one is forced to confront the possibility of a tragic flaw existing in the heart of all humanity—the idea that at any time, given the right set of circumstances, one can be stripped of the clothes of civilization and moral responsibility and run brutal and naked into the forest of human barbarism."[66]

This sobering conclusion seems at odds with the belief system of the Humanist magazine in which it was published. It seems that no matter how unappetizing the idea may be, mankind is flawed. This explanation best squares with reality. Baldoni's assessment is powerful because it reflects the evidence.

Reality Trumps Idealism

Read today's newspaper. Watch tonight's news on TV. Locally or nationally, the names are different, but the story is always the same: murder, abuse, rape.* Internationally, the names are different, but the story is the same: political unrest, territorial disputes, war. "I think it is really easy to ignite the worst in all of us," concluded a human rights specialist about the Rwanda genocide.[67] No matter what the era or locale, it never ends. That something is wrong on planet Earth is painfully clear. Human evil is an ever-present reality.

New Age author Eckhart Tolle, popularized by Oprah Winfrey, has taken a similar view. He said that if all of human history could be boiled down to the life of a single person, the diagnosis for that person would be "chronic paranoid delusions, a pathological propensity to commit murder, and acts of extreme violence and cruelty against his perceived 'enemies.'"[68] He added that this condition would be interrupted by only a few, short-lived periods of lucidity.

Though the Judeo-Christian worldview and the worldviews of others, such as secular humanists, are diametrically opposed on key issues, including the existence of a personal God, the observations of secular humanists about humans is precisely what is taught in the Scriptures—to which we now turn.

---

* According to the U.S. Department of Justice and FBI, violent crime in America is committed every 22.4 seconds. Property crime is committed every 3.2 seconds (United States Department of Justice and Federal Bureau of Investigation, 2008). A review of previous "crime clocks" reveal that these 2007 statistics are very similar to previous years.

Life on Planet Earth
from a Judeo-Christian Perspective

According to the Scriptures, after each day of creation, God looked upon what he had made and declared that it was "good."[69] At the beginning of human history, God and human beings were at peace with one another (Genesis 1-2). All was well on planet Earth. Full and unfettered fellowship between God and his creation, as well as perfect harmony between the sexes, existed. Adam and Eve lived in an environment that provided for their every need. The garden, which was to be tended to, and God's command to the couple to be fruitful and multiply provided purpose. This idyllic picture, however, did not last. Conflict emerged between God and humans. To fully understand the conflict and why it occurred, it is critical that we first examine the nature of the parties involved.

In One Corner, God: Holy and Righteous

In one corner of this conflict is God. He is holy. Theologians often speak of God's holiness as his foremost attribute.[70] God's holiness refers to His "moral perfection...purity unsullied by any breath of evil."[71] God's holiness is so abundantly presented in the Old Testament that by comparison it "overshadows" his other attributes.[72] Clearly, God's holiness is "the central and culminating idea of the Jewish law."[73] This theme continues right into the New Testament.

Closely associated with God's holiness is his righteousness. Because God *is* holy, he *does* what is just and right. "Justice is simply God's holiness in its judicial activity."[74] Said another way, "God always acts in accordance with what is right and is himself the final standard of what is right."[75] Consider a few examples from Old and New Testament texts that refer to the holiness and righteousness of God.[76]

Genesis 18:25
"Shall not the Judge of all the earth do what is just?"

Leviticus 11:45
"I am the Lord who brought you up out of the land of Egypt to be your God. You shall therefore be holy, for I am holy."

Deuteronomy 32:4
The Rock, his work is perfect, for all his ways are justice. A God of faithfulness and without iniquity, just and upright is he.

Isaiah 6:3
"Holy, holy, holy is the LORD of hosts."

Psalm 145:17
The LORD is righteous in all his ways.

Matthew 6:9
"Our Father in heaven, hallowed be your name."[77]

Revelation 4:8
"Holy, holy, holy, is the Lord God Almighty."

In the Other Corner, Mankind: Free and Fallen

If God is in one corner of the conflict, man is in the other. It is in man's corner that evil emerges. Here is the story in brief. God created man and woman in his image.[78] The image of God included free will. Shortly thereafter conflict arose. God had given permission to the first couple to eat freely from all the trees in the garden except one.

Genesis 2:15-17
15 The Lord God took the man and put him in the garden of Eden to work it and keep it. 16 And the Lord God

commanded the man, saying, "You may surely eat of every tree of the garden, 17 but of the tree of the knowledge of good and evil you shall not eat, for in the day that you eat of it you shall surely die."

Adam and Eve were made in the image of God (which is good). They had free will (which is also good). However, they chose to exercise their freedom in a way that was in rebellion to God's command (which is bad). We read:

Genesis 3:6-7a
6 So when the woman saw that the tree was good for food, and that it was a delight to the eyes, and that the tree was to be desired to make one wise, she took of its fruit and ate, and she also gave some to her husband who was with her, and he ate. 7 Then the eyes of both were opened.

The Fall

The fruit was good for it was created by God. Man's corruption and downfall had to do with the act of turning away from God. As Augustine put it, "Man did not therefore strive after an evil nature when he touched the forbidden tree; but by deserting what was better [i.e., God's commandment], he committed an evil deed."[79] Augustine profoundly wrote, "When the will abandons what is above itself, and turns to what is lower, it becomes evil–not because that is evil to which it turns, but because the turning itself is wicked.[80]

A modern-day example of turning away from the good comes from an article about risky gay sex. Warner, a homosexual, concluded that many men are attracted to "queer sex" because it goes against what is considered proper and prudent by most people. The rejection of societal normalcy is what motivates them. He stated, "The appeal of gay sex, for many, lies in its ability to violate the responsibilizing frames of good, right-thinking people."[81] The desire to do wrong is triggered by the entreaty to do right. Exploring what is forbidden is what tantalizes. "Abjection," according to Warner, is homosexuality's dirty little secret.[82]

Warner's statement not only supports Augustine's statement, but it also corresponds to what the apostle Paul wrote about the experience of sin in general. The apostle stated, "I would not have known what it is to covet if the law had not said, 'You shall not covet.' But sin, seizing an opportunity through the commandment, produced in me all kinds of covetousness" (Rom. 7:7b-8a). Sin, regardless of the specific example, involves a person's turning away from the good established by God. Not surprisingly, there are at least twenty different Hebrew and Greek words used to describe this turn. Sin is understood as "missing the mark, badness, rebellion, iniquity, going astray, wickedness, wandering, ungodliness, crime, lawlessness, transgression, ignorance, and a falling away."[83]

The Result of the Fall

As a result of the fall, the biblical picture of humanity is this: What was originally created totally good by God, his image in man and woman, has become corrupted, adulterated, diminished, and weakened. Like the deteriorated sphinx in Egypt, though we can still make out its original form, it is disfigured and marred. Like Mount Rushmore or the Statute of Liberty, which, before restoration, lost the splendor of their original creation, so God's image in us has become a tarnished replica of what it was. It has lost its original integrity and luster. It is not that we have no value or are incapable of doing good and aspiring to great moral heights. Rather, we are incapable of maintaining such goodness in thought and deed. We all deviate. When God calls people "sinners" in the Scriptures, it does not mean that people have no inherent worth or that humans are "rotten through and through." Indeed, the Old and New Testaments both affirm that humankind was created in the image of God and after the fall continued to be created in the image of God.[84] The Old Testament writer of Ecclesiastes put it

38

this way: "God made man upright, but they have sought out many schemes" (7:29 NASB). Tinder summed up our condition as, "all are sacred and none are good."[85] From Cain's murder of his brother Abel to the atrocities we see throughout the world today, ours is a world that is characterized almost as much by its evil as by its good, almost as much by its hatred as by its love, almost as much by its lying, selfishness, and murder as by its truthfulness, selflessness, and empathy.[86] Whether through omission or commission, we all turn away from God's moral order and perfect will for our lives.

No Exceptions

Every human being on earth engages in wrongdoing. No one is exempt.* Civil rights leader Martin Luther King used the metaphor of a civil war to describe the fight between good and evil that takes place within all people.[87] Soviet dissident and Pulitzer Prize winner, Alexander Solzhenitsyn, mulled over the possibility of segregating evildoers from the rest of the population but realized the futility of the effort. With great insight he penned, "If only there were evil people somewhere insidiously committing evil deeds, and it were necessary only to separate them from the rest of us and destroy them.

"If only there were evil people somewhere insidiously committing evil deeds, and it were necessary only to separate them from the rest of us and destroy them. But the line dividing good and evil cuts through the heart of every human being."

---

* Unwitting support for the biblical view that all human beings have inherent deficiencies comes from the father of psychoanalysis and atheist, Sigmund Freud. He argued in 1930 that the Communistic assertion that a change of economic systems, from private ownership (capitalism) to everything held in common (communism), would cure the world of its ill will, greed, etc. was an "untenable illusion" (1962, p. 60). Economic systems do not change man's nature. Romanian Joseph Ton, who lived under Communist rule, confirmed Freud's assertion nearly a half century later. Writing in 1976, Ton observed, "Today, many years after the [Communist] revolution has passed, it is clear that socialist man's character has *not* changed. He has remained as he was in the capitalist society: an egoist, full of vice, and devoid of uprightness" (1976, p. 7).

But the line dividing good and evil cuts through the heart of every human being."[88]   Consider the following biblical texts that affirm the universality of human sin.[89]

I Kings 8:46
There is no one who does not sin

Psalm 130:3
If you, O Lord, should mark iniquities, O Lord, who could stand?

Psalm 143:2
No one living is righteous before you.

Proverbs 20:9
Who can say, "I have made my heart pure; I am clean from my sin"?

Ecclesiastes 7:20 NASB
There is not a righteous man on earth who continually does good and who never sins.

Mark 7:20-23
20 And he [Jesus] said, "What comes out of a person is what defiles him. 21 For from within, out of the heart of man, come evil thoughts, sexual immorality, theft, murder, adultery, 22 coveting, wickedness, deceit, sensuality, envy, slander, pride, foolishness. 23 All these evil things come from within, and they defile a person."

Romans 3:9
For we have already charged that all, both Jews and Greeks, are under sin.

Romans 3:23
For all have sinned and fall short of the glory of God.

The Conflict Between Mankind and God

All Evil Behavior Is First and Foremost Sin Against God

Our sinful behavior puts us in direct conflict with God. According to the Judeo-Christian worldview, the activities people identify as evil because of the pain they cause to others are first and foremost viewed as sins against God.[90] This is analogous to the underlying framework of the U.S. justice system. Criminal behavior is viewed first and foremost as a crime against the State and not against the individual victim.[91] Likewise, "all offenses in Israel had a religious dimension: theft or adultery was not merely an offense against one's neighbor but was a sin against God."[92] Consider the following texts.[93]

> Genesis 13:13
> Now the men of Sodom were wicked, great sinners against the Lord.

> Genesis 39:6-9
> 6 Now Joseph was handsome in form and appearance. 7 And after a time his master's wife cast her eyes on Joseph and said, "Lie with me." 8 But he refused and said to his master's wife, "Behold, because of me my master has no concern about anything in the house, and he has put everything that he has in my charge. 9 He is not greater in this house than I am, nor has he kept back anything from me except yourself, because you are his wife. How then can I do this great wickedness and sin against God?"

> Psalm 51:4[94] (see also 2 Samuel 12:13)
> Against you, you only, have I sinned and done what is evil in your sight.

Luke 15:17-18
17 "But when he came to himself, he said, 'How many of my father's hired servants have more than enough bread, but I perish here with hunger! 18 I will arise and go to my father, and I will say to him, "Father, I have sinned against heaven and before you."

The Scriptures teach that when people engage in evil deeds on a social level, there is a transcendent dimension to their act as well. We simultaneously sin against God.*

This then is the basis of the conflict between God and humanity. In this drama, we are the offenders. God is the offended party. Moreover, because God is omniscient, he is conscious of every human activity[95] and every sin[96] against him. People may hide their wrongs from others, but there is no way they or anyone else can conceal their identities and activities from God.[97]

God Is Angry Over Sins Committed Against Him

More than knowing about our sins, the Scriptures clearly state that God is indignant over them. There are more than twenty different Hebrew words to express such sentiment in the Old Testament alone. Combined, these various words occur over 580 times.[98] Concerning God's anger, one scholar observed, "It is no capricious passion, but the stern reaction of the divine nature towards evil. It is aroused only and inevitably by sin."[99]

Though the number of words describing God's wrath are less varied and found fewer times in the New Testament, the theme remains constant. In fact, the concept of eternal judgment is much more pronounced in the New Testament. The statement by the apostle Paul in Romans 1:18 provides a good summary statement for the

---

* The essential difference between sin and evil is that evil is what is done against people. Sin is what is done against God. (See Chafer, 1947, vol. 2, p. 267.)

entire Bible: "For the wrath of God is revealed from heaven against all ungodliness and unrighteousness of men, who by their unrighteousness suppress the truth." The often-heard statement that the God of the Old Testament is a God of anger but the God of the New Testament is one of love is simply wrong. "The idea that God cannot be angry is found neither in the OT nor in the NT. It is neither Jewish nor Christian."[100]

Croatian-born Miroslav Volf is an individual who struggled with the concept of God's anger. His last resistance against it was overcome when he thought about the civil war that split apart the land of his birth, Yugoslavia. Some 200,000 were killed and over 3 million others displaced. He knew what had happened in Rwanda, where some 800,000 civilians, almost all Tutsi, were slaughtered over the course of 100 days.[101] He knew that these killings were up close and personal. (More often than not, the Tutsis were murdered one person at a time, beaten and hacked to death with clubs or machetes.)[102] He knew about this and other faraway places of woe. But now it was his villages and cities that were being ruined. It was his people who were being bombed day after day. It was his people who were being terrorized. Volf turned 180 degrees in his thinking. "Though I used to complain about the indecency of the idea of God's wrath, I came to think that I would have to rebel against a God who *wasn't* wrathful at the sight of the world's evil."[103]

Overall Summary

According to the Scriptures, God does not shy away from, ignore, or overlook sin. To dilute God's wrath in any way is to diminish God's holiness.[104] "God can no more wink at sin and turn His head than He can cease being holy, perfect, and absolutely unchangeable."[105] To the contrary, God is outraged over our sins and crimes against humanity, because, after all the pain and tears they cause to others, they are ultimately transgressions against him. Given God's holy and righteous nature and the sinful nature of human beings, we clearly are in a state of conflict with our Creator.

Part 3

The 12 Stages of the Judeo-Christian Model of Peacemaking

Chapter 4

The Twelve Stages
of the Model

Chapter 3 examined the barrier that sin created between sinful mankind and a holy God. This scenario establishes the backdrop against which God's peacemaking process with us is established. This chapter delineates this process into twelve stages, stages that can be emulated in social relations, a model I have named the Judeo-Christian model of peacemaking. Using the way God makes peace with us, we now have a blueprint for making peace with each other.

Overview

The Twelve Stages

Stage	In Brief	Like Father, Like Son
1	Initiating the Process	In the same way God, the aggrieved party, initiated the process to make peace with mankind by sending his Son as mediator, so the aggrieved party initiates the process of making peace by contacting a qualified peacemaker.
2	Mediator Immersion	In the same way Jesus was fully immersed in the identity, perspective, and experiences of both God and man as mediator between the two, so the peacemaking mediator immerses himself or herself in the perspective of each side of the conflict.
3	Envisioning Justice	In the same way God set forth a vision of ultimate justice for the sins we commit against him, so the peacemaker learns from the aggrieved party what they would consider a just outcome for the wrong they suffered.
4	Envisioning Shalomic Peace	In the same way God set forth an image of shalomic peace that includes sinful mankind, so the peacemaker helps disputing parties paint a picture of shalomic peace that is inclusive of the other side.
5	Humanizing One Side to the Other	In the same way God created humanity with no essential differences, so the peacemaker helps parties in conflict understand that there are no inherent differences between them.
6	Seeing the Error of One's Ways	In the same way sinners are urged to change the erroneous thinking that has brought them into conflict with God, so the peacemaker helps offending parties see the error of their ways.

Stage	In Brief	Like Father, Like Son
7	Making a Genuine Apology	In the same way a person's confession of sin to God is expected after repentance, so the peacemaker encourages the offending party to follow up the recognition of wrongdoing with a verbal apology to the injured party.
8	Making Reparations	In the same way God expects those who sinned against him and hurt others to make reparations to those harmed, so the peacemaker encourages the offending party to make the aggrieved party materially whole again.
9	Exercising Faith	In the same way people place their trust in Jesus as the mediator to make peace between them and God, so the parties in dispute place their trust in their mediator to make peace between them.
10	Granting Forgiveness	In the same way God forgives repentant sinners, so the peacemaker encourages aggrieved parties to forgive those who express genuine sorrow for the wrong they committed against them.
11	Building on the Spirit of Reconciliation	In the same way God reconciles with those he has forgiven, so the peacemaker encourages the parties to build upon their spirit of reconciliation and work toward a future characterized by shalomic peace.
12	Problem Solving Follow-up	In the same way Jesus continues to serve as mediator for believers even after they have made peace with God, so the parties rely upon the ongoing work of their peacemaker to help them resolve all remaining issues in order for reconciliation to be complete.

Stage 1: Initiating the Process

The Aggrieved Party Initiates the Process by Contacting a Peacemaking Mediator

What Is the Scriptural Basis for this Stage?

God, the Aggrieved Party, Initiated the Peacemaking Process with Mankind

Like Father, Like Son

Stage 1: Initiating the Process

Unresolved Conflicts Need Outside Intervention
  Introduction
  The Twenty Dollar Auction
  Closed Conflicts in Churches
Who Should Initiate the Peace Process?
Who is the Aggrieved Party?
  Conflict Is Messy
  Which Aggrieved Party Should Call Upon the Peacemaker?
Profile in Courage

Specific Application for the Local Church

Overcoming Unrealistic Expectations
The Need for a Proactive Church Conflict Management System
The Outline of a Proactive Conflict Management System
  The System

The journey toward reconciliation and peace, like any other journey, starts with the first step. This section begins by looking at how God initiated the peacemaking process with us: sinners in conflict with him. We will then apply what we learn to breaking the cycle of conflict between people. The section concludes with special application for congregational settings.

What Is the Scriptural Basis for this Stage?

God, the Aggrieved Party, Initiated the Peacemaking Process with Mankind

Had God decided not to initiate and implement a reconciliation process with sinful man, no one would have peace with God.[106] All would experience his judgment. That God was the one who initiated a plan to make peace is widely accepted by evangelical theologians of all stripes.[107] The key observation to be made at this first stage is that the offended party, God, made

52

the first move toward peace with us by sending a peacemaking mediator. Consider these texts.

> John 3:17
> For God did not send his Son into the world to condemn the world, but in order that the world might be saved through him.

> John 6:38
> For I have come down from heaven, not to do my own will but the will of him who sent me.

> Galatians 4:4-5
> 4 But when the fullness of time had come, God sent forth his Son, born of woman, born under the law, 5 to redeem those who were under the law, so that we might receive adoption as sons.

> 1 John 4:9
> In this the love of God was made manifest among us, that God sent his only Son into the world, so that we might live through him.

The biblical record is clear regarding the fact that God, the aggrieved party, created a mediatorial structure by which peace with mankind could be established (see chapter 2) and that he then initiated the peacemaking process. He did so by calling upon Jesus to be the peacemaker between heaven and earth.

Like Father, Like Son

In the same way God, the aggrieved party, initiated the process to make peace with mankind by sending his Son as mediator, so the aggrieved party initiates the process of making peace by contacting a qualified peacemaker.

Stage 1: Initiating the Process

Unresolved Conflicts Need Outside Intervention

Introduction

There is a law of science that Einstein considered the premier law—the second law of thermodynamics.[108] The law states that over time and in closed systems there is an irreversible tendency for energy and matter to move from order to disorder. In other words, everything will eventually decay, deteriorate, and disintegrate.[109] Houses fall into disrepair. Cars stop working. People get sick and die. That which was once in excellent condition becomes nonfunctional. This deterioration can be halted and even reversed if energy from outside the system enters into it; that is, if the closed system becomes open. A reversal of fortunes would occur in the above examples if a carpenter brings energy and skill to rebuild rooms in a dilapidated house, a mechanic replaces a part in a broken-down car, and a doctor successfully prescribes life-saving treatment and medication.

By way of analogy, when peaceful relationships become conflicted, disputants often try to work things out on their own. If resolution fails to occur, the conflict likely will deepen. The two sides lock horns and block out everything else around them. When conflict becomes closed, restraint deteriorates into unrestraint, and civility *Closed systems don't improve; they get worse. They don't evolve; they devolve.* gives way to incivility. Closed systems don't improve; they get worse. They don't evolve; they devolve.

Consider the case of two professional men whose attention became so focused on beating the other in a $20 auction that they lost all sense of objectivity. When it was over, they were humiliated by what had happened.

The Twenty Dollar Auction

The dollar auction game first appeared in 1971. The game is often played as follows: A large group of people gathers and participates. A $20 bill is auctioned off to the highest bidder. Bidding begins at $1. All subsequent bids must be in single dollar increments. The unique twist to this auction is that while the highest bidder wins the $20 bill, the second highest bidder must pay to the auctioneer what he or she bid as well.

By the time the auction reaches $19, most bidders have dropped out. The person who had bid $18 will invariably bid $20 to break even. Presumably, that would bring the auction to a close, right? Wrong! One professor who utilized the dollar auction as a teaching tool for more than twenty years said that the bidding usually continues well past the $20 mark.[110]

There was one auction the professor will never forget. He used the dollar auction while teaching a course for executives in organizational behavior. At the end of the first auction, the "winner" paid $54 for the $20 bill. The loser paid $53. The rest of the class watched the futile bidding war with bewilderment and glee.[111]

The professor then pulled out another $20 bill and asked if anyone wanted to bid on it. (Through the years he had observed that people bid more during the second auction than the first, even though they all just witnessed the losses involved.) There were seventy people in the class that day. A variety of people made bids, some early, others late, right up to a bid of $20. Then, as is commonly the case, only two people remained. One was an engineer. The other was the president of a small company.

Bidding eventually rose to $100. The professor got tired of counting by ones. Bids were now to be made in $5 increments. The auction continued, and the bids quickly grew to $400 with no end in sight. The professor suggested that the bids be made in $10 increments. This caused no hesitation. Neither man was ready to relinquish the bidding war. As the auction continued, members of the class were in an uproar. Some were calling out for their classmates to stop, but the two men weren't paying attention. The tumult of the room was simply part of the background noise that these two men had tuned out. When the bidding reached $700, the professor suggested that each bid be made in $20 increments. When bidding quickly reached $1,200, increments again changed, this time to $50 a bid. The professor's knees were shaking, and the class was in an uproar. When the president of the company bid $2,000, the engineer was silent. He made no reply. The auction finally had come to an end. Everyone was astonished and shocked by what had just occurred. As the adrenaline slowed and the haze of the moment passed, the two bidders felt embarrassed. The professor privately spoke to them during the lunch break to debrief and reassure them that all was well. He also said that they didn't have to pay the full amount. The two men agreed to pay $50 each.

Reflecting on what transpired, the "winner," the company president, noted that he simply got caught up in the moment. He stated, "My ego took over and my competitive juices began to flow."[112] The engineer said much the same. "I was more concerned with 'winning' and 'not giving up.'"[113] Clearly, there came a point in the auction when the money was no longer the issue. Each man's point of concentration was aimed at the other person. It was a "me-versus-you" mind-set and an "I'm-not-going-to-lose-to-you" attitude. In their self-made, closed system, rational thought and self-restraint were reduced to pure emotionalism.

Closed Conflicts in Churches

There comes a point in a conflict when direct, head-to-head discussions between the parties become counterproductive.[114] Resistance against an adversary's proposals is strong, simply because it is one's adversary who proposed them.[115] To put it another way, when the parties are looking at each other down the barrel of what is or feels like a gun, being open to each other's ideas is unlikely![116] Outside intervention is needed.

One senior pastor wrote about a severe, self-contained conflict that he had with his board chairman unbeknownst to the other board members. The conflict eventually became public and spilled out to a shocked congregation with near-disastrous results. The pastor later chided himself, "I should have taken our disagreement to the board from the beginning."[117] That likely would have contained the conflict.

I received a letter from a pastor that was much in the same vein. This minister wrote, "In the end, what had been a growing, vibrant ministry was decimated. My biggest regret as I look back is that I did not contact you earlier. I am writing this note in hopes that other congregations could be encouraged to have the wisdom to seek help before it is too late. The pride of thinking that we can always handle such situations on our own carries too great a price." Closed church conflicts, like any others, need outside intervention to stop and reverse the downward spiral.

Who Should Initiate the Peace Process?

The closed system of conflict should be opened up to the work of an outside peacemaker who will bring new impetus to restoring what was lost: peace. To begin the process, one of the sides is going to have to contact someone from outside the conflict to come in and help facilitate resolution. Who should take that first step? According to the Judeo-Christian model of peacemaking, just as God, the aggrieved party, initiated the peacemaking process with mankind, it is incumbent upon the one who feels improperly treated to make the first move.[118] When parties have become deadlocked in their dispute, the aggrieved party should be the one who initially contacts a peacemaker. The mediator then can connect with the other disputant to learn if that party is interested in resolving the conflict.[119]

Who is the Aggrieved Party?

Conflict is Messy

Though one side may present their case as open and shut in their favor, conflict usually is more complicated than it first appears. Though there may be situations where one side is totally undeserving of the extent and depth of the other's aggression (e.g., the deaths of six million Jewish civilians at the hands of the Nazis in World War II), most situations are not that cut and dried. For example, acts of terror rarely are viewed by the terrorist as a first strike against the enemy. They are viewed as retaliation against the enemy's prior provocative and offensive actions.[120] What may seem like a random act of violence to an outsider is part of a larger story. What if a man lives under severe oppression? He sees his children die slowly from illness or malnourishment while life-saving care is callously withheld. He watches men from his village made sick by an industry that does not value the health or safety of its workers. He learns about missing friends who have been tortured and killed by government-sponsored death squads because they made a critical remark about the government. He sees a vacant pulpit in his church because the preacher was murdered for advocating justice. He cries out with pain and shame as he learns that his wife has been gang-raped by local policemen.[121] What if this man then rises up and commits an act of violence against the ones who are responsible for these atrocities? Can the offender and the aggrieved, the good guys and the bad guys, be so clearly identified and labeled? Terrorists often view their aggressive behavior as acts of self-defense. This is what makes conflict so messy.

Yesteryear's victims become today's aggressors. They justify their actions because of the past indignities they suffered. What one side perceives as aggression the other side perceives as self-defense. This cycle continues so that today's aggressors become tomorrow's victims of today's victims.[122] It has been said, "Nobody is more dangerous than a victim."[123] The more one feels he or she is being treated unjustly, the more one feels justified in giving the perpetrators what they deserve.[124] It is precisely situations like these, when each side blames the other, that a third party peacemaker should be called in.

Which Aggrieved Party Should Call Upon the Peacemaker?

Disentangling the completely innocent from the obviously guilty is hard, if not impossible, to do. How far back in time does one go to determine who took the first hostile action or fired the first shot? It is not unusual for discussions between two groups or representatives of nations to talk about events that occurred prior to the birth of anyone in the room as if they happened yesterday.[125] Current acts of transgression find their justification in the distant, yet ever-present past.

This is unlike the situation presented in the Scriptures between a holy God and sinful people. In mankind's relationship with God, the aggrieved party and offender never reverse roles. But in conflicts between human beings, either side could, in its own mind, legitimately contact the peacemaker because each side truly sees itself as the victim. If that is the case, then either side can and should take the initiate and contact a mediator.

But what about the mediator? How can he or she ever hope to know who is the true victim and who is the perpetrator? The answer is, the peacemaker doesn't need to know or make that judgment. It is likely that each side has played the role of both victim and perpetrator. The mediator therefore should be prepared to begin the peacemaking process as if both sides are victims.

Profile in Courage

One of the most courageous leaders in the second half of the twentieth century is Egypt's President Anwar Sadat. Since its founding in 1948, Israel has been fighting for its survival against the Arab world. In his November 9, 1977 speech to Egypt's parliamentary People's Assembly, President Anwar Sadat shared his frustration in dealing with Israel in preparation for upcoming indirect negotiations in Geneva. He reaffirmed Egypt's position that the lands conquered by Israel in the 1967 War, including Egypt's Sinai desert, still belonged to the conquered Arab nations. He also reaffirmed the rights of the displaced Palestinian people and their right to their own state and self-determination. He remarked to the Assembly, "I am ready to go to Geneva. You must have heard me say that I would go to the end of the world to spare an injury to one of our men, much more the death of one. Israel must be greatly surprised to hear me say that I am even ready to go to the Knesset [Israel's parliament] and discuss with them."[126]

Following the speech, one worried aide asked President Sadat, "Mr. President, what would be our reaction if Israel actually extended an invitation to you?" Sadat calmly replied, "I would accept it immediately. I have declared that I would go to the end of the earth. I would go to Israel, for I want to put before the people of Israel all the facts."[127]

When days later an invitation was indeed extended by Israel's leaders, Sadat stayed true to his word. On November 20, 1977, President Sadat spoke before the Israeli parliament much to the dismay and consternation of most leaders in the Arab world. He spent three days in the land of Egypt's historic enemy. This bold move broke the impasse between Israel and Egypt. In March, 1978, President Carter served as mediator between President Sadat and Israel's Prime Minister, Menachem Begin, to make what started as a bold move a reality. The result was the Camp David Accords (for which Sadat and Begin each won Nobel Peace Prizes). Based on these negotiations, a peace treaty between the two nations was signed in 1979. Sadat was hated by many Islamists for making peace with Israel, and he was assassinated in 1982.

Both Israel and Egypt claimed to be the aggrieved party in their conflict. Yet it was President Sadat who took a bold step to break out of the recurring cycle of hostility that characterized the relationship between the two countries. He exhibited the courage to take what he rightly identified as the "initiative."[128] President Carter later served as the mediator to transform this initiative into a peace accord. In any conflict such an initiative is required to break the cycle of conflict. In the Judeo-Christian model of peacemaking, that first step is contacting a peacemaker.

Specific Application for the Local Church

Overcoming Unrealistic Expectations

When pastors and church members look to a model of the ideal church, they inevitably turn to the snapshot of the newborn church in Acts 2.

> Acts 2:42-47
> 42 And they devoted themselves to the apostles' teaching and the fellowship, to the breaking of bread and the prayers. 43 And awe came upon every soul, and many wonders and signs were being done through the apostles. 44 And all who believed were together and had all things in common. 45 And they were selling their possessions and belongings and distributing the proceeds to all, as any had need. 46 And day by day, attending the temple together and breaking bread in their homes, they received their food with glad and generous hearts, 47 praising God and having favor with all the people. And the Lord added to their number day by day those who were being saved.

This passage is often cited as the kind of loving fellowship that is expected to exist in our congregations. In fact, such love and care is routinely demonstrated today.

The above snapshot, however, is only one moment in time. Reading on through the first half of the book of Acts, we discover the euphoria of those early days gave way to instances of false pretenses and lying (Acts 5:1ff.), to serious conflict between two culturally distinct groups with charges of unequal treatment (Acts 6:1ff.), to theological contention (Acts 15:1ff.), and to an intense personal disagreement (Acts 15:36ff.).[129] The truth is, as Christianity spread, first-century churches had their fair share of internal disputes and problems. They are noted in the majority of New Testament epistles.[130]

Notwithstanding this fact, what makes conflict in churches so difficult to deal with is that it is incongruent with what is anticipated. People expect a different, higher experience in the church where love is extolled as its greatest virtue. Jesus's words to his disciples are well-known: "By this all people will know that you are my disciples, if you have love for one another" (John 13:35). The words of one confused attorney who commented about the prolonged conflict in his church explain the difficulty. "I thought the church was different from other organizations – especially with regard to conflict."[131]

The fact that church conflict exists does not diminish Jesus's words about love. It only acknowledges the realities that churches face when people from different age groups, races, cultures, income brackets, and backgrounds come together to become part of one corporate body. The goal of love remains the same. Our differences simply open our eyes to see what love must overcome to reach fulfillment.

Still, it seems that for a church to admit there is conflict in its ranks is to confess failure. What is the result? It is the underreporting,[132] avoidance,[133] and denial[134] of conflict's existence. One anthropologist, who secretly studied an unnamed evangelical church, noted that acceptable vocabulary for resolving church conflict did not even exist![135] With no predefined and approved means to address frustrations and concerns, a congregant's feelings of frustration remain bottled up. They simmer until they are no longer held back, exploding onto the scene and catching the rest of the congregation off guard. Then the hallmark of Christian fellowship, love, is nowhere to be found. It is at times like these that people scratch their heads and say, "But I thought the church is supposed to be different."[136]

The message that pastors and church leaders should bring to their members is that conflict is to be expected. No researcher has ever found a conflict-free society.[137] Conflict is also endemic to organizational life.[138] This includes the church.[139] It occurs in the best marriages. Why wouldn't it occur in the best churches?

The Need for a Proactive Church Conflict Management System

For churches, such an understanding needs to be followed by a plan of action. After the massively destructive San Francisco earthquake of 1906, how did city officials proceed? Did they say, "Let's remove the cause of earthquakes"? No, that was impossible. Did they say, "Let's assume that another earthquake will not occur and rebuild accordingly"? No, that was unrealistic. Did they say, "It is foreseeable that another earthquake will occur"? Yes! They then put policies into place that reflected their desire for city buildings to withstand large earthquakes in the future. Today, earthquakes that destroy buildings around the world do little damage in San Francisco because the city prepared for them.

Church leaders must be equally prepared. Because of the inevitability of conflict, forward-thinking church leaders should take steps to put into place an in-house conflict management system.* More specifically and based on the Judeo-Christian model (see chapter 2), the system must be one that revolves around the work of peace-making mediators.

The critical factor that must be appreciated is that church leaders are the only ones in a position to institute such a process. They are the only ones who are in a position of authority to sanction the work of designated peacemakers to whom members in conflict can turn. They are the ones who have the responsibility to protect the communal life of their church (Acts 20:28-31). Hence, within a congregational setting, if an aggrieved party is to call upon the services of a mediator in accordance with the Judeo-Christian model of peacemaking, it is incumbent upon leadership to first institute the system that creates that role.

To provide specific guidance in this area, what follows is the outline of a proactive conflict management system for churches that pivots around the appointment and work of in-house church mediators.

The Outline of a Proactive Church Conflict Management System

There are two major components that are needed to create an in-house conflict management process: a specified structure and members who will serve as volunteer mediators.**

---

* Such systems are vital to church growth. Based on the research for his doctoral dissertation, Dr. Jeffrey Gaskins asserted, "The research supports the conclusion that only as churches carefully use conflict management strategies can church growth strategies facilitate sustained growth" (Gaskins, 1999, Abstract).

** The structure that is presented here is comparable to what Moses did in Exodus 18 and what the apostles did in Acts 6. In both of these cases, because existing practices proved to be counterproductive, a more decentralized process was introduced to better meet the needs of those under their care.

The System

Phase One. A problem arises among congregants, board, or staff. Left unattended, a crack emerges in the church's fellowship that can deepen and widen over time. An early attempt by the parties themselves should be made to resolve matters privately. Many disputes will be resolved at this stage, but not all. What then?

Phase Two. Identify church members (typically, anywhere from two to six people) who are to be trained as "first responders." They will be the ones who assume initial responsibility for third-party peacemaking in the church. This is a biblical, nonthreatening, and decentralized approach that fits the culture of the church well. Most disputes will be resolved at this stage. Some will not. What then?

Phase Three. A durable agreement is fashioned by the parties themselves with the help of the church's "director of mediation," who guides the disputants through a more formal mediation process. More disputes will be resolved at this stage. Some will not. What then?

Phase Four. Only the most difficult cases persist to this stage. They are taken to a governing body of the church. After all sides are heard, the governing body renders a final decision.

Note: When conflict has so engulfed church leaders that an executive decision would do more harm than good, a church conflict resolution practitioner should be called in.

Identifying Qualified Mediators

In General. Long lists of qualifications can be found that describe the characteristics of the ideal mediator.[140] Here is a shortened list of what I consider to be the two essential qualifications. The first has to do with the parties. The second has to do with the mediator.

The first qualification is that the person selected must meet with the approval of all the parties. The parties must be satisfied with the person's trustworthiness, competence, and background.[141] The second qualification is that the mediator must be adept at facilitating peace. Toward this end, the mediator should (1) have an understanding of the environment and/or subject matter as it relates to the conflict at hand[142] and (2) understand conflict resolution and problem-solving processes. This includes (a) being impartial, free of any conflict of interests, (b) working toward a win/win outcome, (c) possessing active listening skills, (d) being able to keep confidences, and (e) being supportive and understanding.[143]

Potential Candidates. In light of the above characteristics, who might make the best mediators in the church? Three groups of people come to mind: (1) those who are already trained and experienced in mediation, (2) those in the "listening" business, that is, Christian counselors, social workers, and psychologists, and (3) those who are naturally gifted in relating well with other people.

In addition, selecting those who are embedded in the life of the church is a plus. Those who are an integral part of the congregation are in the best position to understand the context, the idiosyncrasies of the people involved, how things get done and are communicated, etc. They are less prone to misdiagnosis when a problem arises and less likely to suggest unworkable solutions. Deep and broad under-standing of how your church really operates comes with personal involvement within it over time. Such embedded church members make excellent peacemakers.

Co-mediation is a well-established practice that also should be considered. This is when two mediators work together on a given dispute. Personally, I think that a man and a woman who work well together make a very effective team. They each bring their unique qualities and perspectives to the mix, and where one may be weak the other may be strong in helping others work out their differences.

Who It Should Not Be. Mediators should not be selected from among those who hold positions of authority in the church. This would include members of the pastoral staff and governing board. The mere presence of a person of authority so early in the process likely will influence how disputants speak to one another during their dialogue. Instead of trying to resolve their issue, they will be more prone to demonstrate to the person of authority who is right and who is wrong.

By contrast, if the mediator is someone who has no power over the disputants and whose only responsibility is to help the parties resolve their issues, then that will be the sole focus of the discussions. As a general principle, it is more likely the disputing parties will find a solution with which they are both satisfied if the designated peacemakers can resolve the conflict without involving those in power. At this relatively early stage of the conflict, you want the parties to resolve issues without the participation of someone who may later have to make a final decision if the issue is not resolved. Hence, mediators should be selected for their personal qualities and not their organizational authority.

Training for Church Members

There are various levels of training for mediators. The more competent peacemakers are upon entering a conflict situation, the more likely there will be a positive outcome.[144] One workplace study revealed that "the most common denominator to successful conflict resolution is formal training."[145] Various universities and private practices provide mediation training. For the church, in addition to my on-site training, I will be developing an online course to provide conflict resolution and mediation training for congregational peacemakers. To view my latest course offering and schedule, see my Web site: www.HopeInTheFaceOfConflict.com

Establishing a successful mediation ministry in the church is not hard to do. Just consider the success "peer mediation" has enjoyed among students in public schools. Select elementary school children

67

who have been trained in the basics have successfully served as mediators for classmates in conflict. Their success rates, as reported by different elementary schools, range from 71 percent to 100 percent.[146] The point is, if kids can do it, so can adults!

A Word About Church Conflict Consultants

I repeat here the words of a senior pastor who e-mailed me, inquiring about my conflict resolution and reconciliation services rather than seeking help from his own denomination. He wrote in part, "Our denomination has a state staff which is available for mediation and conflict resolution. But my honest opinion is that they know just enough to be dangerous. I've not worked with them because every church I know of where they've 'helped' has ended up worse than before they intervened." This comment should not reflect poorly on the correct process of conflict resolution. Rather, it underlines the need to use someone who is properly trained.

The fact is there are some conflicts, especially those involving leadership, that are too difficult for an untrained person to handle. In such cases, a church conflict resolution specialist should be called in. The qualified professional should be trained and experienced in accurately analyzing six distinct areas related to the conflict: (1) the individual people involved, their thoughts and actions, (2) the interactions between those in conflict, (3) the culture of the church (that is, shared values, unwritten rules, expectations, etc.), (4) organizational structure (specified roles, decision-making authority, policies and procedures, etc.), (5) the theology of the church, and (6) the history of the conflict. Each of these areas impacts the others and must be simultaneously considered.

A strong caution needs to be issued here. If the goal of the consultant's process is to produce a report that assigns blame or renders a verdict, watch out! One pastor, for example, told about a conflict on the board in his church. Staff members from another church were called in to serve as mediators. This pastor wrote, "After listening to both sides, the mediators promised to return with their recommendations in a few days. But when they handed down their verdict, I was stunned."[147]

From my own perspective, it matters not what the verdict read. It is the fact that a "verdict" was offered at all and done so under the umbrella of "mediation" that is of concern. This would be appropriate for an arbitrator, who must make judgments and rulings to bring an ongoing matter to an official close. However, this is not what mediators do! They enter into the fray and develop relationships with each side in order to lead the parties to a peaceful resolution. The difference between mediation and arbitration apparently is not widely understood. Such confusion gives true peacemaking a bad name. So be careful about the kind of "mediators" your church considers hiring. Require them to provide you with an outline of the process they intend to use from beginning to end, the rationale behind it, and its goals. If you are not satisfied with the answers you receive, look elsewhere.

Overall Summary

When there is ongoing, unresolved conflict, the Judeo-Christian model of peacemaking provides the answer to the question, "Who takes the first step?" The answer is the one who feels trespassed against. Those who have been hurt should not wait until the other side "sees the light" and makes a move to correct the error of their ways. That may never happen. The offenders may not even be aware that there is a problem.

What is required is the courage to say, "Enough! No more! There has to be a better way to deal with the increasing trauma of this dispute, and I am going to pursue it!" The aggrieved party breaks the closed system of escalating conflict by calling upon a peacemaker to assist the parties resolve their issues. Although aggrieved parties may not have caused the conflict they are in, it is incumbent upon them to make the first move toward peace. In the same way God, the aggrieved party, initiated the process to make peace with mankind by sending his Son as mediator, so the aggrieved party initiates the process of making peace by contacting a qualified peacemaker.

Stage 2: Mediator Immersion

The Peacemaking Mediator Immerses Himself or Herself in the Perspective of Each Side of the Conflict

What Is the Scriptural Basis for This Stage?

Jesus Was Immersed in the Perspective of Both
Parties to the Conflict

Fully God

Fully Man

Book of Hebrews

First Timothy

Relevance

Like Father, Like Son

Stage 2: Mediator Immersion

Building Rapport

Introduction

Gaining Perspective

John Howard Griffin

Overall Summary

The work of the peacemaker begins by gaining an "insider's view" of the conflict from each disputant's perspective. This stage, like others, never really ends. As time goes on, the peacemaker continues to develop a deeper relationship with and understanding of the parties. This section begins by examining the scriptural basis for Stage 2. It will conclude with a discussion of its real-world application.

What Is the Scriptural Basis for This Stage?

Jesus Was Immersed in the Perspective of Both Parties to the Conflict

One of the cardinal tenets of Christianity is the belief in the coexistent divine and human natures of Jesus while he was on earth. The Scriptures teach that God the Father and God the Son are relationally distinct persons whose essence is one. Hence, Jesus is fully divine. The Scriptures also teach that Jesus was fully human. The divinity and humanity of Jesus have been accepted by all main streams of orthodox Christianity. An authoritative definition of the person of Jesus emerged from the Chalcedon council in AD 451. It states, in part,

> We all with one accord teach men to acknowledge one and the same Son, our Lord Jesus Christ, at once complete in Godhead and complete in manhood, truly God and truly man … recognized in two natures, without confusion, without change, without division, without separation; the distinction of natures being in no way annulled by the union, but rather the characteristics of each nature being preserved and coming together to form one person and subsistence.[148]

The following passages provide the biblical evidence that supports the divine and human natures of Jesus.[149]

Fully God

Luke 1:30-35
30 And the angel said to her, "Do not be afraid, Mary, for you have found favor with God. 31 And behold, you will conceive in your womb and bear a son, and you shall call his name Jesus. 32 He will be great and will be called the Son of the Most High. And the Lord God will give to him the throne of his father David, 33 and he will reign over the house of Jacob forever, and of his kingdom there will be no end." 34 And Mary said to the angel, "How will this be, since I am a virgin?" 35 And the angel answered her, "The Holy Spirit will come upon you, and the power of the Most High will overshadow you; therefore the child to be born will be called holy—the Son of God."

John 1:1-3, 14
1 In the beginning was the Word, and the Word was with God, and the Word was God. 2 He was in the beginning with God. 3 All things were made through him, and without him was not any thing made that was made.... 14 And the Word became flesh and dwelt among us, and we have seen his glory, glory as of the only Son from the Father, full of grace and truth.

John 17:5
"And now, Father, glorify me in your own presence with the glory that I had with you before the world existed."

Philippians 2:5-8
5 Have this mind among yourselves, which is yours in Christ Jesus, 6 who, though he was in the form of God, did not count equality with God a thing to be grasped, 7 but made himself nothing, taking the form of a servant, being born in the likeness of men. 8 And being found in human form, he humbled himself by becoming obedient to the point of death, even death on a cross.

Colossians 2:9
For in him the whole fullness of deity dwells bodily.

The New Testament makes it clear that Jesus was God in the flesh. He left heaven to become a man.

Fully Man

Matthew 8:20
And Jesus said to him, "Foxes have holes, and birds of the air have nests, but the Son of Man[150] has nowhere to lay his head."

Mark 6:2-3
2 And on the Sabbath he began to teach in the synagogue, and many who heard him were astonished, saying, "Where did this man get these things? What is the wisdom given to him? How are such mighty works done by his hands? 3 Is not this the carpenter, the son of Mary and brother of James and Joses and Judas and Simon? And are not his sisters here with us?" And they took offense at him.

John 10:33
The Jews answered him, "It is not for a good work that we are going to stone you but for blasphemy, because you, being a man, make yourself God."

John 19:33-34
33 But when they came to Jesus and saw that he was already dead, they did not break his legs. 34 But one of the soldiers pierced his side with a spear, and at once there came out blood and water.

These and numerous other passages make it abundantly clear that Jesus lived and died as any human being.

Book of Hebrews

The major characteristic of Jesus as mediator is his solidarity and identification with both God and humanity. This fact, along with its implications, finds its fullest expression in the New Testament book of Hebrews.[151] The author of Hebrews compares the office of high priest in the Old Testament to the ministry of Jesus. In the Old Testament, the high priest stood between the people of Israel and God, offering sacrifices to God on behalf of the Israelites for the atonement of their sins.[152] The writer of Hebrews builds upon this concept to demonstrate that Jesus is a superior high priest because of his divinity (compare Hebrews 5:1-3 with 7:23-28) as he stands between God and mankind. Being divine, Jesus has total access to God the Father. Being sinless, no barrier exists that can separate him from the Father's presence. Nevertheless, being fully human, the writer of Hebrews also pointed out that Jesus has full solidarity with mankind.[153]

> Hebrews 4:14-16
> 14 Since then we have a great high priest who has passed through the heavens, Jesus, the Son of God, let us hold fast our confession. 15 For we do not have a high priest who is unable to sympathize with our weaknesses, but one who in every respect has been tempted as we are, yet without sin. 16 Let us then with confidence draw near to the throne of grace, that we may receive mercy and find grace to help in time of need.

First Timothy

Jesus's solidarity with the human race as mediator is also implicit in 1 Timothy 2:5: "For there is one God, and there is one mediator between God and men, the man Christ Jesus." The key word in terms of Jesus's identification with the human race is the word *man*. John Calvin (1509–1564) put it like this:

It is not without cause, therefore, that Paul, when he would set forth Christ as the Mediator, distinctly declares him to be man. There is, says he, "one Mediator between God and man, the man Christ Jesus" (1 Tim. 2:5). He might have called him God, or at least, omitting to call him God he might also have omitted to call him man; but because the Spirit, speaking by his mouth, knew our infirmity, he opportunely provides for it by the most appropriate remedy, setting the Son of God familiarly before us as one of ourselves. That no one, therefore, may feel perplexed where to seek the Mediator, or by what means to reach him, the Spirit, by calling him man, reminds us that he is near, nay, contiguous to us, inasmuch as he is our flesh.[154]

Relevance

Because of Jesus's two natures, human and divine, he was fully immersed in the experiences and perspectives of both. As a result of this dual identification, he is uniquely qualified to serve as mediator between God and mankind. He emptied himself of his divine glory and became a man in order to reach and relate to us. As the quintessential mediator, Jesus serves as a model for those who work as mediators and address conflict between people. Immersing oneself in the experiences and perspectives of both sides in a conflict is foundational to the work of a peacemaker.

Like Father, Like Son

In the same way Jesus was fully immersed in the identity, perspective, and experiences of both God and man as mediator between the two, so the peacemaking mediator immerses himself or herself in the perspective of each side of the conflict.

Stage 2: Mediator Immersion

Building Rapport

Introduction

Peacemaking can be conceptualized as a threefold process: The parties trust (1) the mediator, (2) the mediator's process, and (3) one another. "The parties must trust the mediator before they can trust the process, and must trust the process before they can begin to trust each other."[155] Peacemaking cannot begin if the mediator is unable to gain the confidence of the parties. Therefore, the mediator's first order of business is to develop rapport with each of the disputants.[156]

For insight into developing rapport, peacemakers would do well to reflect on the approach of Dr. Jerome Groopman, a cancer specialist, as he interacted with new patient, Kirk Bains. Bains already had received three bleak diagnoses from three other physicians about his cancer. Even though Dr. Groopman had read over the man's medical history, he told Bains that he wanted to hear the story of his illness directly from Bains's own mouth, and not just from the records. The doctor told Bains that after they discussed everything, he would give him a comprehensive examination. After that they would work through Mr. Bains's condition and treatment options together. The doctor not only learned the facts about his patient, but he also, as Dr. Groopman put it, "became integrated into his experience."[157] The rapport and bond of trust that resulted from this approach was instantaneous. Peacemakers should take a similar approach with the parties involved in a conflict.

Gaining Perspective

There is an old and enlightening Jewish expression that says, "You and I do not see things as they are. We see things as we are."[158] The idea behind this expression is also captured in what is known as

77

Miles's Law: Where you stand depends on where you sit. That is, where you stand on a given issue depends on your beginning vantage point.* Where a person stands on the Israeli-Palestinian issue, for example, in large measure will depend on where he or she was born. It is sobering to consider that an ardent pro-Palestinian would be an ardent pro-Israeli had he been born a Jew instead of an Arab (and vice versa). Or imagine that a college president is considering a proposal to ban alcoholic drinking on campus. What do you think your reaction would be if you were a beer salesperson, a campus security guard, president of your fraternity or sorority, or a parent who is a recovering alcoholic? Our opinions and attitudes will be different depending upon who we are and where we are positioned as it relates to the issue.

Hence, the ability to view reality the way others see it is critically important.[159] For peacemakers, building rapport means demonstrating genuine interest in the disputants. Peacemakers need to ask enough questions to be able to see the world as if in the disputant's shoes,[160] being "empathic" and "on both parties' sides at the same time."[161] As one practitioner put it, "The mediator's sense of self as a separate person needs to be subsumed or melded into each party's perspective."[162] This does not mean that the peacemaker gives up his or her own identity, values, etc. Understanding another person's mind-set does not necessarily mean there is agreement with it. However, understanding does allow the mediator to more fully see the framework and foundations of a person's thinking, which will later help facilitate

The ability to view reality the way others see it is critically important.

---

* Miles coined the phrase while working in the federal government's budget office. One of Miles's coworkers had been very critical of an agency that the budget office supervised. However, his attitude completely changed some six months after he began to work for that agency. Then he started to criticize those in charge of the budget office. Miles had predicted the change in this person's attitude the day his colleague switched jobs. Miles understood that the way we typically evaluate matters depends upon our position in the situation (Miles, 1978, p. 399).

a way to peace with grace and finesse.[163] The apostle Paul took this approach in his role as intermediary to help sinners be reconciled to God. He described his efforts this way:

> 1 Corinthians 9:19-23
> 19 For though I am free from all, I have made myself a servant to all, that I might win more of them. 20 To the Jews I became as a Jew, in order to win Jews. To those under the law I became as one under the law (though not being myself under the law) that I might win those under the law. 21 To those outside the law I became as one outside the law (not being outside the law of God but under the law of Christ) that I might win those outside the law. 22 To the weak I became weak, that I might win the weak. I have become all things to all people, that by all means I might save some. 23 I do it all for the sake of the gospel, that I may share with them in its blessings.

There are no shortcuts to this stage. It takes time, commitment, and an inquiring mind. Consider the lengths John Howard Griffin went to in order to gain a new perspective on race relations in America.

John Howard Griffin

In the late 1950s, John Howard Griffin was a relatively obscure white journalist. During the 1960s and 1970s he became a sought-after peacemaker who helped alleviate racial tensions between whites and blacks. In 2007, twenty-eight years after his death, a Pulitzer Prize winning book critic for the Washington Post wrote a glowing article about Griffin. He stated that it took Griffin, a white man, to really convey what life was like as a black man in America "as nothing else had."[164] How could that be? In 1960, Griffin, published his book entitled *Black Like Me*.

In the late 1950s, Griffin wondered what life was truly like as a black man in the Deep South, where there was an entrenched culture of prejudice against blacks. Communication between the two races was virtually nonexistent. Despite assurances from white legislators that harmony characterized the relationship, Griffin had reason to believe otherwise. But how would he get to the truth of the matter? How could he get the honest perspective of black Americans? He concluded that the only way he could see things from the African American perspective was to become one.

Griffin flew from his Texas home to New Orleans, Louisiana and found a dermatologist who was willing to help him darken his skin. Through a combination of medication, ultraviolet rays from a sun lamp, and a skin staining cream, Griffin transformed his appearance from white to a deep brown in less than a week. On the final day of his treatment, Griffin shaved off his straight hair and applied multiple coats of stain to his skin. After showering and dressing, Griffin looked at himself in the bathroom mirror. He literally did not recognize the image that stared back at him. Griffin was shocked and even distressed by such a complete transformation. He lost his sense of self. Who he had been in terms of appearance was now gone. Even more frightening was the prospect of the new world that waited outside his hotel room.

During the course of his experience as a black man, no one, white or black, suspected Griffin was a white man. He was black and related to as such by all. Even Griffin began to think of himself as a black man. Early on, Griffin told of one episode with one of the few black men he confided in about his true identity. Griffin had spoken to him on various occasions as a white man. After he changed color, he went back to the man. The man did not recognize Griffin and was flabbergasted to learn who he really was. Nevertheless, Griffin recounted that it didn't take long for the black man to treat Griffin as one of his own race. He began to talk about "we" and "our situation." Griffin wrote, "The illusion of my 'Negro-ness' took over so completely that I fell into the same pattern of talking and thinking."[165]

80

It is beyond the scope of this section to highlight all of what Griffin experienced as a black man. Suffice it to say, he was able to gain a depth of perspective on race relations in America that he never would have had otherwise.

In 1977, Griffin added an epilogue to his best-selling 1960 book. It is clear that Griffin's sensitive and accurate portrayal of his experience as a black man gave him entry into the African American community. Blacks trusted him virtually as one of their own. After his book was published, he continued to socialize and live with both groups. In city after city Griffin was called upon to increase communication between the two races. Though the talk of the day among many whites was one of tolerance, the reality for blacks was still one of ingrained prejudice. Griffin took on the role of mediator by sharing the harsh realities and injustices the black community experienced at the hands of the white community. He did this because the whites could not stand to hear it from the mouth of a black man.[166] In light of the tensions between the races, Griffin was given an audience with whites to share the black perspective, an audience that African Americans did not yet have for themselves.

Having experience as a white man and a black man, he was trusted by both sides. Griffin represents an extreme picture of what effective peacemaking mediators do in terms of gaining the trust of parties in conflict. They so immerse themselves in the situation that they are able to see things as each side perceives them in order to be in the best position to facilitate peace.

Overall Summary

The work of a peacemaker parallels the work of an anthropologist or missionary insofar as the peacemaker needs to build rapport if he or she wishes to gain entry into the new community. As time progresses, the anthropologist or missionary begins to understand the world as the indigenous people understand it. Peacemakers likewise must enter into the mind-set of each of the disputing parties. By doing so, they will be in an ideal position to bridge the gap between the parties. In the same way Jesus was fully immersed in the identity, perspective, and experiences of both God and man as mediator between the two, so the peace-making mediator immerses himself or herself in the perspective of each side of the conflict.

Stage 3: Envisioning Justice

The Peacemaker Learns from the Aggrieved Party How Justice Would Best Be Served

What Is the Scriptural Basis for This Stage?
Introduction: The Absence of Justice
God's Justice Will Ultimately Prevail
Old Testament
New Testament
Impact of This Vision in Modern Times
Summary

Like Father, Like Son

Stage 3: Envisioning Justice
How Important Is Justice to Peace?
What Kind of Justice?

What Should the Peacemaker Do?
Addressing the Aggrieved Party's Feelings
Addressing the Aggrieved Party's Mind-set
Summary

Specific Application for the Local Church
Can Injustice Exist Within a Local Church?
The Answer Is Yes
Four First-century Churches

Overall Summary

This stage is a continuation of Stage 2: mediator immersion. The peacemaker's focus is on beginning to paint a picture of justice guided by the needs of the aggrieved party. The main question to be asked of the aggrieved party is how they believe justice would best be served under the circumstances. This section will look at the biblical concept of justice, discuss its relevance in the world today, and conclude with special application to local churches.

What Is the Scriptural Basis for This Stage?

Introduction: The Absence of Justice

Depending upon the severity of the evil, the need for justice in the human experience is so great that a lack of justice in the face of evil can collapse our entire emotional, psychological, and spiritual framework.   Indeed, some would rather give up their understanding of God than relinquish their claim to justice. A survey in the 1970s of almost a thousand Holocaust survivors, for example, found that three times as many people lost their faith in God than gained it because of what they endured.[167]

Depending upon the severity of the evil, the need for justice in the human experience is so great that a lack of justice in the face of evil can collapse our entire emotional, psychological, and spiritual framework.

Consider the sentiments of two of these survivors. Said one, "I can't imagine how anyone can believe in God after what has happened, particularly the Jewish victims but even the rest of mankind, regardless of not being involved personally. How can you believe in a God who can permit that atrocity on such a grand enormous scale?"[168] Said the other, "Five minutes of seeing dead bodies scattered along the road; corpses dangling in grotesque formations from the electrically charged barbed wire fence; living

84

skeletons appearing more like ghosts than humans staggering around and dying at our feet; heaps of the dead and dying, by the hundreds. Five minutes and I knew I could never believe in a God who'd not prevent this. I was positive I'd be an atheist all the rest of my life."[169]

The searing words of Holocaust survivor Elie Wiesel are probably the most well-known. As a young religious teen experiencing his first night at Birkenau, the reception center for the Auschwitz concentration camp, he smelled the burning of human flesh. He saw with his own eyes children and adults being sent to their deaths in pits of fire. Years later he emotionally stated,

> Never shall I forget that night, the first night in camp, which has turned my life into one long night, seven times cursed and seven times sealed. Never shall I forget that smoke. Never shall I forget the little faces of the children, whose bodies I saw turned into wreaths of smoke beneath a silent blue sky. Never shall I forget those flames which consumed my faith forever. Never shall I forget that nocturnal silence which deprived me, for all eternity, of the desire to live. Never shall I forget those moments which murdered my God and my soul and turned my dreams to dust. Never shall I forget these things, even if I am condemned to live as long as God Himself. Never."[170]

Cries for justice are not a modern phenomenon. Thousands of years earlier biblical writers wrestled with the same problem. One such Jewish writer, Asaph, wrote of his spiritual struggle with the injustice of his day. Reading excerpts from the first half of his psalm,

> Psalm 73:1-14
> 1 Truly God is good to Israel, to those who are pure in heart. 2 But as for me, my feet had almost stumbled, my steps had nearly slipped. 3 For I was envious of the arrogant when I saw the prosperity of the wicked.... 5 They are not in

trouble as others are; they are not stricken like the rest of mankind. 6 Therefore pride is their necklace; violence covers them as a garment.... 8 They scoff and speak with malice; loftily they threaten oppression. 9 They set their mouths against the heavens, and their tongue struts through the earth... 13 All in vain have I kept my heart clean and washed my hands in innocence. 14 For all the day long I have been stricken and rebuked every morning...

Like those before and after him, Asaph had difficulty comprehending the impunity of the wicked and the suffering of those such as himself who endeavored to live a moral life. His faith in the God of Israel had almost failed due to the absence of justice in his day. But in the end, his faith did not fail.

Psalm 73:16-26

16 ...when I thought how to understand this, it seemed to me a wearisome task, 17 until I went into the sanctuary of God; then I discerned their end. 18 Truly you set them in slippery places; you make them fall to ruin. 19 How they are destroyed in a moment, swept away utterly by terrors! 20 Like a dream when one awakes, O Lord, when you rouse yourself, you despise them as phantoms.

21 When my soul was embittered, when I was pricked in heart, 22 I was brutish and ignorant; I was like a beast toward you. 23 Nevertheless, I am continually with you; you hold my right hand. 24 You guide me with your counsel, and afterward you will receive me to glory. 25 Whom have I in heaven but you? And there is nothing on earth that I desire besides you. 26 My flesh and my heart may fail, but God is the strength of my heart and my portion forever...

God's Justice Will Ultimately Prevail

Notwithstanding the tragic experience of those who endured the Holocaust or other evils throughout time, the historic response from those who hold to a Judeo-Christian perspective is this: Though justice may not be executed during one's lifetime, this should not be interpreted to mean it will never be. On this point Jewish and Christian theologians are in complete accord. Cohen, summarizing the Jewish view, observed that the doctrine of retribution at the final judgment "was a cardinal belief of the Rabbis."[171] A representative Christian theologian succinctly put it, "evil will yet be defeated (in the future)."[172]

Indeed, one of the most persistent themes throughout all of Scripture is that no evil, no violation of God's righteousness will be left unanswered or go unaccounted for. Through his prophets, God set forth a vision of how those who have violated his standards will be impartially dealt with because "God's righteousness demands it."[173] What follows are illustrative texts from the Old and New Testaments that make it clear that no sin escapes his notice and that every evil act will be brought before his bar of justice whether in this life or the life to come.[174]

Old Testament[175]

> Exodus 32:33
> But the LORD said to Moses, "Whoever has sinned against me, I will blot out of my book...."

> Numbers 32:23
> If... you have sinned against the Lord, be sure your sin will find you out.

> Ecclesiastes 12:14
> For God will bring every deed into judgment, with every secret thing, whether good or evil.

Isaiah 3:10-11

10 Tell the righteous that it shall be well with them, for they shall eat the fruit of their deeds. 11 Woe to the wicked! It shall be ill with him, for what his hands have dealt out shall be done to him.

Daniel 12:2

And many of those who sleep in the dust of the earth shall awake, some to everlasting life, and some to shame and everlasting contempt.

New Testament[176]

Matthew 25:31-33, 46

31 "When the Son of Man comes in his glory, and all the angels with him, then he will sit on his glorious throne. 32 Before him will be gathered all the nations, and he will separate people one from another as a shepherd separates the sheep from the goats. 33 And he will place the sheep on his right, but the goats on the left.... 46 And these [on the left] will go away into eternal punishment, but the righteous into eternal life."

Galatians 6:7-8

7 Do not be deceived: God is not mocked, for whatever one sows, that will he also reap. 8 For the one who sows to his own flesh will from the flesh reap corruption, but the one who sows to the Spirit will from the Spirit reap eternal life.

Hebrews 4:13

And no creature is hidden from his sight, but all are naked and exposed to the eyes of him to whom we must give account.

Hebrews 10:26-27, 31

26 For if we go on sinning deliberately after receiving the knowledge of the truth, there no longer remains a sacrifice

for sins, 27 but a fearful expectation of judgment, and a fury of fire that will consume the adversaries.... 31 It is a fearful thing to fall into the hands of the living God.

Revelation 20:12
And I saw the dead, great and small, standing before the throne, and books were opened. Then another book was opened, which is the book of life. And the dead were judged by what was written in the books, according to what they had done.

Not only do the prophets speak of a time of accountability, a vision of righteousness and healing is also given. Though more will be said about this in Stage 4, consider these two passages, one from the Old Testament, the other from the New.

Isaiah 25:8-9
8 He will swallow up death forever; and the Lord GOD will wipe away tears from all faces, and the reproach of his people he will take away from all the earth, for the LORD has spoken. 9 It will be said on that day, "Behold, this is our God; we have waited for him, that he might save us. This is the LORD; we have waited for him; let us be glad and rejoice in his salvation."

Revelation 21:3-4
3 And I heard a loud voice from the throne saying, "Behold, the dwelling place of God is with man. He will dwell with them, and they will be his people, and God himself will be with them as their God. 4 He will wipe away every tear from their eyes, and death shall be no more, neither shall there be mourning, nor crying, nor pain anymore, for the former things have passed away."

Impact of This Vision in Modern Times

The psalmist asked, "O Lord, how long shall the wicked, how long shall the wicked exult?" (Psalm 94:3). Faced with injustice, it is a question that is asked by every generation in every part of the globe. It was the question asked by Dr. Martin Luther King in 1965 when blacks were still experiencing the harsh and unjust effects of segregation, discrimination, and second class citizenship in the United States. In a speech to fellow marchers near the state capital building in Montgomery, Alabama, Dr. King said,

> I know you are asking today, 'How long will it take?' Somebody's asking, 'How long will prejudice blind the visions of men, darken their understanding, and drive bright-eyed wisdom from her sacred throne?' Somebody's asking, 'When will wounded justice, lying prostrate on the streets of Selma and Birmingham and communities all over the South, be lifted from this dust of shame to reign supreme among the children of men?' ...I come to say to you this afternoon, however difficult the moment, however frustrating the hour, it will not be long, because 'truth crushed to earth will rise again.' How long? Not long, because 'no lie can live forever.' ...How long? Not long, because the arc of the moral universe is long, but it bends toward justice. How long? Not long, because: Mine eyes have seen the glory of the coming of the Lord..."[177]

Such a vision of eventual justice sustained the civil rights movement in America.

Nobel Peace Prize Laureate Bishop Desmond Tutu, a black South African, explained how this understanding of God's justice played a role in his country's eventual transformation in the 1990s. (More will be said about South Africa's "miracle" later in the book.)

90

"During the darkest days of apartheid I used to say to P. W. Botha, the president of South Africa, that we had already won, and I invited him and other white South Africans to join the winning side. All the "objective" facts were against us—the pass laws [laws restricting travel], the imprisonments, the teargassing, the massacres, the murder of political activists—but my confidence was not in the present circumstances but in the laws of God's universe. This is a *moral* universe, which means that, despite all the evidence that seems to be to the contrary, there is no way that evil and injustice and oppression and lies can have the last word." [178]

Summary

As discussed in chapter 3, God's justice is a reflection of his holy character. Therefore, "for him to let sin go unpunished is to approve of it; which is the same as a denial of holiness."[179] Justice will triumph in the end because of who God is. His very nature guarantees it. This anticipation and vision of justice reiterated by the biblical writers has provided hope in the face of injustice for untold numbers of people down through the centuries.

Like Father, Like Son

In the same way God set forth a vision of ultimate justice for the sins we commit against him, so the peacemaker learns from the aggrieved party what they would consider a just outcome for the wrong they suffered.

Stage 3: Envisioning Justice

Broadly defined, and from the recipient's perspective, injustice means being treated unfairly, not receiving an equitable outcome as a result of one's interactions with others, or not having one's rights respected. Injustice exists in every society.

How Important Is Justice to Peace?

Justice is "a basic human need."[180] It is "fundamental to our psychological well-being."[181] Among peacemakers, the expression "without justice there can be no peace" is axiomatic. Journalist Maria Gabriela Carrascalao-Heard of war-torn East Timor stated, "There are a lot of people who can't accept any kind of reconciliation until there is justice."[182] A Christian practitioner who works with victims in the criminal justice system declared, "Justice is a precondition for closure."[183] Over a half century ago, President Dwight D. Eisenhower said in a broadcast to the American people, "Peace and justice are two sides of the same coin."[184] Pope John VI similarly declared, "If you want peace work for justice."[185]

The list of quotes can go on and on. The point is, when injustice occurs, the need for justice by those who have been violated is fundamental. The very idea, for example, that a child abductor would not be prosecuted for his crimes would violate the sensibilities of every law-abiding citizen, not to mention the parents of these children. "I just got home from work, my 5-year-old daughter is gone," blurted out Ronald Cummings, the father of Haleigh Ann-Marie Cummings, to a 911 dispatcher. "I need someone to be here now. I'm telling you, if I find whoever has my daughter before you all do, I'm killing him. I don't care. I'll spend the rest of my life in prison."[186] The emotional reaction to injustice runs deep within the human psyche. Insisting upon justice is essential in the peacemaking process.

What Kind of Justice?

The following story was anonymously posted on a public message board. No names were used. I have edited the story only slightly.

> My girlfriend has been going on and on for months about how super impressed she is with her super smart, handsome, rich, ivy league-educated, married boss. Whatever. It did not matter until she told me they had sex in Las Vegas last month during a business trip. Her digital camera also had 30 or so shots of them naked in the hotel room in various sex acts appearing very drunk and happy. I found the disc last week and she admitted what happened. I told her that our relationship was over. I own the house which we have lived in for a bit over a year. I told her to pick up her stuff today.

> Over the weekend I forwarded the digital pics to her boss, his wife (after I told her what happened over the phone), and her boss's boss. Well ... everyone who got the pics ain't too happy. My now ex-girlfriend's boss called me on Sunday and told me I ruined his marriage, job, and life. He said he was going to sue me after he beat the stuffing out of me and gouged out my eyes. Then he started to cry over the phone. I laughed and told him he can come over to my house any time he likes. I had a cop friend of mine call him back and scare the daylights out of him regarding the threatening phone calls. He left 3 threatening messages on my machine before I picked up. My ex-girlfriend took the day off from work today to pick up her stuff. Well ... she loves clothes and shoes. She likes good names too like Chanel, Gucci, Versace, etc. All her good things I took to an upper class consignment store so I can make a little cash. Every other piece of her clothing from underwear to gym clothes were burned in a beautiful bonfire fueled with gasoline last night. I gave her back all her other

stuff but not ONE stitch of clothing. For numbers.... 60 or so pairs of shoes and the designer duds.... 40 or so dresses/suits. When she asked for her clothes this morning I pointed to the remains of my bonfire. I thought she had a heart attack. I told her to get off my property and never speak to me again. I also told her if she or her boss decide to seek revenge on me her digital pics from Vegas as well as the 10 or so homemade porn films we personally made together could accidentally end up at her parents' house or get splashed all over the Internet. She left numb. I feel much better now than I did last Friday. Now it's time to move on. I will still watch my back for a while. If they try anything I will be ready. Thanks for letting me rant. It has been a crummy 5 days.

This account (of which more will be said below), like countless others, demonstrates how visceral the need for justice really is. This should not be surprising. As God's demand for justice is unwavering, we find the same desire among those he made in his image. Among people, of course, what that picture of justice looks like will depend upon who is casting the vision. One's vision of justice may look like heaven to that person, but to others who might be asked to live in that vision, it is a picture of hell.

What Should the Peacemaker Do?

Address the Aggrieved Party's Feelings

The venting of strong feelings inevitably will be part of this process, and the peacemaker should not discourage it, especially in the beginning.* Venting in a private setting where the disputants have not yet been brought together does not further escalate the conflict. The peacemaker becomes a safe haven

---

* There is nothing wrong with the expression of emotions. Jesus, for example, was not hesitant to express his throughout his ministry, emotions such as frustration (Matt. 17:17), anger (Mark 3:5), and sorrow (John 11:35).

for the aggrieved party to express thoughts and feelings that are bottled up. Experienced peacemakers know that people's raw emotions will so color their immediate thinking that what is demanded for justice is simply "overkill." After a period of time, people are able to cool down, and they usually understand that what they said in the heat of the moment should not be acted upon. This was the case in the abduction of Haleigh Ann-Marie Cummings noted above. Ronald Cummings, the girl's father "later made a public plea for Haleigh's return and promised not to seek revenge, if whoever stole her would just bring her home safely."[187] When emotions calm down, the peacemaker will learn from the aggrieved side how justice can appropriately be pursued and accomplished in that setting.

If, on the other hand, the parties remain fixed in a mind-set of revenge, the peacemaker should use his or her persuasive powers to help them avoid knee-jerk retaliatory action. Such reactions typically go beyond justice. They inevitably escalate the conflict and lead to further injustice. Such was the case of the boyfriend in the opening story of this section. Here was a man who was stung by his girlfriend's infidelity. As a victim he felt justified to victimize both his girlfriend and the other man. His sense of injustice and outrage was expressed by actions that, in part, were criminal. Breaking off the relationship with his girlfriend was one thing. Torching thousands of dollars worth of clothing and shoes was something else. It is interesting to note that the jilted boyfriend apparently knew he had crossed over the line because he was prepared for retaliation. Yet, since he had additional retaliatory options of his own, he believed his threats would contain the conflict. The injustice the boss and ex-girlfriend each felt, however, may have been great enough for them to develop their own act of revenge. If executed, the conflict would inevitably escalate and get even nastier. Such is the way of conflict and why peacemakers are so important early on.

Addressing the Aggrieved Party's Mind-set

At this stage in the process, the peacemaker needs to ascertain from the aggrieved party what would satisfy that person's sense of fair play. The peacemaker learns from the person whose world has been wrongfully violated what justice looks like for him or her.

Consider the case of Bernard Madoff who became a household name shortly after his arrest on December 11, 2008. He was the mastermind "investor" who was behind what has been characterized as the largest Ponzi scheme in the history of the world. He bilked clients and charities out of an estimated 50 billion dollars. Mr. Madoff was not immediately thrown into jail but remained for months under house arrest in his multimillion-dollar New York City apartment. One called it a "gilded penthouse incarceration."[188] This was incongruent with people's sense of justice. The picture seemed so wrong. Many would wholeheartedly agree with one New Yorker, who said, "Other people go to jail for much less severe offenses, while he is sitting in the lap of luxury. It's almost as if he's being rewarded for what he's done. I think it's a disgrace."[189]

So what would justice look like for Bernie Madoff? Nobel Peace Prize winner and Holocaust survivor, Elie Wiesel, whose foundation, the Elie Wiesel Foundation for Humanity, lost 15.2 million dollars to Madoff, outlined his vision of justice: "I would like him to be in a solitary cell with a screen, and on that screen, for at least five years of his life, every day and every night there should be pictures of his victims, one after the other after the other, always saying, 'Look, look what you have done to this poor lady, look what you have done to this child, look what you have done.' But nothing else – he should not be able to avoid those faces, for years to come."[190]

Justice can take many forms. What does a fair and just picture look like for divorced parents who still must raise their children? Wealth succession is a major concern for aging parents who own a successful, thriving business and want to pass it on to their children.

96

Many a family has experienced deep conflict because the children can't agree who does what or who gets what. What does a just solution look like for them? What does justice look like between nations where atrocities have been perpetrated against one another? There is not a uniform answer for any of these. We can only endeavor to strive toward true justice and hope that as finite beings our answers mirror those of a righteous God.

Summary

The peacemaker should individually encourage the parties to talk about the injustice that occurred and the outcome they believe needs to happen for justice to prevail. This is an important first step in establishing justice. Expressing outrage and/or grief over injustice is a healthy and moral response to it.[191] The peacemaker needs to listen to the pain a person is experiencing with an ear toward learning and discerning how justice can best be achieved. Such a conversation, however, is only a starting point. Talking about what one would like to see done, no matter how "over the top" it is, is not the same as implementing those ideas. Over time, immediate thoughts commonly change and evolve. The peacemaker may be instrumental in this maturation of thought.

Specific Application for the Local Church

Can Injustice Exist Within a Local Church?

The Answer Is Yes

As stated earlier, injustice means being treated unfairly, not receiving an equitable outcome as a result of one's interactions with others, or not having one's rights respected. Injustice exists in every society. It is a reflection of our sinful natures (see chapter 3). Christians are not exempt from engaging in it.*   Indeed, when they are not obedient to God,[192] they are as capable of perpetrating as much injustice as any pagan (cf. Gal. 5:19-21).   In the church, disputants can devolve into mutual destruction with the ability to "bite and devour one another" and be "consumed by one another" (Gal. 5:15).   Pastor Joe McKeever, referring to his church, which had split five ways in the two years prior to his accepting the call to pastor that congregation, recollected, "I was especially careful during my first four or five years here.   We spent a lot of time addressing the issues of guilt and disappointment.   Many felt guilty for their actions.   The rest were disappointed–in their friends, their pastors, themselves, even God."[193]

In 1 Corinthians 6:8, the apostle Paul makes reference to Christians in the Corinthian church who "wrong," that is, "treat unjustly"[194] (and "defraud") their brothers.   Many are unaware of the full meaning of "unrighteousness" mentioned in 1 John 1:9, a passage that applies to Christians: "If we confess our sins, he is faithful and just to forgive us our sins and to cleanse us from all unrighteousness."   The word *unrighteousness* conveys "the quality of injustice" and can be translated, "unrighteousness, wickedness, injustice."[195]   Thus, 1 John 1:9 could be rendered, "If we confess our sins, he is faithful and just to cleanse us from all injustice," that is, the injustice we consciously and unconsciously bring into the world.[196]

Four First-century Churches

What follows are four illustrative passages from four different New Testament books that record injustices that occurred in four different first-century churches.

---

* To cite just one example, on its 150th anniversary in 1995, the Southern Baptist Convention apologized for its support of slavery and prejudicial attitudes toward blacks.   It stated, in part, "Racism has led to discrimination, oppression, injustice, and violence, both in the Civil War and throughout the history of our nation ... Many of our congregations have intentionally and/or unintentionally excluded African-Americans from worship, membership and leadership" (1995, para. 6 and 8).

Acts 6:1
Now in these days when the disciples were increasing in
number, a complaint by the Hellenists [Greek-speaking
Jews] arose against the Hebrews because their widows were
being neglected in the daily distribution.[197]

Commentary on Acts 6. Friction between Hebrew-speaking Jews
(Jews native to Palestine) and the Hellenistic Jews (Jews who came
from outside of Palestine and whose first language was Greek) had
historical roots that predated the birth of the church. Even though
both groups acknowledged Jesus as Messiah, prior cultural tensions
spilled over into the Christian assembly.[198] The grievance about
the inequitable way the food was being distributed was the latest
flashpoint.

James 2:1-4
1 My brothers, show no partiality as you hold the faith in our
Lord Jesus Christ, the Lord of glory. 2 For if a man wearing
a gold ring and fine clothing comes into your assembly, and
a poor man in shabby clothing also comes in, 3 and if you
pay attention to the one who wears the fine clothing and
say, "You sit here in a good place," while you say to the
poor man, "You stand over there," or, "Sit down at my feet,"
4 have you not then made distinctions among yourselves
and become judges with evil thoughts?

Commentary on James 2. One scholar observed that the total
amount of space James devoted to this issue (read vv. 1-9) "suggests
that discrimination was a problem among his readers."[199] The rich
were treated with greater deference than the poor. They were given
the best seats in the house while the indigent were given the worst.

1 Corinthians 11:17, 20-22, 33-34
17 But in the following instructions I do not commend you,
because when you come together it is not for the better but
for the worse. ... 20 When you come together, it is not the

Lord's supper that you eat. 21 For in eating, each one goes ahead with his own meal. One goes hungry, another gets drunk. 22 What! Do you not have houses to eat and drink in? Or do you despise the church of God and humiliate those who have nothing? What shall I say to you? Shall I commend you in this? No, I will not. .... 33 So then, my brothers, when you come together to eat, wait for [or, share with] one another— 34 if anyone is hungry, let him eat at home—so that when you come together it will not be for judgment.

Commentary on 1 Corinthians 11. The "inequality of the proceedings"[200] was at the heart of what Paul condemned. On the very occasion when the church members should have demonstrated unity, coming to the Lord's Table, they demonstrated an "I-have-mine-and-too-bad-for-the-rest-of-you" attitude. The rich, who hosted these gatherings, had "first dibs" on the food and beverages they prepared. They feasted until they were satiated and drunk, while the poor went away hungry. They were treated as second-class citizens of the kingdom. The whole event only deepened ill will in an already divided church.[201] No wonder Paul said these gatherings did more harm than good (v. 17).

3 John 9-10
9 I have written something to the church, but Diotrephes, who likes to put himself first, does not acknowledge our authority. 10 So if I come, I will bring up what he is doing, talking wicked nonsense against us. And not content with that, he refuses to welcome the brothers, and also stops those who want to and puts them out of the church.

Commentary on 3 John. Diotrephes was "a local church leader of Asia Minor."[202] He loved to put himself first, which, according to the Greek word, included the inclination to control others.[203] He also sharply broke from the apostle John. Diotrephes questioned John's authority. He made spurious accusations against John.

Diotrephes did not receive the traveling missionaries who fellow-shipped with John. In fact, he excommunicated church members who wanted to welcome these Christian brothers.[204] To put it bluntly, Diotrephes was an authoritarian who not only attacked John's apostolic authority and integrity but autocratically cut off relations with anyone in the church who demonstrated loyalty to the apostle or those associated with him.[205] The unjustified pain and suffering he caused to those he removed from the church was an outcome that was of little concern to him.[206]

These illustrations, and the previous discussion about injustice in the church, are not meant in any way to eclipse the love, joy, and fellowship that are routinely found in any body of believers where Jesus is Lord and Savior. What the biblical record tells us, however, is that churches are not exempt from the same tendency toward selfishness that all humans have. The well-known bumper sticker is right: "Christians are not perfect. Just forgiven." Because sin leads to a violation of the second greatest commandment, "to love your neighbor as yourself," injustice occurs in local congregations.

This is all the more reason churches should establish a process that involves members who have been trained to serve as in-house mediators (see Stage 1). They can take parties through a peacemaking process that includes an understanding of how justice can be restored and thus move the work of the church forward. According to both the Old and New Testaments, God requires that those who trust in him uphold justice wherever they are. Jesus was critical of the religious leaders of his day because they failed to do this: "But woe to you Pharisees! For you tithe mint and rue and every herb, and neglect justice and the love of God. These you ought to have done, without neglecting the others" (Luke 11:42).[207]

Overall Summary

Stage 3 is a continuation of Stage 2 in that the peacemaker digs deeper into the aggrieved party's world to uncover the injustice they have experienced. God's holy character requires that justice will ultimately triumph over sin and evil. In like manner, an aggrieved party requires that justice reign in his or her world. As God's demand for justice cannot be overlooked, so the just claims of an aggrieved party should not and must not be given short shrift. In the same way God set forth a vision of ultimate justice for the sins we commit against him, so the peacemaker learns from the aggrieved party what they would consider a just outcome for the wrong they suffered.

Stage 4: Envisioning Shalomic Peace

The Peacemaker Helps the Parties Envision the Shalomic Peace That Could Be

What Is the Scriptural Basis for This Stage?

Introduction: Insight from Augustine
The Concept of Shalomic Peace
    Letter from Captain Sir Edward Hulse
Passages That Envision Shalomic Peace Under
the Rule of God

Like Father, Like Son

Stage 4: Envisioning Shalomic Peace

Practical Examples
    A Positive Approach for Troubled Marriages
    Positive Example from Cambodia
    A Negative Example from the Middle East

What Should the Peacemaker Do?

Specific Application for the Local Church

Does the Church's Vision of Fellowship Embrace
    Imperfect People, Including Its Leaders?
Jesus's Vision for Peter in the Midst of Failure
    Peter's Devotion to Christ
    Peter's Preeminence Among the Disciples
    Peter's Failure
    The Case Against Peter

Specific Application for the Local Church (continued)

Jesus's Vision for Peter
The Aftermath
The Lesson To Be Learned
Reaction to the Fall of Ted Haggard
Lesson Continued

Overall Summary

This stage, like Stage 3, is also a continuation of Stage 2: mediation immersion. After addressing justice, the peacemaker helps the disputants develop a vision of "shalomic peace," a peace that is inclusive of the other side. This section will begin by examining the meaning behind the biblical concept of peace and its practical value in various scenarios. The discussion will conclude with specific application in churches today.

What Is the Scriptural Basis for this Stage?

Introduction: Insight from Augustine

In AD 426, Augustine made the following profound statement about the goals and aspirations of those who wage war.

> Whoever gives even moderate attention to human affairs and to our common nature, will recognize that if there is no man who does not wish to be joyful, neither is there anyone who does not wish to have peace. For even they who make war desire nothing but victory ... And when this is done there is peace. It is therefore with the desire for peace that wars are waged, even by those who take pleasure in exercising their warlike nature in command and battle. And hence it is obvious that peace is the end sought for by war. For every man seeks peace by waging war, but no man seeks war by making peace. For even they

who intentionally interrupt the peace in which they are living have no hatred of peace, but only wish it changed into a peace that suits them better. They do not, therefore, wish to have no peace, but only one more to their mind [i.e., liking].[208]

Augustine observed that even people who wage war are guided by their own vision of peace. War has no integrating power in and of itself. There must be a greater purpose and vision that unites people to fight. Therefore it follows that if people are going to stop battling one another, there must be a common vision that unites them. In the Scriptures, the highest form of peace is "shalomic peace."

The Concept of Shalomic Peace

The concept of "shalomic peace" found in the New Testament originates in the Old Testament.[209] It is based on the Hebrew word for peace, *shalom*. Though *shalom* can mean the absence of strife and war (known as negative peace), it is also rich with a wide range of affirmative meanings (known as positive peace). Nuances of the word include: "fulfillment, completion, maturity, soundness, wholeness (both individual and communal), community, harmony, tranquility, security, well-being, welfare, friendship, agreement, success, and prosperity."[210] In the Old Testament in particular, *shalom* signified peace in a relational and social sense.[211] That is, the emphasis was not on inner peace but on peace with others.[212]

Various authors have sought to succinctly summarize the essence of the concept behind the word *shalom*. Suggestions include: "the way things ought to be,"[213] "unimpaired relationships with others and fulfillment in one's undertakings,"[214] "the end of fragmentation,"[215] and "the presence of justice."[216] Shalomic peace "is a state of existence where the claims and needs of all that is are satisfied, where there is a relationship of communion between God and man and nature, where there is fulfillment for all creation."[217] The following account illustrates the emergence of shalomic peace, if but for one day.

Letter from Captain Sir Edward Hulse

"My Dearest Mother, Just returned to billets [quarters] after the most extraordinary Christmas in the trenches you could possibly imagine. Words fail me completely in trying to describe it, but here it goes!" [218] So began an amazing letter dated Monday, December 28, 1914, by British soldier Captain Sir Edward Hulse in the midst of World War I. The letter received wide circulation both in England and in the U.S.[219] Sadly, the captain was killed in action two and a half months later in France.

It was Wednesday, December 23, when the captain and his troops were ordered to the front line against German troops. The exchange of fire between the warring armies was intense. However, early Friday morning, on December 25, the shooting by the Germans began to subside. By 8:00 a.m., they were not firing at all. At 8:30 Captain Hulse was startled by an unexpected sight. Unarmed, four Germans left their protected positions and began walking toward the British side. Unsure of their intentions and not wanting them to get too close, the captain and one of his men headed out to meet them. Weapons from both sides were pointed at them.

As the men huddled together, Captain Hulse questioned their purpose. "What orders do you have from your officers?" "None," the Germans replied. They came out from their trenches out of goodwill. They wanted to wish their British counterparts a merry Christmas. This is why the German soldiers ceased firing. They said that unless ordered otherwise they were going to withhold their fire.

After thirty minutes, the English party escorted the Germans back to their line of barbed wire. They parted after a friendly exchange of British cigarettes and German cigars. Then Captain Hulse went immediately to headquarters to report the incident.

Returning at 10 a.m., he couldn't believe what his eyes saw in the open space between the two armies: "I saw, to my amazement, not only a crowd of about 150 British and Germans ... [in front of] my lines, but six or seven such crowds, all the way down ... extending toward the 8th Division on our right." The only things left in the trenches were the weapons.

Stunned, Hulse observed that the soldiers "were fraternizing in the most genuine possible manner. Every sort of souvenir was exchanged ... photos of families shown, etc." The captain exclaimed, "It was absolutely astounding, and if I had seen it on film I should have sworn that it was faked!" A British soldier captured the prevailing sentiment. "It's only right that we should show that we could desist from hostilities on a day which is so important in both countries."

The captain went on to describe the day itself. "From foul rain and wet, the weather had cleared up the night before to a sharp frost, and it was a perfect day, everything white, and the silence seemed extraordinary, after the usual din. From all sides birds seemed to arrive, and we hardly ever see a bird generally. Later in the day I fed about 50 sparrows outside my dug-out, which shows how complete the silence was."

During this lull in hostilities, an agreement for the care of the dead was reached. Soldiers who had been killed near the opposing side were carried out to the halfway line where they were honored and buried. Personal effects of the dead were exchanged. The sounds of war were stilled, and shalomic peace emerged for a day among soldiers who were otherwise locked in a struggle for life and death.

Passages That Envision Shalomic Peace Under the Rule of God

Given that we already have discussed the meaning of the word *shalom*, let us turn to sample passages that illustrate the concept. Though he lived in troubled times, around 700 BC, the prophet Isaiah beautifully set forth the vision of shalomic peace at the time when the Messiah will reign over the earth. A picture of social connectedness with God, people, and nature is evident throughout.

Isaiah 2:1-4
1 The word that Isaiah the son of Amoz saw concerning Judah and Jerusalem 2 It shall come to pass in the latter days that the mountain of the house of the Lord shall be established as the highest of the mountains, and shall be lifted up above the hills; and all the nations shall flow to it, 3 and many peoples shall come, and say: "Come, let us go up to the mountain of the Lord, to the house of the God of Jacob, that he may teach us his ways and that we may walk in his paths." For out of Zion [Jerusalem] shall go the law, and the word of the Lord from Jerusalem. 4 He shall judge between the nations, and shall decide disputes for many peoples; and they shall beat their swords into plowshares, and their spears into pruning hooks; nation shall not lift up sword against nation, neither shall they learn war anymore.* [220]

Isaiah 9:6-7
6 For to us a child is born, to us a son is given; and the government shall be upon his shoulder, and his name shall be called Wonderful Counselor, Mighty God, Everlasting Father, Prince of Peace. 7 Of the increase of his government and of peace there will be no end, on the throne of David and over his kingdom, to establish it and to uphold it with justice and with righteousness from this time forth and forevermore. The zeal of the Lord of hosts will do this.

---

* Former secretary-general of the United Nations, Boutros Boutros-Ghali, stated that the words in the latter part of Isaiah 2:4, "They shall beat their swords into plowshares, and their spears into pruning hooks; nation shall not lift up sword against nation, neither shall they learn war anymore," are "the creed of the United Nations" (Boutros-Ghali, 1996, second to last para.).

Isaiah 11:5-9

5 Righteousness shall be the belt of his waist, and faithfulness the belt of his loins. 6 The wolf shall dwell with the lamb, and the leopard shall lie down with the young goat, and the calf and the lion and the fattened calf together; and a little child shall lead them. 7 The cow and the bear shall graze; their young shall lie down together; and the lion shall eat straw like the ox. 8 The nursing child shall play over the hole of the cobra, and the weaned child shall put his hand on the adder's den. 9 They shall not hurt or destroy in all my holy mountain; for the earth shall be full of the knowledge of the LORD as the waters cover the sea.

God's revealed vision of shalomic peace is found in the New Testament as well. The most vivid image is found in the book of Revelation.

Revelation 21:1-4

1 Then I saw a new heaven and a new earth, for the first heaven and the first earth had passed away, and the sea was no more. 2 And I saw the holy city, new Jerusalem, coming down out of heaven from God, prepared as a bride adorned for her husband. 3 And I heard a loud voice from the throne saying, "Behold, the dwelling place of God is with man. He will dwell with them, and they will be his people, and God himself will be with them as their God. 4 He will wipe away every tear from their eyes, and death shall be no more, neither shall there be mourning, nor crying, nor pain anymore, for the former things have passed away."

Like Father, Like Son

In the same way God set forth an image of shalomic peace that includes sinful mankind, so the peacemaker helps disputing parties paint a picture of shalomic peace that is inclusive of the other side.

Stage 4: Envisioning Shalomic Peace

Practical Examples

Let's consider this stage by first viewing different scenarios where imagining a more holistic future with one's adversary paves the way for such a future to become reality.

A Positive Approach for Troubled Marriages

John Gottman, a leading marriage researcher, discovered that couples locked in perpetual conflict and headed for divorce can alter that outcome if they better understand and respect each other's aspirations and dreams. He has demonstrated that many long-standing marital conflicts are not so much about a specific issue. They are more the result of the non-communicated framework through which each spouse thinks and acts. Since the link between a given dispute and one's ideal picture of the world are inseparable, Gottman advises each spouse to become "a dream detector."[221] Each spouse is to simultaneously share and discover his or her mate's highest values and ideals. What does the dream marriage relationship look like for each spouse? Based on years of research and counseling, Gottman found that the mutual understanding, accommodation, and merging of the idealistic dreams of a husband and wife will reduce conflict in their daily interactions and produce a more satisfying marriage.

A Positive Example from Cambodia

Peacemaker John Paul Lederach told of his experience in war-torn Cambodia. He was working in an educational setting with officials who represented all the factions that formed the government in 1994. The genocide that occurred in Cambodia during the years 1975 to 1979 resulted in the death of approximately 1.7 million people, 21 percent of the nation's population.[222] This slaughter came at the hands of its former ruler, Pol Pot, and ruling political party, the Khmer Rouge. It "combined extremist ideology with ethnic animosity and a diabolical disregard for human life to produce repression, misery, and murder on a massive scale."[223] The people at this gathering had all lost family members and friends and/or participated in the killing. Both victims and oppressors were now part of the new government. Lederach wondered how these people were able to work with those who previously were their mortal enemies. The answer was the same. "I do it so my children and grandchildren will never have to suffer as we did." "We must keep our eyes on the children."[224] It was this shared desire for future peace and social harmony for their children that was instrumental in resolving conflict in the present.

A Negative Illustration from the Middle East

In 2006, Mahmoud al-Zahar, cofounder of the Palestinian group Hamas and its newly appointed foreign minister, gave an exclusive interview to the Chinese newspaper *Xinhua*. During the interview he stated, "I dream of hanging a huge map of the world on the wall at my Gaza home which does not show Israel on it. … Our dream [is] to have our independent state on all historic Palestine (including Israel). This dream will become real one day. I'm certain of this because there is no place for the state of Israel on this land."[225]

In a 2007 press conference with the Japanese foreign minister, Israel's foreign minister, Tzipi Livni, stated, "The ideology of Hamas is an extreme ideology and they are not fighting for the national aspirations of the Palestinians. Rather, they are fighting to deprive others of their rights–and the others are us."[226] Obviously, if such divergent visions are not altered, there will be no peace between Israel and the Palestinians. If the Hamas dream for the future denies the existence of Israel as a nation, there will be constant conflict in the region (unless one side annihilates the other). The fundamental conflict is not over any given incident, such as rockets launched from Gaza into Israel or a military incursion by Israeli soldiers into Gaza. The fundamental conflict is over clashing visions of the future. This situation amply demonstrates that if the ideals and dreams are mutually exclusive, permanent peace will be impossible to achieve.

What Should the Peacemaker Do?

At this stage, the peacemaker should probe the ideals anchoring the conflict. The idea here is that if two parties are locked in conflict because of opposing positions on an issue, the way to break the stalemate is to uncover the unspoken vision that guides each side. What is the unexpressed vision behind the stated position? The mediator needs to ask each side what the ideal outcome looks like, one without a hint of conflict, one where positive relationships characterize the picture. "Having a shared vision of the future relationship between the contending communities is critical."[227] Since it is only an understanding of the whole that gives meaning to the parts, an understanding of the ideal future for each side is a prerequisite to negotiating meaningful and long-lasting agreements. The parties "would be able to deal with their differences in the present in light of that perceived future."[228]

By contrast, it is futile for one side to constantly argue over specific details when the other side has rejected the whole picture within which the argument is taking place. That would be like a salesman asking a customer, "Would you like delivery of this large-screen TV by the tenth or the fifteenth of the month?" when the customer, who came into the store to buy an extension cord, has indicated that he has absolutely no interest in making such a purchase.

The peacemaker, therefore, must ask each side what the big picture is for them. It is the peacemaker's task to see if there are any grounds for a common vision and, if there are, to help the parties merge their competing frameworks into a vision large enough to accommodate the other side. Such forward-looking visioning of peace in the midst of conflict has been referred to as exercising "moral imagination." It is exercising the ability "to imagine responses and initiatives that, while rooted in the challenges of the real world, are by their nature capable of rising above destructive patterns and giving birth to that which does not yet exist."[229] Relating to one's current adversary in a positive and affirming way needs to be part of the picture if shalomic peace is to materialize.[230]

Specific Application for the Local Church

Does the Church's Vision of Fellowship Embrace Imperfect People, Including Its Leaders?

There is no question that it is difficult for people to envision peace with those they have negative feelings toward. It is not uncommon for me to hear a church member or lay leader remark with respect to their pastor, "I have lost all respect for him," "I don't trust him," or "He needs to leave." Many congregations have become sharply divided over the senior pastor, whether he should stay, resign, or be removed. How can a church experience harmony when a pastor, whether justified or not, falls short of people's expectations? Does Jesus provide us with a general orientation we should have toward leaders (as well as each other)? The answer is yes.

Jesus's Vision for Peter in the Midst of Failure

Let's look into the life of the apostle Peter, remembering that in the end it is not Peter in whom I am most interested. Rather, it is the mind of Christ. It is Jesus's vision for Peter (and by extension for the church as a whole) in the midst of moral failure that I want us to ponder.

113

Peter's Devotion to Christ

The first thing we learn about Peter is that he was devoted to Jesus. For example, after a number of superficial followers had deserted Jesus, "Jesus said to the Twelve, 'Do you want to go away as well?' Simon Peter answered him, 'Lord, to whom shall we go? You have the words of eternal life, and we have believed, and have come to know, that you are the Holy One of God'" (John 6:67-69). Peter stated, in essence, "Others may leave you but not me!" His commitment to Jesus, witnessed by the other disciples, was unwavering. The night before Jesus's death, Peter said to Jesus, "Though they all fall away because of you, I will never fall away. ... Even if I must die with you, I will not deny you!" (Matt. 26:33, 35). There should be no question about the reality of Peter's devotion to Jesus.

Peter's Preeminence Among the Disciples

The second thing we learn about Peter is that he was a prominent member of Jesus's team. Not only was he one of three members in Jesus's inner circle (see Mark. 5:37; 9:2; 14:33; cf. 3:3), but he was also, in essence, the "captain" of the team of twelve disciples. Of this, there are numerous indications. Every time you find the disciples listed together, Peter's name is mentioned first. For example, in Matthew 10:2 we read, "The names of the twelve apostles are these: first, Simon, who is called Peter, and ..." His prominence is also seen in the fact that his name appears in the New Testament far more than any of the other disciples. Additionally, it was Peter, in distinction from the other disciples, to whom Jesus said He would give "the keys of the kingdom of heaven" (Matt. 16:19). Peter is presented as the leading figure among the disciples in the Gospel accounts as he was moving in lockstep with Jesus.

Peter's Failure

But during the last night of Jesus's life, after the Last Supper, Peter got turned around. Jesus had been arrested and was now being interrogated by Israel's religious leaders during the night. Peter gained entry into the courtyard of the high priest's residence, where the interrogation of Jesus was taking place. We pick up the story in Matthew 26.

> Matthew 26:69-75
> 69 Now Peter was sitting outside in the courtyard. And a servant girl came up to him and said, "You also were with Jesus the Galilean." 70 But he denied it before them all, saying, "I do not know what you mean." 71 And when he went out to the entrance, another servant girl saw him, and she said to the bystanders, "This man was with Jesus of Nazareth." 72 And again he denied it with an oath: "I do not know the man." 73 After a little while the bystanders came up and said to Peter, "Certainly you too are one of them, for your accent betrays you." 74 Then he began to invoke a curse on himself and to swear, "I do not know the man." And immediately the rooster crowed. 75 And Peter remembered the saying of Jesus, "Before the rooster crows, you will deny me three times." And he went out and wept bitterly.

The key question to ask in all this is, how serious was Peter's denial? How serious was his infraction? It was very serious. Just consider Jesus's words. Jesus taught, "Everyone who acknowledges me before men, I also will acknowledge before my Father who is in heaven, but whoever denies me before men, I also will deny before my Father who is in heaven" (Matt. 10:32-33). The Greek word for "deny" that Jesus used here is the same Greek word used to describe what Peter did. Peter's denials of knowing Jesus cannot be lightly dismissed.[231]

115

Think about it. If a person today said, "I have nothing to do with Jesus Christ, I do not confess Him as my Savior, I do not acknowledge Him as special to me in any way," what would we say about such a person? Such an individual has no part in the Christian hope of salvation. To deny Christ is a serious matter, and if that denial reflects the reality of a person's heart, then according to Jesus's own words, that person has no hope of heaven. Peter's denials mirrored what an enemy of Christ might say. This point should not be softened or lost. In addition to this, Peter lied once. Then he lied again. Then, he lied a third time. Peter gave false testimony about what he knew to be true, and he did so with an oath. He committed a serious sin.

Beyond all this, Peter was disloyal to his friend. There is a most poignant moment in this scene that is recorded only by Luke. While Jesus was out in the courtyard of the high priest, apparently being shuffled from one room to another, Jesus saw and heard Peter's last denial. "But Peter said, 'Man, I do not know what you are talking about.' And immediately, while he was still speaking, the rooster crowed. And the Lord turned and looked at Peter. ... And he [Peter] went out and wept bitterly" (Luke 22:60-62).

Peter blew it big time. Earlier that evening, Peter was not alone in his insistence that he would never deny Jesus. All the disciples said the same thing (Matt. 26:35). But the truth of the matter is, only Peter actually disavowed his relationship with Jesus. Only Peter publicly declared that he had no knowledge of Jesus. Only Peter did what everyone said they wouldn't do—only Peter, the captain of the team.

The Case Against Peter

A strong case can be made against Peter's fitness for leadership. Given the fact that during their time with Jesus the disciples had disputes about who was the greatest among them (Luke 9:36-48; 22:44ff; cf. Matt. 20:20ff), it is easy to imagine one of the other disciples readily stepping into Peter's leadership role. Indeed, after

116

his failure to stand strong, it is not at all clear that he was still "in" with the others. Judas, who had betrayed Jesus, was clearly "out." He hung himself (Matt. 27:5). But what about Peter? What role, if any, could he be envisioned to play in the future?

Jesus's Vision for Peter

On Easter morning, when some women came to visit Jesus's tomb, they were met by an angel who told them that Jesus had risen from the dead. Then the angel said to the women, "Go, tell his disciples and Peter that he is going before you to Galilee. There you will see him, just as he told you" (Mark 16:7). Peter was singled out. Why? Peter was given the reassurance he needed that he was not to be excluded from the company of the disciples. Peter received that message, and after he arrived in Galilee, Jesus had this dialogue with him.

> John 21:15-17
> 15 When they had finished breakfast, Jesus said to Simon Peter, "Simon, son of John, do you love me more than these?" He said to him, "Yes, Lord; you know that I love you." He said to him, "Feed my lambs." 16 He said to him a second time, "Simon, son of John, do you love me?" He said to him, "Yes, Lord; you know that I love you." He said to him, "Tend my sheep." 17 He said to him the third time, "Simon, son of John, do you love me?" Peter was grieved because he said to him the third time, "Do you love me?" and he said to him, "Lord, you know everything; you know that I love you." Jesus said to him, "Feed my sheep."

Biblical scholar Leon Morris commented,

> There can be little doubt but that the whole scene is meant to show us Peter as completely restored to his position of leadership. He has three times denied his Lord. Now he has three times affirmed his love for Him, and three times he has been commissioned to care for the flock. This must

117

have had the effect on the others of a demonstration, that whatever had been the mistakes of the past, Jesus was restoring Peter to a place of trust.[232]

Indeed, Jesus always had envisioned Peter being brought back into the fold and restored to his leadership role. This was made unmistakably clear during the Last Supper, when Jesus said to Peter in Luke 22:31-32, "Simon, Simon, behold, Satan demanded to have you, that he might sift you like wheat, but I have prayed for you that your faith may not fail. And when you have turned again, strengthen your brothers."

What Jesus tells us about Peter is that it wasn't Peter's faith that died that night. It was his courage. The critical factor about Peter's denials was that they were more an unfortunate reaction under the pressure of the moment than an accurate reflection of his true heart and allegiance. Jesus told Peter that when he turned back from going down that wrong path, when he retraced his steps, Peter was to strengthen his companions. He was to encourage and lead them once again. What Jesus did here was to give Peter encouragement in advance of the fact. All that Peter would need to do is recall Jesus's words when he was weeping bitterly for what he had done wrong.

The Aftermath

Given Jesus's words to Peter, it should come as no surprise to us what follows in the book of Acts, the New Testament book that provides us with the history of the early church. What we find from the earliest chapters is the unquestioned prominence and leadership of Peter as the one who takes the helm in preaching the good news of the gospel. It was Peter who unlocked the doors to the kingdom of heaven for the Jews in Acts 2, the Samaritans (half-Jews) in Acts 8, and the Gentiles in Acts 10. Only when Peter was present did the Holy Spirit initially come upon each of these three groups. Indeed, if we were to outline the book of Acts biographically, we would find that the book has two major personages. In the second division of the book (chapters 13-28), the apostle Paul is the major personage. At the emergence and foundation of the new church, in chapters 1-12, the major personage is Peter.

The Lesson To Be Learned

Unlike Judas, whose betrayal of the Lord revealed that he was not a true follower of Christ (John 6:70-71; Luke 22:3; Acts 1:25), Peter's momentary lapse did not reflect his abiding, heartfelt commitment to Jesus. Jesus saw Peter in a leadership role, both before Peter's embarrassing episode and after. Jesus's vision of the future was inclusive of Peter, the one who denied him. In the midst of his moral failure, Peter was not true to his own calling and beliefs. Who is, in the midst of sin? Yet, the shalomic peace and fellowship Jesus envisioned for his small company of disciples was inclusive of Peter.

The lesson to be learned is that such an inclusive mind-set ought to be the controlling attitude when it comes to thinking about those in the church who fall short of our expectations and/or disappoint us. Shalomic peace and fellowship in a local assembly are not achieved through separation and exclusion* but through acceptance, encouragement, and grace. Given Jesus's mind-set, this should be a controlling vision for the church.

Reaction to the Fall of Ted Haggard

In 2006, Ted Haggard, senior pastor of the Colorado Springs megachurch, New Life Church, and president of the thirty-million-member National Association of Evangelicals, lost both positions because of immoral behavior unbefitting someone in those positions. He had engaged in homosexual sex and bought methamphetamines.

---

* This was something Jesus constantly battled the Pharisees over. Whereas these religious leaders separated themselves and excluded sinners from their company, Jesus included them (cf. Luke 15:2; 19:7).

119

In November 2008, Haggard was invited by a long-time pastor friend to speak at his 350-member church. An audiotape of Haggard's sermon was briefly posted on the internet.[233] What was of particular interest was not what Haggard had to say about his fall, the shame he brought upon his family, and his remorse and repentance, but the statements that were posted online about his remarks by people from all over the country. There was one comment that not only summarized other postings but also displayed the same kind of attitude Jesus displayed toward Peter. With some minor editing, here is what this person wrote.

> I see three different kinds of anti-Haggard opinions emerging here. Some are anti-Christians who are simply glad to have some basis to "prove" that Christianity is "false." Some are genuine seekers after God who are turned off by what they see as Christian hypocrisy. Some are offended Christians who simply think Haggard is washed up, never to return to ministry. But I remind you that the primary mission of the church is redemptive and restorative. It is explicitly the function of the church to take a total failure like Haggard and seek to restore such a one back into fellowship and into productive work for the kingdom of God. Were we unable to do that, what possible hope could we offer to all the other failures of the world? People fall down. That is a fact of life. The function of the church is to offer them hope that they can get back up again.[234]

In his first broadcast-news interview since the scandal broke, Haggard bluntly stated in a January 2009 *Nightline* interview, "I am a failure." Yet despite his inadequacies, his biological family, his wife and five children, stuck by him. But this was not the case with his spiritual family, that is, people from his former church. Recalling those broken relationships, Haggard sadly reflected, "I thought we were a family. Now, I violated the rules, no question about it. I am responsible. I just never dreamed that the family would throw me out."[235]

Lesson Continued

For Christians who sin, lie, and live hypocritical lives and then repent, the question is this: In the mind of Christ, is there an "after" after the "before and after"? What I mean is: The importance of conversion is huge in terms of the change in direction that occurs in a person's life. Where matters get sticky is how we view those who have come to a saving knowledge of Christ but then get turned around and start heading back in the wrong direction. There is the spiritually blind "before" picture, and then there is the spiritually awakened "after" picture. But how are Christians supposed to react when someone's "after" picture begins to look like his or her "before" picture? I am not talking about those who renounce Christ. I am not talking about a person who has given up his or her faith. I am talking about a Christian who takes the wrong path, brings shame on the name of Christ, and embarrasses one's family, as well as the church of which he or she is a member. The question is, is there recovery and restoration for the repentant Christian? In light of how Jesus responded to Peter, the answer is yes. As one theologian put it, "God is disposed to restore the fallen. His goal is to restore every believer to perfect Christlikeness."[236] Accordingly, peacemakers working in the church should encourage parties in conflict to paint a vision of the future that is inclusive, one that does not seek to amputate but reconnect.

Overall Summary

Even though mankind is in conflict with God and one another, God set forth a future vision of peace when war will be no more. It will be a time of global reconciliation within families, between neighbors, among nations, with the environment, and of course, with God. Until that time arrives, the peacemaker needs to uncover and discuss each disputing party's vision of shalomic peace. The mediator needs to discover the superordinate values and goals of each. Are they large enough to include their adversary? Such a vision is required for peace to emerge. This does not mean that various conditions don't have to be met before peace can be achieved. However, without a preexisting picture of what could be, it will be difficult for real peace to become a reality.[237] God's desire to love and embrace us in a vision of shalomic peace existed prior to setting his peacemaking process into motion for us. In the same way, the peacemaker helps disputing parties paint a picture of shalomic peace that is inclusive of the other side.

Face-to-Face Meetings Versus Shuttle Diplomacy

Face-to-Face Meetings

From Stage 5 onward, the format of the meetings will depend upon the specific conflict. As a general guideline, I recommend that the parties process through the stages together in the same room. This allows for clean, unencumbered communication.

Consider the first summit between U.S. President Ronald Reagan and Mikhail Gorbachev, general secretary of the USSR, which occurred in Geneva in 1985. As each leader spoke with his respective delegations present, tensions in the room began to rise. To bring some relief, Reagan suggested to Gorbachev that just the two of them talk together in private. Gorbachev agreed. The PBS narrative picks up the story: "Narr[ator]: As they walked to a less formal house by the lake, they chatted about Reagan's movie career–the first time they had talked as human beings. Bessmertnykh: Gorbachev immediately ah, started to like Reagan. That was a very surprising thing. I think Reagan had something which was so dear to Gorbachev and that was sincerity. Tarasenko: This human vision and human touch. And when he [Reagan] talked with our leaders, he talked very emotional. And he came across. This is a human being. He is trying to explain himself to you. So maybe for the first time our leaders started to think that on the other side it's not a machine. It's not some robot."[238] Once these two cold war leaders began to more fully communicate to each other as individuals, not merely as negotiators, a warming of the relationship took place. Eventually, this led to a dramatic arms control agreement between the two countries and the end to the cold war.

General Guidelines for Face-to-Face Meetings

Since the goal of the Judeo-Christian model is reconciliation, having the parties successfully work out their issues face-to-face serves to bolster that end. Prior to the peacemaking process, communication between the parties likely has dwindled. Unless the emotions of the parties are so volatile that they would obstruct progress, having the parties meet together enables each side to more fully understand the other. On most occasions, before the issues relating to the conflict are discussed, ground rules are reviewed and agreed upon in order to ensure productive interactions.

Caucusing

The face-to-face approach does not mean that the mediator cannot meet in private with either side at any given point in the process. In fact, such relatively short breaks from group discussion, known as "caucusing," are very useful. Caucusing involves a private meeting between the mediator and one or more people on a given side. It enables the disputant to privately express concerns, ideas, or emotions to the mediator. The conversation may involve clarifying issues, perceptions, positions, or interests. It may involve discussing issues or solutions that one party is not yet ready to discuss in front of the other. It may involve inquiring about possible options to find common ground. It may involve the mediator offering encouragement or even admonishment. In this private setting, the mediator is free to openly express his or her opinions toward the larger goal of moving the process to resolution. Three common guidelines for caucusing are: (1) any party may request one, (2) when the mediator completes his caucus with one side, he or she will offer to meet in private with the other side, and (3) what is discussed during the caucus will remain confidential unless the mediator and the caucusing party decide otherwise.

Caucusing with each party is itself a form of shuttle diplomacy. The difference is that the private meetings the mediator holds with each side are ancillary to the main sessions, where the parties are together. Most of the work is still accomplished when the parties are together. Direct dialogue helps lay the foundation of trust. By working behind the scenes with one side and then the other, the peacemaker helps ensure that the face-to-face meetings are as productive as possible.

Shuttle Diplomacy

Shuttle diplomacy is defined as "the use of a third party to serve as an intermediary or mediator between two parties who do not talk directly. The third party travels frequently back and forth (that is, 'shuttles') between the two primary parties."[239] While the practice of shuttle diplomacy is said to have originated with Henry Kissinger, when he was working for peace in the Middle East in the early 1970s,[240] the practice is actually an ancient one.[241]

Shuttle diplomacy was successfully used during the September 5–17, 1978 meetings between President Carter of the U.S., President Anwar Sadat of Egypt, and Prime Minister Menachem Begin of Israel. Because of the starkly divergent views of the two heads of state, Carter ended up working with each side separately. During the last ten days of the meetings, Sadat and Begin never personally met.[242] All communications went through Carter and his staff.

For mediators, shuttle diplomacy is a fallback approach that keeps parties engaged in the peacemaking process when direct, face-to-face discussions would be counterproductive. The mediator may not realize the need for this until after the parties are in the same room together. Shuttle diplomacy at the beginning of negotiations does not preclude bringing the parties together after progress has been made.

Stage 5: Humanizing One Side to the Other

The Peacemaker Helps Parties in Conflict Understand That There Are No Inherent Differences Between Them

What Is the Scriptural Basis for This Stage?

Like Father, Like Son

Stage 5: Humanizing One Side to the Other
Insights into Human Nature
Obedient Citizens Acting Inhumanly
Dehumanization and Conflict

What Should the Peacemaker Do?
Humanize One Side to the Other
The Reframing Process
Described
Two Specifics
John Howard Griffin

Specific Application for the Local Church
Dehumanization as It Relates to Church Conflict

Overall Summary

Whereas in Stages 1 to 4 the peacemaker's attention is primarily devoted to discovering the perspective of the disputants, in Stage 5 the peacemaker begins to share each disputant's perspective and experience with the other side. People in conflict tend to stereotype their opponents in ways that are unproductive for resolving conflict. The peacemaker seeks to correct false assessments and provides increased understanding of one party to the other. This section will conclude with its relevance for the local church.

What Is the Scriptural Basis for this Stage?

The textual basis for this stage is presented in chapter 3, and I refer you there. In those pages you will see that not only are we all created in the image of God, but because of our moral deficiencies, we also all stand equally condemned. "For there is no distinction: for all have sinned and fall short of the glory of God" (Rom. 3:22b-23). God sees all people in the exact same light because we all share in the same fallen nature.

The apostle Paul spoke of our shared heritage when he stated, "And he [God] made from one man[243] every nation of mankind to live on all the face of the earth" (Acts 17:26). The apostle Paul affirmed "the unity of the human race with a common origin and with God as the Creator."[244] The point here is that there are no inherently superior races and no inherently inferior races. There are no essential differences among us. We are all one and the same and thus equal.

Like Father, Like Son

In the same way God created humanity with no essential differences, so the peacemaker helps parties in conflict understand that there are no inherent differences between them.

Stage 5: Humanizing One Side to the Other

Insights Into Human Nature

Obedient Citizens Acting Inhumanly

The television program, *60 Minutes,* aired a segment entitled, "The Devil Is a Gentleman." The story was about Adolf Eichmann, one of the chief architects of the Holocaust. Reporter Mike Wallace posed a number of questions at the beginning of the piece. Wallace wanted to know what kind of person Eichmann was. Was he a madman or a monster? Or was he something even more frightening? Was it possible that he was simply normal?

The answer came during Wallace's riveting interview with Yahiel Dinur, a concentration camp survivor. He was called to testify against Eichmann at Eichmann's 1961 trial in Jerusalem, almost two decades after the Nazi personally sent him to Auschwitz. Wallace observed that Dinur was thunderstruck simply seeing Eichmann. A film clip of the trial was replayed on the broadcast. Dinur walked into the courtroom. At the sight of Eichmann, Dinur was overtaken by emotion and collapsed.

Why did Dinur crumble? From what he learned in his conversation with Dinur, Wallace reported that at that very moment in time, Dinur suddenly realized that Eichmann was not the godlike figure he had always imagined. Though he was instrumental in the persecution and annihilation of millions of Jews, Eichmann was a plain, ordinary man. At the realization that Eichmann was, in essence, everyman, Dinur recognized that what Eichmann did any other human could do, even himself. Dinur dramatically asserted, "I saw I am capable to do this. I am capable exactly like he."[245]

This is an extraordinary statement made by a Holocaust survivor. Yet it was no exaggeration. Writing about Eichmann and his trial, Hannah Arendt coined the phrase "the banality of evil"[246] to convey the idea that evil is not found in a clearly identifiable human monster who is qualitatively different from the rest of us. Eichmann was an average, even bland man, who lacked the imagination or independence to question the Nazi machine of which he was but a cog. In this vein, author, C. P. Snow, soberly concluded, "When you think of the long and gloomy history of man, you will find more hideous crimes have been committed in the name of obedience than have ever been committed in the name of rebellion."[247]

The truth is that countless thousands of loyal German citizens were involved in their country's campaign of annihilation against the Jews. What can be said about them? "It was not crazed lunatics who created and managed the Holocaust, but highly rational and otherwise quite normal bureaucrats."[248] Nazi physicians during the Hitler era were loving husbands and fathers at home, even though they were cruelly torturing and murdering Jews as part of their professional lives.* As *60 Minutes* correspondent Morley Safer reminded viewers in a different Holocaust story, "Evil can have a very ordinary face."[249] Indeed, those who engage in committing atrocities look like you and me.** The

---

* One human rights worker who spent 14 years studying the Rwanda holocaust similarly observed that it was not "monsters" who carried out the deaths of 800,000 people in 100 days. They included pillars of the community. "Doctors, politicians and teachers were as brutally complicit as everyone else" (quoted in Cose, 2008, para. 8). Education is no firewall against engaging in evil.

** For decades, until 1990, blacks in South Africa suffered under a prejudicial, oppressive, and murderous system known as apartheid. (For more information, see the section entitled, "The South Africa Experience," located after Stage 12.) Bishop Desmond Tutu served as the chairman of the Truth and Reconciliation Commission in South Africa, which investigated atrocities during that period. People came in droves to testify. Tutu remarked about those who caused incalculable harm and sorrow, "They did not grow horns on their foreheads or have tails hidden in their trousers. They looked just like you and me" (Tutu, 1999a, p. 144).

uncomfortable truth is that we are all the same.*

Dehumanization and Conflict

There was one difference between the Nazis and the Jews. The Nazis dehumanized the Jews. That is, they considered the Jews less than fully human. They considered them a sub-race of people who were not worthy of the same respect, rights, and treatment one would offer a person who is considered an equal.[250] With this belief firmly fixed in the Nazis' thinking, one can better understand the resultant inhumane treatment and slaughter of six million Jews. Ironically, by imagining they were so superior, the Nazis plummeted to the depths of human depravity.**

The road that leads to ill-treatment and violence against others has been described as a threefold process: (1) clump members of the opposition into a single, indistinguishable group, (2) become harshly critical of the entire group by amplifying and exaggerating differences from your group, and (3) demonize the other group as evil. Then, attacking the out-group seemingly becomes justifiable.[251]

---

* Forensic psychiatrist Dr. Robert Simon, after forty years of work, concluded that there is no discernible difference in the mental life between the criminal and the law-abiding citizen. The only difference between the two groups is succinctly captured in the title to his book, *Bad Men Do What Good Men Dream* (2008). That is, whereas a good man may daydream about hurting an adversary, the less restrained man does it. Otherwise, in terms of thought process, there is no difference. Another psychologist reported that studies "clearly show how the histories of men and women who perpetrate terrible deeds are rooted in the same moral humanity as the rest of us" (Gobodo-Madikizela, 2002, p. 27).

** Consider the social experiment Bandura and colleagues conducted to test the effects of dehumanization among college students. Subjects were told that they would be evaluating the answers of other students and would give these students varying degrees of electrical shocks for giving wrong responses. (There were no shocks actually delivered, but the subjects did not know this). One set of subjects inadvertently heard (which was actually by plan) that the students they would be evaluating were a "perceptive, understanding, and otherwise humanized group." By contrast, other subjects were told that the students were "an animalistic, rotten bunch." It was found that subjects in the dehumanized group received much higher levels of electrical shock when they gave wrong answers compared to the shock levels given to the humanized group for the same wrong answers (Bandura, et. al., 1975, p. 258).

That this phenomenon of differentiation leads to dehumanization is readily seen by anthropologists, even when no conflict
is involved. "That is, we are all raised to believe that our ways
are 'normal' and other ways are therefore, by definition, different.
Each culture thinks its own ways are superior."[252] This translates
into the universal tendency to perceive other/different ethnic
groups in an unflattering and derogatory manner.[253] When
conflict is added to this natural tendency, it is likely that each
side will perceive the other in an increasingly less human and
relatable fashion.

Indeed, it has been argued that ethnicity is the cause of
the bloodiest, most destructive, and most enduring conflicts
on earth, more so than national interests or religion.[254] Here's
why. The victors of war often expand their national boundaries,
incorporating the territory of the defeated foes. The victors
may disallow the practice of the native religion and promote
the indoctrination of the victor's religion or, as in the case in
Communist countries, suppress religious expression and teach
atheism. What cannot be changed, however, is the ethnicity of
the vanquished foe. Borders can be changed. People can be
forced to practice a different religion. But the ethnic identities of
the defeated cannot be altered. Hitler wanted to create a super
race of blond, blue-eyed Aryans. That could occur only through
extermination. The consequences were devastating. In the end,
he failed. But his attempt clearly demonstrates why conflicts
centered on the denigrated identity of the enemy are the most
destructive of all. The only way to vanquish such enemies is to
destroy them.

What Should the Peacemaker Do?

Humanize One Side to the Other

Clearly, as long as people on one side of a dispute view those on the other side as significantly different from themselves in a negative way, there is little possibility of a trusting relationship.[255] The peacemaker is therefore called upon to break any dehumanizing perceptions because, at root, they are patently false. The peacemaker must work to reveal the mutual humanity of each side to the other.

Consider the story of Robert Desnos, a French poet known for his vivid imagination. In 1944, he was arrested by the German Gestapo and sent to a Nazi concentration camp because of his work with the French Resistance. One day Desnos and other camp prisoners were ordered to board the back of a truck. The packed vehicle drove away from the barracks. The riders suspected they were being taken to be killed. The mood was somber. As the truck arrived at its destination, the prisoners got out and stood in line. Everyone was silent, even the guards. Suddenly, Desnos seized the hand of the prisoner next to him. He began to read his palm out loud with exuberance. He exclaimed, "Oh, I see you have a very long lifeline. You are going to have three children." Everyone was dumbstruck. Undeterred, Desnos went to the next hand and then to the next. He enthusiastically predicted abundant lives of longevity, joy, and children. The mood quickly lightened. From foreboding and gloom, there was animation and unexpected levity. Remembrances of the past and hopes for the future surfaced. A change also took place in the guards, so much so that they were unable to carry out this particular mission. They saw in the aspiration of the prisoners their own hopes and dreams for the future. For a penetrating moment, the guards could not deny the humanity of the prisoners they were supposed to murder. The men in uniform saw that those in prison garb were no different than they. Unexpectedly,

133

they packed the prisoners back onto the truck and returned them to the barracks. Although Desnos was not among them, at least one of these prisoners survived to tell the story.[256]

The Reframing Process

Described

In order to help parties in conflict to see the other side in more relatable terms, peacemakers will need to employ a process known as "reframing." Framing relates to the way we perceive things, someone or something, in a good light or a negative one. Reframing refers to a change in one's earlier perception. One comes to see the same situation or another person in a different way. It can have a transformative impact.

A helpful illustration of how reframing works can be gleaned from a "Dear Abby" letter. A seventy-four-year-old woman wrote about her experience as a bashful, fourteen-year-old teenager living in a Catholic boarding school. The sisters suggested that she take a class in drama to overcome her shyness. The course required students to stand before fellow students and recite poetry. The woman recalled that her cheeks burned red every time she had to perform. Eventually, she shared her sense of embarrassment about her blushing with one of her teachers. The teacher told the young girl that there were thousands of women in the country who would love to have rosy cheeks to beautify their complexion. Something clicked for the teen. The words had their intended effect. From that time forward, she looked at her flushed cheeks in a completely different manner. Reality didn't change. Her perspective did. So significant was the impact of the teacher's words and her own change of perception, that she vividly and gratefully recalled the moment sixty years later!

In settings involving conflict, reframing doesn't change who the other person is or what the other person has done. It simply changes the way the aggrieved party views that person or behavior. "Reframing is, among other things, a process whereby the wrongdoer can be regarded as someone over and above the wrong he has committed, a means of 'separating' the wrongdoer from the wrong he has done."[257] On this point, C. S. Lewis famously wrote,

> I remember Christian teachers telling me long ago that I must hate a bad man's actions, but not hate the bad man: or, as they would say, hate the sin but not the sinner. For a long time I used to think, this is a silly, straw-splitting distinction: how could you hate what a man did and not hate the man? But years later it occurred to me that there is one man to whom I had been doing this all my life – namely myself. However much I might dislike my own cowardice or conceit or greed, I went on loving myself. There had never been the slightest difficulty about it.[258]

There is likely not a person on the planet who cannot identify with such words. We have all established in our minds a wall that separates who we are from what we do. Why? Because who we consider ourselves to be and what we do at a given moment are not necessarily the same. Yet how many of us equate the person and the action when thinking of the one with whom we are in conflict? As hurt individuals, we often shrink a person down to the size of the act that was committed against us. The worse the offense, the more reductionistic and simplistic the description. "He is nothing more than a 'rotten apple.'" "She is nothing more than a 'chronic liar.'" Every such description only serves to diminish one's ability to relate to that person. The person becomes known, totally and completely, by what he or she did wrong.[259]

The fact is, we are all more than any bad act we commit. In 1726, Joseph Butler advised against such reductionism when he said, "Resentment should surely, at least, be confined to that particular part of the behaviour which gave offence, since the other parts of a man's life and character stand just the same as they did before."[260]   Convict Charles Diggs, who is serving a life sentence, aptly remarked, "What a guy's in jail for probably only took a few seconds. That's not the whole person. That's just a couple of minutes out of the person's life. There are more dimensions to that person."[261]   Indeed, people are referred to as criminals, not because they are committing a crime every waking moment of their lives, but because of the comparatively short time frame in their lives when they were breaking the law. Each one of us is more than a given instant or even period in our lives.

An article published by NASA's Career Management Office, tells the story of an old woman who died in the geriatric ward of a small hospital near Dundee, Scotland. After her death, the nurses went through the woman's belongings and came across an eloquent poem, now widely distributed, entitled, "A Crabbit Old Woman." It poignantly captures the truth that human beings are more than the negative reducing assessments we tend to make about each other based on a relatively brief period in a person's life. The poem is reproduced below.

> What do you see, nurses, what do you see?
> What are you thinking when you're looking at me?
> A crabby old woman, not very wise,
> Uncertain of habit, with faraway eyes?
> Who dribbles her food and makes no reply,
> When you say in a loud voice, "I do wish you'd try!"
> Who seems not to notice the things that you do,
> And forever is losing a stocking or shoe.
> Who, resisting or not, lets you do as you will,
> With bathing and feeding, the long day to fill...
> Is that what you're thinking? Is that what you see?
> Then open your eyes, nurse; you're not looking at me.
> I'll tell you who I am as I sit here so still,
> As I do at your bidding, as I eat at your will.
> I'm a small child of ten ... with a father and mother,

Brothers and sisters, who love one another.
A young girl of sixteen, with wings on her feet,
Dreaming that soon now a lover she'll meet.
A bride soon at twenty – my heart gives a leap,
Remembering the vows that I promised to keep.
At twenty-five now, I have young of my own,
Who need me to guide and secure a happy home.
A woman of thirty, my young now grown fast,
Bound to each other with ties that should last.
At forty, my young sons have grown and are gone,
But my man's beside me to see I don't mourn.
At fifty, once more babies play round my knee,
Again we know children, my loved one and me.
Dark days are upon me, my husband is dead.
I look at the future, I shudder with dread.
For my young are all rearing young of their own,
And I think of the years and the love that I've known.
I'm now an old woman … and nature is cruel;
'Tis jest to make old age look like a fool.
The body, it crumbles, grace and vigor depart,
There is now a stone where I once had a heart.
But inside this old carcass a young girl still dwells,
And now and again my battered heart swells.
I remember the joys, I remember the pain,
And I'm loving and living life over again.
I think of the years ... all too few, gone too fast,
And accept the stark fact that nothing can last.
So open your eyes, nurses, open and see,
Not a crabby old woman; look closer, see ME!![262]

This is a poignant and excellent example of reframing.

Two Specifics

Peacemakers must do at least two things when it comes to reframing. First, they need to try to remove the use of negative stereotyping from the discussion, both in private and in public. Let an aggrieved party vent all they want. Let them find fault in what the other party said or did or didn't say or do. Allow the parties to be as verbal and expressive as they must. The only thing they must agree not to do is call or use names in order to pigeonhole others by one- or two-word descriptors. Sweeping statements that reduce the other person's or group's entire identity to a label must be contested.

Second, the mediator needs to help the injured party begin to see "the offender's underlying humanity masked by the offense."[263] Henry Wadsworth Longfellow wrote, "If we could read the secret history of our enemies, we should find in each man's life sorrow and suffering enough to disarm all hostility."[264] Peacemakers should gather every argument, fact, and illustration they can assemble to unfreeze the perspective of those parties who have framed their opponents in a narrowly denigrated fashion.

Reframing is essential in the conflict-resolution process. If the two parties do not have a more empathetic understanding and humanized view of each other, negotiating shalomic peace is near impossible. This is not to say or mean that justice in a given situation is not required. It is. But it is to say that beyond the condemnable act there is a human being who, at core, is just like you and me. It is little wonder that the expression, "There but for the grace of God go I," has been around for almost five hundred years. It has resonated down through the centuries because people know it to be true.

John Howard Griffin

John Howard Griffin provides an outstanding case in point.[265] Griffin, a white man, darkened his skin and lived as a black man in the South for six weeks. The time was the late 1950s, and prejudice against blacks by whites in the Deep South was strong.

He tells of the days when he was walking and hitchhiking from Biloxi, Mississippi to Mobile, Alabama. During the day, no one gave him a ride. However, after the sun went down, on one night alone, a dozen or so white drivers gave him a lift as they drove him closer to his destination. Why did they pick Griffin up at night but not during the day? It was because they wanted to talk about the sex life of black men and black women. In the darkness of night, there was a sense of anonymity. Men would talk about and inquire about things they would never say in the light of day—topics that Griffin considered degenerate. Why would these white men have a conversation with a black man that they would not consider having with their own friends? Griffin explained that they viewed the Negro as a species significantly different from and lower than their own.

Griffin told of one particular ride. The man who picked him up along the road was fifty-three. He was married and had children and grandchildren. No doubt, he was a respected man in his community, perhaps even a civic leader. Yet the salacious nature of his conversation and his arrogant and cavalier attitude toward blacks belied his respectability. He boasted that no Negro woman would be hired for work in his home or in his business without first having sex with him. If they wanted the job, if they wanted to put food on the table, they accommodated his sexual desires. Toward the males, his attitude was much more belligerent, explaining how easy it would be to get troublemakers shipped off to prison or killed without anyone raising an eyebrow. Griffin surmised that no one ever saw this cruel and ugly aspect of the man, not his white friends, and certainly not his wife. It was a side that only his black victims saw.

Why do I share this account? It is because of the rather amazing attitude Griffin adopted in trying to properly think about this man (and others like him). He refused to deny the driver's humanity. He refused to make a global assessment solely on the way this man viewed and treated blacks. Griffin recounts that he forced himself to see this man in his other, more commendable roles in life. "I saw him as he played with his grandchildren, as he stood up in church with open hymnal in hand, as he drank a cup of coffee in the morning before dressing and then shaved and talked with his wife on the front porch Sunday afternoons."[266] Reframing the picture of the man required real effort on Griffin's part. Yet he was right in expending the effort because there was truth in seeing the driver as more than he revealed in that conversation.

A peacemaker must work on challenging the perspective of a disputant who says, as one man said about another, "Let's get this straight. We're dealing with a subhuman species here—this is not a human being we're dealing with."[267] Only by moving both sides toward recognizing the other's humanity will the parties be in a better position to resolve their conflict.

Specific Application for the Local Church

Dehumanization as It Relates to Church Conflict

The phenomenon of classifying opponents in spiritually unflattering terms is not unfamiliar to congregational settings. Consider two popular books on church conflict. The first one is entitled *Well-Intentioned Dragons*. It specifically creates all kinds of categories to describe church members who are problem people. Such well-intentioned "dragons" are further labeled as the "Bird Dog," Superspiritual Bird Dog," "Wet Blanket," "Entrepreneur," "Captain Bluster," "Fickle Financier," "Busybody," "Sniper," "Bookkeeper," "Merchant of Muck," and "Legalist."[268]

The second book, *Antagonists in the Church*, takes an even less sympathetic approach. The individuals described in this book are anything but well intentioned. Antagonists are categorized in three ways: as (1) "hard-core," (2) "major," and (3) "moderate." Hard-core antagonists are individuals who are mentally disturbed, psychotic, and discon-nected from reality. Major antagonists are not as severely unbalanced as hard-core ones. They simply choose to be unreasonable. They possess deep-seated personality and character disorders. Moderate antagonists have problem personalities that are simply less severe than the first two groups. Yet, regardless of which category an antagonist falls into, they are all motivated by malevolence.[269]

The problem with clumping individuals into either set of predefined categories is that it is counterproductive to pastoral ministry. It does nothing to add to a mind-set that is oriented toward social harmony. To the contrary, it subtracts from it. As soon as a given individual reminds the pastor of some category he read in a book, that person is now so classified; such reframing becomes a hindrance, not a help. Such labels vilify by narrowly defining who a person is. In essence, they dehumanize. Not only are such labels a blot on a person's identity, but they also lead to intolerance. It sets up a defensive "me-versus-them" paradigm. Once people are negatively labeled, it is relatively easy for the pastor to write them off and treat them dismissively. This is not to say that pastors don't deal with people who cause them real problems, or for that matter, that staff, lay leaders or church members don't have real problems with pastors.[270] Resolution, however, will not be found in reducing people to their most negatively perceived characteristics and then globalizing those characteristics to describe the whole person. Such an approach is never helpful in terms of making peace. It is erroneous. The image of God in each one of us is far bigger than that!

Overall Summary

The conclusion to be drawn from this chapter is that even though we may act differently, in our essence we are all the same. This simple truth gets lost in the pain and suffering one endures at the hands of others. Coming to grips with this truth will not resolve conflict. But, as we shall see, it is an important building block to making peace. Monsters and demons don't make peace. Only people do. In the same way God created humanity with no essential differences, so the peacemaker helps parties in conflict understand that there are no inherent differences between them.

Monsters and demons don't make peace. Only people do.

Stage 6: Seeing the Error of One's Ways

The Peacemaker Helps Offending Parties See the Error of Their Ways

What Is the Scriptural Basis for This Stage?

Repentance
  Definition
  A Negative Illustration
  Repentance with Respect to God
Summary

Like Father, Like Son

Stage 6: Seeing the Error of One's Ways

The Story of Facilitated Communication

What Should the Peacemaker Do?

Address Factors That Contribute to Making Wrong Assessments
  Subjectivity
  Self-centeredness
  Nonrational Emotionality
Address Factors That Help the Parties Get It Right
  Veil of Ignorance
  Appeal to Deeper Beliefs
  Amplify Entrenched Thinking to Highlight Risks
  Raise Doubts
  Look to Objective Sources of Authority or Standards of Practice
  Gain Insight from an Impasse

Overall Summary

This stage addresses what can be the arduous process of helping parties see the error of their ways. The peacemaker has entry into the disputant's life at the point of contention that few others have. As a nonthreatening presence, the peacemaker asks the disputant to entertain ideas that would be rejected if presented by the other side. This section begins by looking at the biblical concept of repentance. It then looks at reasons why people sometimes get it wrong. This is followed by an extended discussion on ways people's thinking can be altered to see things in a new, more accurate light.

What Is the Scriptural Basis for this Stage?

Repentance

Definition

The foundation for this stage is based on the biblical concept of repentance. The Greek word for "repent" literally means "to perceive afterwards."[271] It means to change one's mind, to see things differently. In the New Testament, the change is always for the better.[272] Perception becomes clearer and more accurate.

In his commentary on Matthew 3:2* and his discussion of the word *repent*,[273] Greek scholar A. T. Robertson recalled the comments of Broadus, who said that the translation "repent" for the Greek word that is used in this verse was the "worst" translation in the New Testament. Robertson explained, "The trouble is that the English word 'repent' means 'to be sorry again' from the Latin *repoenitet* (impersonal). John [the Baptist] did not call on the people to be sorry, but to change (think afterwards) their mental attitudes and conduct."[274] The emphasis is on reflection in order to change course. In the New Testament, the focus is not on contrition, but on "the total change, both in thought and behavior, with respect to how

---

* Matthew 3:1-2 reads, "In those days John the Baptist came preaching in the wilderness of Judea, "Repent, for the kingdom of heaven is at hand."

one should both think and act."[275] "The decision by the whole man to turn round is stressed."[276] The need for repentance implies that what a person has been thinking (and doing) has been wrong.

A Negative Illustration

Some people are unable to admit error because their past judgments are so closely identified with who they are. Take the case of Sergei Akhromeyev. After a lifetime of military service and rising to become chief of staff over the Soviet Union's armed forces, Akhromeyev proudly retired in 1988. Soon thereafter, however, he was aghast to witness dramatic waves of political upheaval. The Soviet Union was breaking apart into independent states, East Germany was unifying with West Germany, and the Warsaw Pact was dissolving. At the core of all these changes was the demise of Akhromeyev's beloved Communist Party. Almost overnight, Akhromeyev found himself swimming against the tide of public opinion. One day when he was walking down the street in his military uniform, people started throwing things at him and spitting at him. This wave of public opinion even included his own family. "My daughter doesn't understand me," he complained. "She thinks I'm all wrong. She thinks I ought to shut up and get out of the way. I'm outdated."[277] Akhromeyev could not bring himself to admit that so much of what went wrong in the Soviet Union was due to the communist system itself (i.e. state ownership, totalitarian rule, atheism, etc.). It was too self-condemning a realization. Akhromeyev became despondent. He remarked, "Isn't it depressing to conclude that what you've worked and fought for for fifty years is wrong, and even more depressing to find out at my age that you have to start all over."[278] Rather than accept this as reality, rather than reflect back on his life's work and admit that much of it was for naught, rather than repent (change his thinking), he committed suicide. He could not face the truth that for a lifetime he believed in and defended the system of communism that ultimately brought his country to ruin.

Repentance with Respect to God

The focus of repentance in the Bible is for people to turn away from sinning against God. "The sinner consciously forsakes the old sinful life and turns to a life in communion with and devoted to God."[279] Feelings of remorse and shame are likely to be a consequence of one's new thinking. Such feelings by themselves, however, do not constitute repentance.[280] It is the realization that the path one has been on is wrong in the eyes of God and then acting accordingly.[281]

The apostle Paul is an excellent case study of repentance at work. Before he made peace with God, he was a violent persecutor of the church. We read,

> Acts 8:1-3
> 1 And Saul* approved of his [Stephen's] execution. And there arose on that day a great persecution against the church in Jerusalem, and they were all scattered throughout the regions of Judea and Samaria, except the apostles. 2 Devout men buried Stephen and made great lamentation over him. 3 But Saul was ravaging the church, and entering house after house, he dragged off men and women and committed them to prison.

Shortly thereafter, however, Saul had an encounter with the risen Christ and came to realize the error of his ways (Acts 9:1-9; see also Acts 22:1-21; 26:1-23). He turned 180 degrees in his thinking and behavior. In fact, it was so dramatic a turnaround that others took immediate notice. We read,

> Acts 9:20-22
> 20 And immediately he [Saul] proclaimed Jesus in the synagogues, saying, "He is the Son of God." 21 And all who heard him were amazed and said, "Is not this the man who made havoc in Jerusalem of those who called upon this

---

* Saul was the apostle's Hebrew name. Paul was his Roman name.

name? And has he not come here for this purpose, to bring them bound before the chief priests?" 22 But Saul increased all the more in strength, and confounded the Jews who lived in Damascus by proving that Jesus was the Christ.

Later in life Paul looked back to this time and wrote, "And I was still unknown in person to the churches of Judea that are in Christ. They only were hearing it said, 'He who used to persecute us is now preaching the faith he once tried to destroy'" (Gal. 1:22-23). Paul provided a graphic picture of repentance with respect to God. He came to realize that what he was doing and the thinking that was behind it were wrong and that he was fighting, not for God, but against God (see Acts 26:14). His new thinking led him to experience peace with God.

Passages that call for repentance in the New Testament include the following texts.[282]

Luke 3:7-8, 10-14
7 He [John the Baptist] said therefore to the crowds that came out to be baptized by him, "You brood of vipers! Who warned you to flee from the wrath to come? 8 Bear fruits in keeping with repentance. ... 10 And the crowds asked him, "What then shall we do?" 11 And he answered them, "Whoever has two tunics is to share with him who has none, and whoever has food is to do likewise." 12 Tax collectors also came to be baptized and said to him, "Teacher, what shall we do?" 13 And he said to them, "Collect no more than you are authorized to do." 14 Soldiers also asked him, "And we, what shall we do?" And he said to them, "Do not extort money from anyone by threats or by false accusation, and be content with your wages."

Matthew 4:17
From that time Jesus began to preach, saying, "Repent, for the kingdom of heaven is at hand."

Luke 15:10
"Just so, I [Jesus] tell you, there is joy before the angels of God over one sinner who repents."

Acts 3:17, 19-20
17 "And now, brothers ... 19 Repent therefore, and turn again, that your sins may be blotted out, 20 that times of refreshing may come from the presence of the Lord."

The following passages are representative texts found in the Old Testament that call for repentance. The New Testament perspective on this subject is simply a continuation of what is found in the Old Testament.

Isaiah 55:6-7
6 Seek the Lord while he may be found; call upon him while he is near; 7 let the wicked forsake his way, and the unrighteous man his thoughts; let him return to the LORD, that he may have compassion on him, and to our God, for he will abundantly pardon.

Ezekiel 18:30b-32
30 "Repent and turn from all your transgressions, lest iniquity be your ruin. 31 Cast away from you all the transgressions that you have committed, and make yourselves a new heart and a new spirit! Why will you die, O house of Israel? 32 For I have no pleasure in the death of anyone, declares the Lord God; so turn, and live."

Daniel 9:3, 5-6 (what repentance in prayer looks like)
3 Then I turned my face to the Lord God, seeking him by prayer and pleas for mercy with fasting and sackcloth and ashes. ... 5 we have sinned and done wrong and acted wickedly and rebelled, turning aside from your commandments and rules. 6 We have not listened to your servants the prophets, who spoke in your name to our

kings, our princes, and our fathers, and to all the people of the land.

Summary

The first word of the gospel message from both John the Baptist and Jesus is *repent.* The theme is carried throughout the rest of the New Testament, a theme that is firmly rooted in the Old Testament. Within rabbinic tradition, repentance was such a necessary component of one's relationship with God that it was viewed as one of seven things created before the beginning of the world.[283] According to the Bible, changing one's estranged relationship with God begins with a change in one's thinking. For things to be right with God, man has to first recognize that he has been wrong. This then will be reflected in a change of behavior. The road to experiencing peace with God begins when people recognize the error of their ways, see things from God's perspective as revealed in the Scriptures, and act in light of their new understanding.

Like Father, Like Son

In the same way sinners are urged to change the erroneous thinking that has brought them into conflict with God, so the peacemaker helps offending parties see the error of their ways.

Stage 6: Seeing the Error of One's Ways

The Story of Facilitated Communication

Robert* drove home from his job as a pharmacist at a veteran's hospital one day and was met by his wife, who frantically came rushing out of the house. She told her husband that he could not enter their home. Nor was he allowed anywhere near their seventeen-year-old autistic son. A warrant had been issued for the man's arrest. Authorities alleged that this father had sexually abused his son. The language used to detail the abuse was graphic. The father protested his innocence. The mother knew the charges were false. Nevertheless, for the next six months Robert was forced out of his home. He was allowed no contact with his son. His family life was in tatters and his future unclear.

But we are getting ahead of ourselves. Let's go back to a happier time, one of unabashed optimism. In January 1992, Diane Sawyer hosted a segment of the television program *Primetime*. She began, "And now a story about hope. For decades, autism has been a dark mystery, a disorder that seems to turn children in on themselves. ... Tonight, however, you are going to see something that has changed that. Call it a miracle. Call it an awakening."[284] Call it facilitated communication (FC for short).

For the first time ever, autistic children, who historically had been diagnosed with a brain development disorder, were showing the world that it was wrong. Many such children were now doing algebra, diagramming sentences, writing poetry, and expressing their feelings. They did this through the help of facilitators who held up and supported their arms. The autistic children would then touch letters or numbers on a keyboard to spell out their thoughts.

---

* This is not his real name.

Interest in this new discovery began to spread like wildfire. By 1994, thousands of people were being trained as facilitators, and millions of dollars were being spent to help autistic children communicate in ways never dreamed of before.[285] Parents who had long wished to converse with their noncommunicative children had new hope that they would be able to do just that. When one mother saw the first words her daughter spelled out, she exclaimed, "I just felt like I was looking down into a well and my daughter was there, down at the bottom of the well, and I was seeing her for the first time."[286] In fact, so amazing was the output of some of these youngsters that people began to wonder whether it was the child or the facilitator who was responsible for the typing. It was not uncommon for an autistic child to type out words without looking at the letters on the keyboard. How could this be?

Then came an unexpected development. As this new communication technique for autistic children spread throughout the country, so did allegations of sexual abuse. Children were alleging that a parent or a teacher was sexually abusing them. Some parents were forced to leave their homes and have no contact with their children. Others were jailed. Still other parents had their children taken from them. Families were being ripped apart as the state stepped in to insure the safety of these children. Yet parents were tearfully insisting upon their innocence. Definitive answers about the validity of facilitated communication were needed.

Tests were set up. For example, the facilitator and child would sit side by side at one end of a long, rectangular table, facing the other end. Running down the middle of the table was a partition so that the facilitator could not see what the child saw and the child could not see what the facilitator saw. Initially, both facilitator and child were shown the same pictures, and the child, with the facilitator's help, correctly typed out what was shown to both. Then, the child was shown one picture and the facilitator was simultaneously shown another. What was typed was the name of the item the facilitator saw, not the item that only the child saw.

At the O. D. Heck Center for the Developmentally Disabled in New York, where facilitated communication had been enthusiastically practiced, there was not a single valid communication after 180 such trials. Ray Paglieri, director of the autism program at the center, had to tell well-meaning facilitators that the children were not typing the words. The facilitators were. The relationships the facilitators thought they had with the children were, in reality, conversations that they had with themselves.

The reaction? Mr. Jim Maruska, a facilitator at the Heck Center, admitted that he cried and likened the discovery to the death of a close friend. Suddenly, what was so real no longer existed. "I centered a lot of things around this and now, all of a sudden, 'No, it's not.'"[287] Marian Pitsas, a speech pathologist and facilitator at the Heck Center, was distraught. She had to tell parents that facilitated communication "wasn't real."[288] She had to acknowledge to herself that she was "dead wrong" about the whole thing.[289] For months, she could not breach the subject without dissolving into tears. As time passed, she came to recognize how the emotionality of the situation overwhelmed her rational thinking. The experience of Heck Center psychologist Dr. Doug Wheeler was much the same. He said he should have discerned that facilitated communication was flawed, but, because he "was so caught up in the emotionality of it," he didn't.[290]

In the case of the pharmacist who was accused of sexually abusing his son, he had to make nine court appearances. During this time, an independent test on facilitated communication was performed. It was determined that the son did not and could not type out words on a keyboard, let alone make accusations of sexual abuse. The case was finally dropped. Father and family were reunited. The facilitator left the state.[291]

By the end of 1993, not one of over a dozen studies could demonstrate that the facilitated communication ever originated with the child. Instead of unlocking the hidden thoughts of autistic children, the technique uncovered instead the unconscious thoughts of the facilitators. The media got hold of the story. Morley Safer's *60 Minutes* report examined claims that facilitated communication worked brilliantly. The program concluded with these words, "So far, there is no convincing objective evidence to support those claims."[292] Hugh Downs on ABC's *20/20* came to a similar conclusion. A PBS documentary went so far as to describe an institute at Syracuse University "dedicated to facilitated communication as, researching, teaching, and promoting a technique that all the scientific evidence says is not real."[293] In 1994, the Council for the American Psychological Association (APA) passed the following motion: "Be It Resolved that APA adopts the position that facilitated communication is a controversial and unproved communicative procedure with no scientifically demonstrated support for its efficacy."[294] In 2003, the association reaffirmed its position, stating, "Study after study showed that facilitated communication didn't really work."[295] In June 2008, the American Academy of Child and Adolescent Psychiatry reaffirmed its earlier 1993 policy statement, stating, "Studies have repeatedly demonstrated that FC is not a scientifically valid technique for individuals with autism or mental retardation. In particular, information obtained via (FC) should not be used to confirm or deny allegations of abuse or to make diagnostic or treatment decisions."[296]

There is nothing to suggest that the hundreds of educated and dedicated facilitators were given to delusions, which only makes this story all the more amazing. What is so striking is that those who were doing the facilitation were unaware that they themselves were the ones who were typing out the messages. They were the source of the communication, not the children. What these cases make clear is how a person's emotionality, coupled with the baseless conviction that he or she already has the right answer, can produce an error of major proportions.[297] Where this case differs from most others is that the facilitators were not only wrong about what facilitated communication could do, but they also were wrong about the very thoughts and thought processes going on inside their own heads. They were not only wrong about the program itself but also, incredibly, wrong about their own role in it.

153

If such could be the case with normal, well-adjusted people, what does that say to us when we enter into a conflict absolutely certain of the rightness of our position? The truth is that some may be "dead wrong" in their thinking. De-escalation of a conflict will occur when there is a change of thinking.[298] Without it, deadlock is inevitable, and a basis for the conflict will remain. The question is: How can people be convinced that the way they have been thinking has in fact been wrong? We take up this discussion below.

What Should the Peacemaker Do?

Address Factors That Contribute to Making Wrong Assessments

Subjectivity

The peacemaker should discuss with each side the reality of human subjectivity; that is, that our judgments are based on personal impressions and feelings, not necessarily the verifiable facts of the matter. Simply put, we can be wrong in our thinking. Certainly each side would have little problem saying that the other side is wrong in the dispute at hand. The assumption that the other side has gotten it wrong means it is possible we too can get it wrong. Acknowledging the reality of the lack of human objectivity is foundational to getting things right. Getting all those involved to accept this premise is fundamental to the overall peacemaking process.

Self-centeredness

The peacemaker should discuss with each side not only that human beings are subjective and therefore often wrong in their assessments, but also that we are innately self-centered and think, act, and argue accordingly. We are naturally biased toward ourselves and our own group. When we determine what is fair and right, whether consciously or unconsciously, we do so in light of what is best for ourselves, those we love, or those we represent.

For example, this question was put to a thousand Americans: "If someone sues you and you win the case, should he [the plaintiff] pay your legal costs?" The answer was "yes" 85 percent of the time. The next question was the same as the first but from another perspective: "If you sue someone and lose the case, should you pay his costs?" The answer was "yes" only 44 percent of the time.[299] The disparity in responses is dramatic and highlights how our sense of fair play is skewed by self-interest when we become part of the equation.

Even when committed to serving a higher purpose than ourselves, we are unable to transcend our self-centeredness. The United Nations is a global institution comprised of staff from all over the planet who are united in their goal to make peace in the world. Yet, at a 2008 closed-door meeting, United Nations Secretary-General Ban Ki-moon expressed his frustrations about the organization's internal workings. He stated to the institution's chief officers:

> Here at the UN, unfortunately, I see people too often putting their own interests first. I see too many turf fights, too much intramural wrangling, too much protectiveness of the status quo. ... Department heads squabble among themselves over posts and budgets and bureaucratic prerogatives, as though they somehow owned them. But our departments, agencies and programmes are not personal fiefdoms. We are just passing through. We are temporary caretakers. Always, we must keep the larger interests of the organization at the forefront of our minds. We must work together and compromise to reach solutions that are in the best interests of the UN and the global public good. ... [People] are thinking of their own position or benefit, not the larger interest of the UN, or what we are trying to accomplish as a team.[300]

Acknowledging the reality of human self-centeredness is foundational to getting things right. Getting all those involved to accept this premise is fundamental to the overall peacemaking process.

Nonrational Emotionality

Negotiator Herb Cohen was involved in such cases as the Iran hostage crisis, arms control negotiations with the Soviet Union, and the National Football League strike. He wrote a book entitled *Negotiate This*, with the subtitle *By Caring, But Not T-H-A-T Much*. This subtitle is most intriguing. What Cohen meant was that if we become personally involved and invested in a negotiation, achieving one's goals will be less likely. "You're caring too much and with that you lose the requisite detachment for success."[301] Little wonder that Cohen believes that the worst person who can negotiate for you is you.[302] We become so fully absorbed in the matter at hand that we lose all objectivity and default to our emotional ways of thinking and acting.* We vividly saw that in the "$20 Dollar Auction" described in Stage 1. When all sides do this, the basis for agreement and peace evaporates. Acknowledging the reality of nonrational emotionality is foundational to getting things right. Getting all those involved to accept this premise is fundamental to the overall peacemaking process.

Address Factors That Help the Parties Get It Right

If de-escalation of the conflict is to occur, new ways of thinking have to emerge.[303] Subjective, self-centered thinking and emotionality needs to be balanced with a more objective, dispassionate approach. Assuming that the parties are acting in good faith and therefore

If de-escalation of the conflict is to occur, new ways of thinking have to emerge.

---

* Cohen humorously recalled successfully negotiating complex deals with foreign governments (with whom he had little emotional connection) while being bested at home when "negotiating" with his children, who had emotional buttons to push.

would allow their assumptions, reasons, or conclusions to be open to examination, this section describes six different ways the peacemaker can help parties change wrong thinking that contributes to the continuation of the conflict.

Veil of Ignorance

Twentieth-century philosopher John Rawls coined the phrase "veil of ignorance." The concept behind it provides people a way to see things in a less biased, more objective manner.[304] To imagine a better society, for example, a person should be led to make decisions about the ideal society without knowing his or her role or position in it. As we have seen (Stage 2), people normally take a particular stand on an issue depending upon where they are situated. To counteract this natural bias, a veil of ignorance is inserted between the person's identity and the environment in which he or she would live. The idea is to think about creating the governing rules, principles, and guidelines of a society without knowing in advance one's sex, status, role, abilities, disabilities, strengths, weaknesses, wealth or lack thereof, educational level, and the like. Since no one would want to end up in an intolerable situation, one is more likely to create a society with greater equity for all.

Stepping behind the "veil of ignorance" also can be useful in the midst of conflict, especially where injustice is involved.[305] Consider the classic case involving David, the king of Israel. In this famous historical account, David had one of his loyal soldiers, Uriah, killed so that he could take Uriah's wife, Bathsheba, for his own. While his army was off to war, the king became smitten by Bathsheba's beauty. David committed adultery with her and she became pregnant. To keep the affair hidden, the king quietly ordered that Uriah be positioned in the fiercest part of the hottest battle, where it was anticipated he would be killed. That is what happened. King David then married Bathsheba. Months later the baby was born. No one voiced any suspicions that foul play had occurred—except one man, a prophet named Nathan.

When Nathan learned what had taken place, he was not only troubled by it but also was determined to speak out. He would bring his concerns directly to the king. But what would be his approach? Would he rail against the king as an adulterer and murderer? No. He adopted another strategy, one that, in essence, inserted a veil of ignorance between the king and a scenario the king was asked to judge. Nathan told David the following story.

> "There were two men in a certain town. One was rich, and one was poor. The rich man owned a great many sheep and cattle. The poor man owned nothing but one little lamb he had bought. He raised that little lamb, and it grew up with his children. It ate from the man's own plate and drank from his cup. He cuddled it in his arms like a baby daughter. One day a guest arrived at the home of the rich man. But instead of killing an animal from his own flock or herd, he took the poor man's lamb and killed it and prepared it for his guest" (2 Sam. 12:1-4 NLT).

When king David heard this story, he became furious. The king "ordered that the man must repay four lambs to the poor man for the one he stole and for having no pity" (2 Sam. 12:6 NLT). At that moment, Nathan firmly announced to the king, "You are that man!" (v. 7 NLT). David acknowledged his guilt on the spot.

What is instructive about this story is that the king lived for about a year with full knowledge of what he had done. Yet there is no historical record that he was troubled by his selfish actions. Being so entangled in the situation, David did not fully appreciate the injustice he perpetrated. It wasn't until he considered a parallel scenario, one in which he had no part or stake, that he was able to perceive reality free of his subjective biases. It was only by condemning another in a fictitious story that the king realized it was he who stood condemned. The veil of ignorance, which separated personal identity from the narrative, proved to be very effective in changing King David's thinking.

The peacemaker can employ the same kind of approach to help identify wrong thinking in conflict settings today. The mediator can create or call to mind a parallel but different story or case that the disputants can view more objectively than their own. A youth pastor, for example, had a worship leader in his youth group who chose not to participate in the youth pastor's spiritual growth program. The pastor wanted those teens who played a leadership role to exemplify a spiritual commitment as well. It was becoming a source of contention. The pastor might have taken a hard line with this young man. He could have said, "You either participate, or you can't lead worship any longer." Instead, he shared a story with the young man that was outside of their situation. The pastor asked what a basketball coach should do with a starting player who didn't do as the coach asked or attend team practice sessions. The story had its intended effect. After reflecting upon the analogy and its relevance, the young worship leader changed his thinking and behavior.[306]

Because people often stake out their position in light of their role and situation in the conflict, seeing things from an objective perspective is difficult. To the extent that perspective can be widened by stepping behind a veil of ignorance and considering an analogous situation, the less subjective, self-centered, and emotional the new evaluation will be. There may be a change of thinking that in turn will positively impact the course of the conflict.

Appeal to Deeper Beliefs

When battling an outdoor fire, firemen sometimes create another fire, a controlled one. The purpose is to burn a strip of ground in advance of the fire they want to put out. With fuel for the fire gone, the burnt ground becomes a boundary and barrier to keep the previously unmanaged fire in check. In these instances, they literally fight fire with fire.

There is value in taking this type of approach when dealing with conflict that emanates from a person's subjective thinking. How does one bring greater reason to bear when emotions are guiding the ship? The answer is to go to an even deeper level of subjective thought that would naturally counteract the self-centered perspective. That is to say, call people back to their own bedrock beliefs from which they have strayed in the midst of the conflict.

In the civil rights struggles during the 1960s, this is exactly what Dr. Martin Luther King did. The scene was Birmingham, Alabama, which had become known as "Bombingham." Since the end of World War II, at least fifty black homes and churches had been bombed by white supremacists.[307] In April 1963, Dr. Martin Luther King described the city as likely the most segregated city in the U.S., with a horrid record of brutality against blacks and more unsolved cases of bombings of black homes and churches than anywhere else in America.[308]

It was in this tense and hatred-filled atmosphere that King and his followers began his nonviolent civil rights campaign of sit-ins in white-only restaurants, boycotts of downtown merchants, marches on city hall, and the like in April of 1963. Then Student Nonviolent Coordinating Committee chairman, John Lewis, explained, "It was our hope that our efforts in Birmingham would dramatize the fight and determination of African American citizens in the Southern states and that we would force the Kennedy administration to draft and push through Congress a comprehensive Civil Rights Act, outlawing segregation and racial discrimination in public accommodations, employment and education."[309] The campaign began on April 3, 1963. On April 12, Dr. King was arrested. Also on April 12, a statement from eight Alabama clergyman was published in a local newspaper.[310] While in jail, King replied with a long letter known as the "Letter from a Birmingham Jail."

The eight clergymen were unhappy about "outsiders coming in." Dr. King reminded his fellow clergymen of their Scriptures and the examples and principles taught in them. "Just as the prophets of the eighth century B.C. left their villages and carried their 'thus saith the Lord' far beyond the boundaries of their home towns, and just as the Apostle Paul left his village of Tarsus and carried the gospel of Jesus Christ to the far corners of the Greco Roman world, so am I compelled to carry the gospel of freedom beyond my own home town."[311] In response to the appeal these eight clergy made to "observe the principles of law and order," Dr. King cited the words of Saint Augustine, who stated that "an unjust law is no law at all."[312] He went on to explain, "A just law is a man-made code that squares with the moral law or the law of God."[313] He reminded them of the divinely approved civil disobedience described in the book of Daniel, where it "was evidenced sublimely in the refusal of Shadrach, Meshach and Abednego to obey the laws of Nebuchadnezzar, on the grounds that a higher moral law was at stake."[314] The eight clergy said that although Dr. King's actions and those of his supporters were "technically peaceful," they incited in others "hatred and violence" and therefore were not productive. Dr. King responded by asking, "Isn't this like condemning Jesus because His unique God-Consciousness and never ceasing devotion to His will precipitated the evil act of crucifixion?"[315] The eight clergy asserted that the demonstrations were "extreme measures" and were not "justified in Birmingham." To this Dr. King reminded these men of the cloth of the immovable convictions of Jesus, the Old Testament prophet Amos, the apostle Paul, Martin Luther, and John Bunyan. The real issue, according to Dr. King, wasn't about being an extremist, but about the nature of the stand one took. To be an extremist for love, to be unyielding against injustice puts one in noble and honored company.[316]

What should be clear is that Dr. King countered the sentiment of these eight clergymen, not by dismissing them, but by taking these clergy deeper into their own faith. If they could be shown that they were the ones who were being inconsistent with the tenets of their own religion, then they should be open to change in order to remain consistent with their most deeply held convictions.

This is what Gandhi did in India to help secure India's independence from Britain. In taking the path of nonviolent resistance to British rule, Gandhi "wanted to appeal to the British conscience, and so to make them feel that they were violating their own principles if they moved forcibly against him."[317] After years of struggle, both men's efforts were successful.

When the pressure of conflict leads one or both sides to hold fast to positions that seem to make sense in the moment, it is worthwhile for the peacemaker to delve deeper into their core beliefs. By delving deeply into a given side's thinking, the peacemaker can probe for inconsistencies between position and personal convictions and help change thinking.

Amplify Entrenched Thinking to Highlight Risks

Before trying to move the parties in a positive direction, the peacemaker may choose to encourage each side to think through their worst-case scenarios. Rather than immediately trying to change the disputants' thinking, the peacemaker asks each side to take their thoughts about the current conflict down the most destructive paths imaginable. Questions might include: How could you take this bad situation and make it worse? What would have to happen if you wanted to make your pain and losses even greater? How could you become more entrenched and immovable in your current position? Then the peacemaker should ask how strongly they want to steer clear of such a potentially devastating escalation of the conflict. This exercise brings into focus the very real dangers of the situation, with the goal of providing additional motivation to the parties to take a path that will avoid it. Research shows that people are averse to loss.[318]

Raise Doubts

While I was working my way through seminary years ago, I was asked by an atheist coworker and friend, "What would have to happen for you to give up your faith?" In other words, he was asking me what it would take for me to acknowledge that what I believed was wrong. My succinct answer was and still is, "I'll consider giving up my faith when Jews stop existing." I had (and have) good reason for believing this.*[319] But people do not always have good reason for what they believe, not only in matters of faith, but in matters of conflict as well.

It is appropriate for a peacemaker to ask questions that raise doubts in the minds of the disputants about their positions or assessments.[320] "Effective mediators create and maintain doubts by raising questions about alternatives and implications that the [parties] may not have considered or fully appreciated."[321] If the peacemaker doesn't introduce uncertainty into a party's fixed way of thinking and if he or she doesn't introduce alternative interpretations, especially if the consequences of the current course of the conflict are destructive, who will?

Uncertainty is a common ingredient to the resolution of civil cases. The majority of cases get settled before they ever get to court for the simple reason that people would rather accept certain gains or losses through their own negotiations than face an uncertain outcome in a courtroom. In one such case, for example, "the mediator determined that the best way to move the mediation along was to sow seeds of doubt about their options among all the participants."[322] This brought an out-of-court settlement that each party could live with.

The peacemaker can effectively aid in helping the parties better examine their positions by raising doubts about them to see if they can withstand scrutiny. The goal here is not to embarrass. It is to help the parties see things in a truer, fuller light that will move them closer to the resolution of the conflict.

---

* I provide my reason in the endnote.

Look to Objective Sources of Authority or Standards of Practice

Researchers have found that there comes a point when the parties in conflict refuse to be influenced by the other side, even if it has a productive idea.[323] The disputants relate to each other in a far too emotional and subjective way. A battle of the wills is not always grounded in reason. There is, however, a greater willingness to consider ideas that will bring resolution if the bases of those ideas reside outside of the parties themselves. The peacemaker can assist the parties to find solutions rooted in mutually accepted objective criteria or standards, fair and unbiased processes, or objective sources of authority. These include the Golden Rule, evidence, independent tests, opinions from specialists, recommendations from a mutually trusted third party, market value, industry standards, legal precedent, cultural and religious traditions, and even a random process (e.g., flipping a coin). The general guideline here is that the more independent these sources of authority, standards of practice, or fair processes are from the parties themselves, the more likely they will be accepted by both sides as acceptable criteria.[324] In the case of facilitated communication discussed at the beginning of this chapter, it was indisputable facts from independent studies that were instrumental in changing the thinking of the facilitators.

Gain Insight from an Impasse

Facilitator Sam Kaner and his team have given a name to an unpleasant phenomenon groups commonly experience when trying to resolve a difficult problem. It is called the "groan zone." The groan zone is characterized by divergent ideas, lack of a shared frame of reference, confusion, repetition, misunderstanding, tension, frustration, and annoyance because of an overall lack of progress in finding common ground. It is an unpleasant experience that most people would prefer to cut short. However, it is a very important part of the process. Why? Because "a group's most significant breakthroughs are often preceded by a period of struggle."[325]

Psychologists and neuroscientists more formally call this "the insight experience."[326] Translated, this means that "before there can be a breakthrough, there has to be a mental block."[327] What scientists have also found is that between the impasse and insight there must be a period of relaxation, when the mind is in an unclenched state. That is why the answer to the problem we were struggling with yesterday comes to us as we are lying in bed the next morning. Warm showers also have been identified as a place where insight comes because of the relaxing nature of the experience. Google has installed ping-pong tables at its headquarters for much the same reason. Commenting on Google's approach one cognitive neuroscientist remarked, "If you want to encourage insights, then you've got to also encourage people to relax."[328]

Knowing about the insight experience provides hope and a constructive approach to deal with conflict when the parties have come to an impasse in attempting to find a needed solution. One mediator called it the "work hard-get frustrated-stop the session" technique.[329] After some time has elapsed, the disputing parties are called back into session. They may return with new intuition on how to break the impasse. Although there are no guarantees that a breakthrough will come, the fact that fresh insights do come after a period of mental struggle followed by rest is useful for peacemakers to know in helping parties see things in a new way.

Overall Summary

When it comes to the laws of nature on planet Earth, it does not matter where one is situated. The laws operate the same way at all times and in all places. Apples fall down from apple trees. Water freezes at 32 degrees Fahrenheit. And the speed of light is the same. This is not the case when it comes to people. If we were totally objective in our thinking and not influenced by our self-centered biases, our sense of fairness would not be affected by our positions or roles. However, since this is not the reality, the peacemaker must work hard to change minds and conform them to the truth when necessary.

This is no easy task, but it is doable. Having sought to humanize each side to the other in the previous stage, the mediator now encourages each side to be open to the claims of the other. When the aggrieved side's complaints and sense of injustice has merit, when their perspective is an accurate portrayal of reality, the mediator needs to gently help the offending side to see and accept it for themselves. In the same way sinners are urged to change the erroneous thinking that has brought them into conflict with God, so the peacemaker helps offending parties see the error of their ways.

Stage 7: Making a Genuine Apology

The Peacemaker Encourages the Offending Party to Verbally Apologize to the Aggrieved Party for Their Problematic Behavior

Stage 7: Making a Genuine Apology (continued)
An Apology Lies at the Heart of Reconciliation
Why Is Offering a Genuine Apology So Hard?
Fear
Shame (Not Guilt)
How Do You Know If Someone Is Really Sorry?

What Should the Peacemaker Do?

Overall Summary

This section delves into a challenging and delicate part of the peacemaking process: verbal apologies. Once a person has seen the error of his or her way, a verbal acknowledgment of the wrongs that person has engaged in naturally follows. We begin by examining what the Scriptures say on the matter. This is followed by a discussion about apologies, both inadequate and genuine. The role of the peacemaker in dealing with people when there is a need to apologize also is discussed.

What Is the Scriptural Basis for This Stage?

Confession

There is no Hebrew or Greek word in the Old or New Testaments that has as its basic meaning "apology" or "to apologize." Consequently, it should come as no surprise that if you look up either of these two words in a standard Bible dictionary or encyclopedia, you will not find an entry. What you will find instead are the words "repent" (Stage 6) and "confess" (this stage). Though neither word inherently conveys the thought of remorse, this emotion naturally accompanies the recognition of having done wrong.

Consider the case of Peter who filled with recriminations and regret, wept bitterly after denying Christ (Luke 22:62). Consider Jesus's parable about the repentant tax collector. When this man came to God in prayer, he was so ashamed of his sins that he "would not even lift up his eyes to heaven, but beat his breast [a sign of contrition and sorrow],[330] saying, 'God, be merciful to me, a sinner!'" (Luke 18:13). Jesus said it is this kind of attitude that finds favor with God (Luke 18:14). Consider the words of the apostle Paul, who spoke concerning one repentant believer, "You should rather turn to forgive and comfort him, or he may be overwhelmed by excessive sorrow" (2 Cor. 2:7). Paul also wrote to members of the Corinthian church, "You were grieved into repenting" (2 Cor. 7:9).[331] The same thing is found in the Old Testament. For example, Psalm 38:18 reads, "I confess my iniquity; I am sorry for my sin." In the Scriptures, sorrow and remorse are natural emotions that are present with repentance and confession.[332] Today, the word *apology* is a useful term that describes the combination of the two.

Private Confession

In the New Testament, to confess sin is to make "admission of wrongdoing/sin, confess, admit."[333] It is an act of speech. More specifically, the word in the Greek is a compound verb that literally means "to speak or say the same thing."[334] Hence, when sinners utter their sins to God, they are agreeing with him that what they did was wrong.

> 1 John 1:8-9
> 8 If we say we have no sin, we deceive ourselves, and the truth is not in us.[335] 9 If we confess our sins, he is faithful and just to forgive us our sins and to cleanse us from all unrighteousness.[336]

The confession of sin in verse 9 "means saying about our sins what God says about them, namely, that they are indeed sins, offenses against Him."[337] With a changed mind and attitude toward one's sinful habits and ways, we say to God, "I agree with you. You were right, and I was wrong. I am sorry."

In the Old Testament, to confess sin to God was to quietly acknowledge it in the privacy of one's own prayers.[338]

> Psalm 32:1-5
> 1 Blessed is the one whose transgression is forgiven, whose sin is covered. 2 Blessed is the man against whom the LORD counts no iniquity, and in whose spirit there is no deceit. 3 For when I kept silent,[339] my bones wasted away through my groaning all day long. 4 For day and night your hand was heavy upon me; my strength was dried up as by the heat of summer. *Selah*[340] 5 I acknowledged my sin to you, and I did not cover my iniquity; I said, "I will confess my transgressions to the LORD," and you forgave the iniquity of my sin. *Selah*

There are times when confession of sin occurs privately between God and the repentant sinner, as in Psalm 32 and 1 John 1:9 cited above.

Public Confession

There are other times when confession to God takes place in front of other people. The same Greek word that means "to confess" sin privately occurs in the following texts, with the addition of the prefix *ek*, which means "out."[341] The sense is to confess "out loud"[342] or in "public."[343] This form of the word underscores the fact that confession is a speech act. Confession chronologically follows repentance and is evidence of it.[344] Confession is but a reflection of what already has taken place privately between the repentant sinner and God. The prevailing mind-set among Jews during and prior to the first century was that "penitence and confession go together."[345] For example, in the gospel of Matthew we read,

Matthew 3:1-6[346]
1 In those days John the Baptist came preaching in the wilderness of Judea, 2 "Repent, for the kingdom of heaven is at hand."... 5 Then Jerusalem and all Judea and all the region about the Jordan were going out to him, 6 and they were baptized by him in the river Jordan, confessing their sins.

Weymouth observed that the people were "making open confession."[347] Louw and Nida have suggested, "In translating Mt 3.6 in some languages, it may be useful to restructure the expression somewhat, for example, 'they admitted to people that they had sinned' or 'they admitted publicly to God ...'"[348] This practice of public confession of sin in the New Testament mirrors what occurred in the Old Testament.[349]

Summary

Repentance and confession of sin are closely related. As we saw in the prior stage, repentance signifies seeing the error of one's ways. Confession follows it. Truthful confession is the sincere expression of an internal change, whether it is said privately to God or in front of others. The sinner not only comes to the realization that he or she has sinned against God, but says so. Remorse and contriteness are the emotions that naturally accompany repentance and confession.

Like Father, Like Son

In the same way a person's confession of sin to God is expected after repentance, so the peacemaker encourages the offending party to follow up the recognition of wrongdoing with a verbal apology to the injured party.

Stage 7: Making a Genuine Apology

Confession Should Crown Repentance

A Positive Example

In 1989, twenty-eight years after its construction, the Berlin Wall, which physically separated communist East Germany from democratic West Germany, was torn down. In April 1990, East Germany held its first free elections. A new democratic parliament was installed to govern the country. Changes were taking place at breakneck speed. Members of the parliament had many important issues to consider, including reunification with West Germany. Yet despite such pressing concerns, East Germany's first order of business and very first act of parliament was to vote on passing the following declaration.[350]

> We, the first freely-elected parliamentarians of East Germany, admit our responsibility as Germans in East Germany for their history and their future and declare unanimously before the world: Immeasurable suffering was inflicted on the peoples of the world by Germans during the time of National Socialism. Nationalism and racial madness led to genocide, particularly of the Jews in all European countries, of the people of the Soviet Union, the Polish people and the Gypsy people. Parliament admits joint responsibility on behalf of the people for the humiliation, expulsion and murder of Jewish women, men and children. We feel sad and ashamed and acknowledge this burden of German history. We ask the Jews of the world to forgive us. We ask the people of Israel to forgive us for the hypocrisy and hostility of official East German policies toward Israel and for the persecution and degradation of Jewish citizens also after 1945 in our country. We declare our willingness to contribute as much as possible to the

healing of mental and physical sufferings of survivors and to provide just compensation for material losses.[351]

The parliament, composed of four hundred members, passed without dissent this statement of guilt and remorse made before the world. After the vote, members rose to their feet and gave a standing ovation. The applause was then followed by a moment of silence to remember the millions of men, women, and children who were killed in the Holocaust during World War II by a previous generation of Germans.

A Negative Example

Although repentance and confession are logically and sequentially related, they are not the same. They are not always linked. In fact, the gulf between repentance and confession may be huge. This was dramatically illustrated in the Woody Allen film *Crimes and Misdemeanors*.[352] One of the movie's story lines is about a wealthy Jewish doctor who is married but has an affair. After two years, the mistress says she can't go on in such a state of limbo. She wants the man to divorce his wife and marry her. The man tells the woman that he has no intention of leaving his wife of twenty-five years. In fact, he wants to break off the illicit relationship. The woman becomes hysterical and threatens to ruin the man's reputation.

A few days later, the doctor, fearful of what could happen, speaks to his brother, the black sheep of the family. This brother has ties to the underworld. After weeks of deliberation, a "hit" is ordered. The woman is killed, as if by a burglar. After the crime is committed, the doctor begins to drink heavily. He becomes irritable. He is mortified by what he has done. His conscience is killing him, and he can't live with himself. He is thinking about going to the police, but that would also implicate his brother. The situation seems untenable. What will he do?

The scene breaks. Another part of the story line takes center stage. Time elapses. Finally, near the end of the movie, during the festivities after a wedding ceremony, the doctor happens to have a conversation with the character played by Woody Allen. The doctor tells Allen that he has a wonderful fictional story dealing with murder. After he recounts the background and details of what took place, the doctor picks up the story where it left off—with feelings of unbearable guilt.

Teachings from this man's religious instruction as a child, he tells Allen, come to mind, especially those of his father. A man not given over to a belief in God now all of a sudden is concerned that God's eyes are constantly upon him. The sense of his violation takes on even greater burden against the backdrop of God's absolute righteousness. He can't handle the burden of guilt any longer. He is ready to confess his crime, in all its gory details, to the police.

But then he awakens one morning. The sun is brightly shining. Inexplicably, the burden seems lighter. The doctor no longer feels the need to confess. His pangs of guilt don't seem as oppressive. He is surrounded by those who love him and have no idea what he has done. He basks in the constancy of their love and the comfort of his privileged world. The murder is attributed to another man, a killer responsible for other murders. What's the addition of one more to the list? He decides to leave his troubles behind and take his family on an extended European vacation. When they return, everything is as it was before: safe and secure. He returns to his thriving practice, and he is at peace with the world, hardly troubled by a conscience that before was eating him alive. Confession never came, and repentance was forgotten. End of story.

If repentance is to be made complete, confession must crown it. Without confession, repentance remains impotent. If a person truly has turned around in his thinking, it must be expressed in the light of day. Yet this is easier said than done. Even when we do attempt to confess our guilt, our efforts often fall short.

Inadequate Apologies

Broken relationships often fail to heal because what is actually said is insufficient. The following are five apologies that are inadequate.

The Non-Communicated Apology

Dear Brenda,[353]

I am sorry for lying and cheating on you, the girl who gave me her full heart with full trust. It was a tender and precious gift, which I did not properly value. I am sorry that I slept with prostitutes at risk of getting diseases that may have damaged your health and put your life in danger. I am sorry that I tried to cover up my lies and deceptions because I was too afraid to face up to the consequences. I am sorry for the pain I have caused. I am sorry for manipulating the situation in order to gain control. My fear was that I would be deserted, that I would be abandoned if I shared my truth. Now I am on an island. Alone. I desire to shine in the truth once again. I am so so sorry. Neil[354]

This confession sounds sincere. The problem is that it was not shared with the person for whom it was written. Instead, it was posted online in the "Apology Room," a Web site that allows people to anonymously publish those things for which they are sorry. These are confessions without recipients. This is an example of what I call a "non-communicated apology." Whether posted online, shared with another person to whom an apology is not owed, or just felt privately in one's mind and heart, if it is not communicated, it is inadequate and no apology at all. As has been said, "Repentance contemplated, but not verbalized, is valueless."[355] For this apology to be effective, it would need to be made directly to the aggrieved person.

The "Get-Out-of-Trouble" Apology

Consider the written apology of the former governor of Illinois, George Ryan. In April 2006, the jury found him "guilty on all 18 counts of racketeering conspiracy, mail fraud, lying to the FBI, obstructing the Internal Revenue Service and filing false tax returns."[356] On November 6, 2007, the day before he entered prison to serve a six and a half-year sentence, the seventy-three-year-old Ryan stood before reporters and said, "Tomorrow I embark on a new journey in my life ... But I do so with a clear conscience. And I have said since the beginning of this 10-year ordeal that I am innocent and I intend to prove that."[357]

In light of his clear conscience and to prove his innocence, Governor Ryan appealed his case. However, on August 21, 2007, a federal appeals court in Chicago upheld the conviction, declaring that the evidence against Ryan was "overwhelming."[358] Ryan then appealed to the U.S. Supreme Court. His appeal was rejected on May 27, 2008. U.S. Attorney Patrick Fitzgerald stated, "Mr. Ryan has exhausted every legal avenue and argument afforded him but the verdict stands that he was guilty of corrupting the highest office in the state."[359] The governor's wife, who twice appealed to President Bush to pardon her husband, gave a newspaper interview, published November 26, 2008. Mrs. Ryan reiterated, "His conscience is as clear as his mind."[360]

On December 1, 2008, U.S. Senator Dick Durbin from Illinois wrote a letter to President Bush, asking that the president commute the former governor's sentence to time served.[361] On December 12, imprisoned former Governor Ryan offered his first public apology. The apology was read to the press through his lawyer. Here is what the governor wrote.[362]

I must say something that I have known in my heart has been a long time coming. And that is a truly heartfelt apology to the people of Illinois. It has been a difficult journey for me to get to this point, as I truly believed in my service to the people, but it was less than my best, and for that I am sorry.

I want to make things right in my heart with God, with my family, and with those that I have hurt. As a former public official, a husband, a father, and a grandfather, I apologize. Even though I cannot undo my mistakes, I hope I can restore some faith in your hearts and minds by opening up and sharing these thoughts. And even though it took time for me to come to this place, in the end my goal is to do the right thing, no matter how tardy or flawed.

I sincerely hope that by coming forward today, my words in some way might help in the healing process of restoring the people's faith in their government and others that want to serve. In addition to damaging the public's trust and confidence in government, I realize my mistakes had other implications and tangible effects on my constituents and the citizenry. I know that Reverend and Mrs. Willis suffered such effects—an unimaginable pain and loss—from mistakes made in my administration, both by me and others on my watch. My heart has and always will go out to the Willis family.* They, like all of the people of Illinois, deserved far better than I gave them.

Opinions from Chicago newspaper readers were expressed on a Web site sponsored by the Chicago Tribune and other news outlets. The vast majority of responses were negative. Here is a representative sampling.[363]

---

* The Willis family "lost six children in a fiery 1994 crash involving a truck whose driver obtained a license in exchange for a bribe to officials in Ryan's administration" (Schmadeke, 2008, para. 4). More will be said about the incredibly tragic event that befell this family in Stage 10.

Tell inmate Ryan to save his meaningless apology. It is just an attempt to bolster the ongoing attempt for early release. An apology with any level of sincerity would have come long, long ago. This criminal needs to serve his full sentence, regardless of the suffering he has caused his family. He should have thought of the consequences before he abused his position and broke the law.

This apology is totally contradictory to every single statement about his conviction made until now. He has not been the LEAST bit contrite until now. Therefore any reasonable person can conclude this apology is insincere and completely self-serving.

I think it is hard to believe in the sincerity of an apology coming at the time when commuting of his sentence is being considered.

Wonderful apology. I'll accept it when he's released from prison, having served his full term. Until then, his apology means nothing. It sounds like a pathetic and insulting attempt to get out of prison early. If he truly is sorry to all the people he hurt, he can tell us in five-and-a-half years.

Good. Now let him demonstrate just how really sorry he is, by being a man and serving his entire sentence without so much as another peep out of him.

Ryan's apology was offered only after claiming to have a clear conscience, only after proclaiming his innocence for so many years, only after every legal means to have his conviction overturned failed, and only after a formal request was made to President Bush to commute his sentence. (President Bush did not commute the ex-governor's sentence.) Many people from Illinois who followed this case concluded that the ex-governor expressed remorse at a time when the president was being asked to commute his sentence, only because there was no other way out of jail. His incarceration was causing a hardship upon his family, and he wanted out. Such a nebulous apology for unnamed mistakes, not addressed to anyone specific, and offered when release from prison was the goal falls far short of being genuine. To make this kind of apology effective, embrace the just consequences of your wrongdoing.

The Conditional Apology

A common refrain when someone apologizes is, "If I offended you by my actions, I am sorry," or "I am sorry if you were upset by what I said." The key word in such statements is the conditional word *if.* The *if* in these sentences changes the whole tenor of the "apology." Without it, the above apologies would read, "I am sorry for my actions. I am sorry for what I said." The focus would be on the person offering the apology. The problem with "if" statements is that they place the focus not on the offender's words or actions but on the other person's reaction. It is like saying, "I am not actually sorry for what I said but by how you interpreted it." (What's the matter with you?) The conditional *if* is like stealing someone's car, getting caught a week later, and saying to the vehicle's owner, "I am sorry if you were inconvenienced" (but not sorry for the theft). If you pay close attention to many of the apologies you hear today, you may be surprised at how many times the word *if* is used. To make this kind of apology effective, remove the *if.*

The Excuse-filled Apology

When we do something we shouldn't, we tend to hide behind excuses. Excuses separate us and our identity from the acts we commit. Maintaining a positive self-image motivates us to cover our shortcomings with justifications. We blame our misdeeds or inappropriate words on something or someone else. "I'm sorry I cursed you out. I had too much to drink." "I'm sorry I stole clothes from your department store, but I have an impulse-control disorder." "I'm sorry I wasn't faithful to you, honey, but you were not meeting my needs." "I'm sorry that I cheated on the exam, but

179

my parents were pressuring me to get good grades." "I'm sorry I lied on my application, but times are tough and I needed this higher paying job." "I'm sorry I hit you, sweetheart, but you got me so mad." Since excuses have the practical effect of negating responsibility for one's actions, there is little point in offering them. It would likely be more prudent not to offer such an "apology" at all. To make this kind of apology effective, remove the *but*.

The Bulletproof Vest Apology

To better appreciate what is involved with this kind of an apology, let us briefly look at the forty-second president of the United States, William Jefferson Clinton. When allegations were surfacing about his relationship with a White House intern, Monica Lewinsky, President Clinton forcefully asserted on January 26, 1998, "I want to say one thing to the American people. I want you to listen to me. I'm going to say this again: I did not have sexual relations with that woman, Miss Lewinsky. I never told anybody to lie, not a single time. Never. These allegations are false.[364]

As the evidence mounted that there was a sexual relationship, on August 17, 1998 President Clinton felt compelled to make a brief televised speech to the nation. He said, in part,

> Indeed, I did have a relationship with Ms. Lewinsky that was not appropriate. In fact, it was wrong. It constituted a critical lapse in judgment and a personal failure on my part for which I am solely and completely responsible. ... I know that my public comments and my silence about this matter gave a false impression. I misled people, including even my wife. I deeply regret that. I can only tell you I was motivated by many factors. First, by a desire to protect myself from the embarrassment of my own conduct. I was also very concerned about protecting my family. The fact that these questions were being asked in a politically inspired lawsuit, which has since been dismissed, was a consideration, too.[365]

On Sept. 11, 1998 President Clinton was scheduled to give a speech during a White House prayer breakfast. At this time, impeachment proceedings for perjury and obstruction of justice against the president were underway in the U.S. Congress. At the prayer breakfast, President Clinton rose to speak. He said, in part,

> I don't think there is a fancy way to say that I have sinned. It is important to me that everybody who has been hurt know that the sorrow I feel is genuine—first and most important, my family, also my friends, my staff, my Cabinet, Monica Lewinsky and her family, and the American people. I have asked all for their forgiveness. But I believe that to be forgiven, more than sorrow is required. At least two more things: First, genuine repentance, a determination to change and to repair breaches of my own making. I have repented. Second, what my Bible calls a broken spirit. An understanding that I must have God's help to be the person that I want to be. A willingness to give the very forgiveness I seek. A renunciation of the pride and the anger, which cloud judgment, lead people to excuse and compare and to blame and complain.
>
> Now, what does all this mean for me and for us? First, I will instruct my lawyers to mount a vigorous defense using all available, appropriate arguments. But legal language must not obscure the fact that I have done wrong. Second, I will continue on the path of repentance seeking pastoral support and that of other caring people so that they can hold me accountable for my own commitment."[366]

In his reaction to the speech, Dan Thomasson, bureau chief of the Scripps Howard News Service, responded with bewilderment: "At the same time he is asking us to forgive a poor sinner he is announcing he will launch a 'vigorous' defense of his actions. ... Wait a minute! How can you have it both ways?" [367] Thomasson

181

went on to say that if the president was truly sorry, he should go before Congress with hat in hand, i.e., with contrition, and not with a legal defense team.

People can debate the path President Clinton took or could have taken. The legal considerations undoubtedly complicated this case.[368] The larger point to be made here, however, is that true apologies are incompatible with simultaneous attempts to shield one from the consequences of his or her offenses. To apologize and then defend against attempts to bring accountability to bear is a "sorry" that is not sorry enough. It is like the driver who hit a parked car and put a note under the windshield wiper that reads, "I have just backed into and damaged your car. I am really sorry. The people who witnessed the accident are watching me. They think I am writing down my name and address. I'm not. Good luck!" Expressions of regret that deny the opportunity for justice fall short of being genuine.

A Genuine Apology

Three Essential Components

Having looked at what a genuine apology is not, let us consider what a true apology actually is. At its irreducible core, an apology is a "speech act."[369] "The offender must not only *be* sorry but also has to *say* so."[370] (This is just what we found in the study above of the biblical word for "confess".) Unlike other words that accompany actions, the words of an apology actually are the action.[371] To apologize is to plead mea culpa, that is, "through my fault." "To apologize is to declare voluntarily that one has no excuse, defense, justification, or explanation for an action (or inaction) that has insulted, failed, injured, or wronged another."[372]

A genuine apology is made up of three essential components. The person offering it (1) acknowledges and specifically names the wrong done, (2) takes responsibility for engaging in it, and (3) expresses regret and remorse for the harm that resulted.[373]   For example, "I betrayed you when I talked against you behind your back. I have no excuse for my behavior. I am sorry for the hurt and pain that I caused."

It Needs To Be Made in Person

Given that an apology is a speech act, it naturally follows that it should be made in person. The idea, for example, that someone can make an apology on behalf of the offending party is unacceptable. "Part of the obligation that comes with being accountable and taking responsibility for one's wrongdoing is to apologise personally for it."[374]

Consider the dramatic case when an anticipated face-to-face apology did not occur. The context was one of sexual abuse that occurred to boys at a Canadian religious school by one of the adult Brothers. Years later an official apology was offered by the archbishop. In the midst of his apology to a gathering of people, one man yelled out, "I don't want an apology from you. I want an apology from the Brother that did me. He ruined my life, that dog! I don't need an apology from you. You had nothing to do with what he did to me. I want an apology from him!"[375]

The harm inflicted by one person upon another is, by nature, a social act, even if antisocial. For an apology to be effective and to begin to repair that broken relationship, it must mirror that social dimension.[376] "An apology requires communication between a wrongdoer and a victim: no apology occurs without the involvement of each party."[377] It requires direct communication from the wrongdoer to the injured party. "If the offender is sincerely remorseful and is painfully aware of the hurt and damage he has caused, it will be difficult for him to look into the pained, and even vengeful eyes of his victim. Being ashamed of his behavior, he will naturally try to avoid the accusatory stare of the wounded one. Therefore, his willingness to look her in the face, when his guilt is authentic, testifies to his sincerity."[378] The fact that apologies need to be spoken directly to the other person is a critical element of the process that must not be bypassed.

To Illustrate: New Development in Medical Malpractice

Let's discuss the practice of withholding or offering apologies in the medical malpractice arena.

The Traditional Approach: No Apology. Adhering to the traditional approach, one attorney told about a young widow he represented in a medical malpractice suit. The case eventually settled, and the widow and her children were to receive financial compensation for their loss. The attorney recalled,

> As we left the courthouse after the hearing, she began to rage. I thought she was disappointed in the apportionment ordered by the court or that she regretted settling rather than trying the case. But she denied that either of these feelings was the source of her hostility. She was angry that none of the doctors had ever said he was sorry that his conduct had contributed to her husband's death. She experienced this omission as another injury, moral harm added to professional malpractice. She said that if the doctors had apologized, she would have felt more able "to heal."[379]

Why was an apology absent from the process? Medical malpractice lawyers in the U.S. have commonly advised clients to "deny and defend": deny any wrongdoing and defend against all charges.[380] Why? Admission of wrongdoing and acceptance of responsibility increase the chances of a defendant being held liable for damages.[381] The fear is that to admit, "We committed a medical error that has caused the death of your loved one for which we are responsible and very sorry," will result in an increase in the amount awarded to the family in a lawsuit. Because admissions of culpability can be used against a defendant, attorneys have for decades advised their clients not to take that track.[382] To

184

take responsibility and apologize leaves oneself open to subsequent attack. It can even imperil one's medical career. The disclosure comes at too great a cost to the doctor. Fearing the outcome of an apology, there is a strong history of lawyers advising their clients, "Don't do it!"

The More Recent Transparent Approach. In recent years, there has been a new development in the arena of medical malpractice. Instead of taking a posture of not admitting mistakes, hospitals are taking the opposite approach. The Sorry Works! Coalition, founded in 2005, has become "the nation's leading advocacy organization for disclosure, apology (when appropriate), and upfront compensation (when necessary) after adverse medical events." [383] Until just the last few years, "doctors who wanted to apologize for medical errors were not allowed to do so. They were told an apology can be interpreted as an admission of guilt." [384] That mind-set, however, has begun to change. "The practice of apologizing for medical errors is gaining ground across the country, and helping hospitals avoid costly lawsuits." [385]

One such place is the University of Michigan Health System. In one case, university interns failed to provide a proper diagnosis for a woman named Jennifer, who developed a cancerous lump in her breast. It went untreated for twenty-one months from the first time she saw a Health System doctor. By the time a mammogram was ordered, the cancer had spread to other parts of her body. She will likely die prematurely as a result. Rather than deny the error and enter into a costly and protracted legal battle, the hospital acknowledged their error. All relevant parties (hospital administration, doctors, lawyers, the patient, and her husband) came together in a face-to-face meeting to discuss the matter. Jennifer recalled, "My husband and I both left that meeting feeling like a million bucks. I was heard that night. That's all I really wanted. I wanted them to know that this was not right what had happened to me." [386] Soon after that, Jennifer's lawsuit was settled out of court.

Since adopting this approach, malpractice lawsuits at the University of Michigan Health System have dropped by two-thirds, saving the health care system millions in legal and insurance expenses.[387] More to the point, patients are finally hearing the words they have longed to hear, "I am sorry. What has happened to you was wrong." Aspects of shalomic peace were becoming a reality for people willing to honestly engage with each other instead of going through a court system that would only deepen the social rift between them.

An Apology Lies at the Heart of Reconciliation

It has been said that an apology lies at the very heart of the reconciliation process,[388] that it is the key that opens the door to healing.[389] Indeed, it has been argued that "healing from the personal devastation of abuse cannot occur without apologies."[390] This is consistent with the Judeo-Christian model of peacemaking. There is no healing of the relationship between sinners and God until the sinner confesses his or her sins to God. Socially, apologies are not only the impetus for restoring harmony, but they also are a means to reestablish dignity to the parties,[391] including the offender.*

Why Is Offering a Genuine Apology So Hard?

The human inclination to avoid being identified as a wrongdoer is incredibly strong. We deny and lie about what we have done. We blame others. We make excuses. We minimize the injury. Why? The succinct answer is twofold: fear and shame.

---

* Poet Alexander Pope (1688-1744), wrote, "A man should never be ashamed to own he has been in the wrong, which is but saying, in other words, that he is wiser to-day than he was yesterday (1977, p. 103).

Fear

Fear is a strong motivator for people not to admit their guilt. People fear what other people will think of them or what will happen if they confess. The truth is, a man may engage in an activity he knows in his heart is wrong. He understands what he is doing is completely opposite to the way people have come to know him. He is convicted about the dissonance between his private life and his public life. One rabbi described it: "A man lies awake at night and thinks about it [his sin]; his soul cries out in the darkness; but in the light of day, in the eyes of others, he seems happy and content." Yet despite the inner turmoil, these are matters "he does not dare bring to his lips."[392]

The trusted accountant with a secret gambling problem who is embezzling funds from his employer says nothing. What would happen to him if he did? What would those who respect him think? The forty-year-old man who has an affair, even if for one night, says nothing. Would his wife divorce him and shatter his comfortable lifestyle if she knew? How would his children, who admire him now, begin to view him? The elementary school student who broke an apartment window says nothing, even when she learns that a classmate is being accused by the angry resident for having done it. The fear of voluntarily putting herself in front of this angry adult, even to clear her classmate, is too great.

The apprehension of being found out, the dread of facing accusations, the thought of placing our fate in the hands of another is what frightens us so. Moreover, if we confess, we lose control over our image and how those who know us will now view us. If we confess, we lose control of what might happen to us, socially and even legally. Out of fear, people will go to extraordinary lengths to resist being reduced to such nakedness. Fear is what stops us from admitting our guilt and apologizing. Fear is what prevents us from experiencing shalomic peace.

Shame (Not Guilt)

Shame, not guilt, is the second reason an unconditional apology is so hard to make. Based on years of empirical research,[393] psychologists have made a clear distinction between shame and guilt. Whereas guilt focuses on one's behavior, shame focuses on one's self-identity. The difference between guilt and shame can be succinctly captured as, "I did a horrible thing" (guilt) versus "I am a horrible person" (shame). With guilt, the focus is on the transgression. "Look what I *did.*" With shame, the focus is on the transgressor. "Look what *I* did." Shame is the more painful emotion because there is little separation between the person and the act. Not only is a bad deed uncovered, but a bad person is exposed as well.

Individuals who experience guilt are better able to separate what they have done from who they are. The discomfort of their guilt motivates them to accept responsibility and confess that they were in the wrong.[394] Empathy for those they have hurt motivates them to resolve the breach in relationship and seek the other's healing. Moreover, to sincerely admit wrongdoing suggests that they want to move toward a future that is more consistent with who they perceive themselves to be. The very act of confession only serves to separate their past action from their identity.

By contrast, those who experience shame are very concerned about what others think about them. They don't have the inner strength to withstand negative evaluations and condemnation without breaking down. Such people go to extreme lengths to avoid feeling shamed. Responses to being called into account range from becoming defensive, making excuses, finding another person or source to blame (e.g., the circumstances), becoming physically withdrawn or angry, making cutting comments and spreading lies about the other party, and otherwise becoming verbally or even physically aggressive.[395] The thought of being "unmasked" and becoming an object of scorn, contempt, or ridicule is unbearable. The seemingly visceral need to cover up is intense. The reactions, whether flight or fight, will almost certainly cause an escalation in the conflict or end the relationship altogether.

Not surprisingly, the research shows that a person experiencing shame is less able to resolve conflict constructively than a person experiencing guilt. Persons experiencing shame focus their energy and attention on themselves instead of on the person they have hurt. Whereas guilt seeks forgiveness, healing, and freedom based on acknowledgement of the sin, shame experiences an ever-shrinking and isolated world. The person is not able to separate himself from his sinful behavior.

How Do You Know If Someone Is Really Sorry?

Given all the difficulties people have in earnestly apologizing, how do you know when someone is really sorry? The hallmark of a genuine apology is that there is a full acceptance of the wrong committed. This means the one apologizing stands utterly defenseless. It means putting one's less than honorable, embarrassing side on display. It also means placing oneself at the mercy of the other.[396] When polled, it is no wonder that several groups of high school students, medical students, and professional colleagues asserted that the two major reasons they have difficulty apologizing is fear of the other side's reaction and personal embarrassment.[397] Yet, "any diversion from accepting responsibility is not an apology."[398]

The reality is that as soon as an apology is offered, our immediate destiny no longer rests solely with ourselves. It is impacted and controlled by the other, the one who was hurt. Thus, an apology represents a complete reversal of roles and power.[399] Weakness and vulnerability shift from the injured party to the one who caused the injury, while the injured party assumes a position of ascendancy and strength. How the offended party might use his or her newfound power is anything but certain. This is why so many people avoid apologizing without at least some defense or excuse.

189

The genuineness of an apology is directly related to the extent one is willing to acknowledge that one's words or actions have caused harm, even if the self-disclosure makes one vulnerable to criticism and attack. The degree to which I, the guilty party, am willing to surrender self-determination over the legitimate consequences of my sin indicates the extent to which I am sincerely repentant for the wrong I have committed. The more willing I am to subjugate

A sorry without vulnerability, a sorry without the willing surrender of control concerning the outcome of my misdeed or careless words, a sorry that doesn't yield my immediate fate and judgment into the legitimate hands of another, is not sorry enough.

myself to the offended party and suffer the due penalty of my transgression, the more willing and genuine others will consider my apology to be. To put it another way, a sorry without vulnerability, a sorry without the willing surrender of control concerning the outcome of my misdeed or careless words, a sorry that doesn't yield my immediate fate and judgment into the legitimate hands of another, is not sorry enough.

Jesus's most famous parable, the parable of the prodigal son, epitomizes what a genuine, heartfelt apology looks like. A portion of the parable is reproduced below.

Luke 15

11 And he said, "There was a man who had two sons. 12 And the younger of them said to his father, 'Father, give me the share of property that is coming to me.' And he divided his property between them. 13 Not many days later, the younger son gathered all he had and took a journey into a far country, and there he squandered his property in reckless living. 14 And when he had spent everything, a severe famine arose in that country, and he began to be in need. 15 So he went and hired himself out to one of the citizens of that country, who sent him

into his fields to feed pigs. 16 And he was longing to be fed with the pods that the pigs ate, and no one gave him anything.

17 "But when he came to himself, he said, 'How many of my father's hired servants have more than enough bread, but I perish here with hunger! 18 I will arise and go to my father, and I will say to him, "Father, I have sinned against heaven and before you. 19 I am no longer worthy to be called your son. Treat me as one of your hired servants."' 20 And he arose and came to his father. But while he was still a long way off, his father saw him and felt compassion, and ran and embraced him and kissed him. 21 And the son said to him, 'Father, I have sinned against heaven and before you. I am no longer worthy to be called your son.' 22 But the father said to his servants, 'Bring quickly the best robe, and put it on him, and put a ring on his hand, and shoes on his feet. 23 And bring the fattened calf and kill it, and let us eat and celebrate. 24 For this my son was dead, and is alive again; he was lost, and is found.' And they began to celebrate."

Was the prodigal son really sorry? Absolutely. He saw the error of his way (verse 17). He rehearsed and then started to directly state to his father his confession of sin. Given what he had gone over in his mind to say (vv. 18-19), the son came back to his father expecting no special benefit. Rather, he said, "I am no longer worthy to be called your son. Treat me as one of your hired servants" (v. 19; cf. v. 21). There was no defense or excuse. Instead, he put his fate into the hands of him against whom he had sinned. The son, in essence, said, "In light of my actions, I have relinquished my position in the family. Would you simply consider treating me as an outsider, a non-family member, and servant?" Morally naked, the son threw himself at his father's mercy. In this parable, Jesus links the admission of sin and the voluntary surrender of self-determination. He links true repentance with complete defenselessness.

The contrite son put his fate into the hands of his father without reservation because he was truly sorry. It is an excellent example of what every truly apologetic person should do.

What Should the Peacemaker Do?

Given the sensitivity of the subject matter, the peacemaker will seek to have a private conversation with the offending party prior to attempting an open conversation with the aggrieved party. One specialist in international conflict explained, "For the high power group, exposing oneself to the not-so-righteous aspects of one's identity can be extremely difficult and embarrassing. The first phase is to break one's denial that one is capable of inflicting injury upon the other. ... Perpetrators would have to engage in a slow process of exposure before they could be able to expose themselves to those whom they have injured. Exposing too much too soon can be psychologically devastating." [400] The process of self-examination can be conducted in a safe environment with the peacemaker. It will take time. Only after the perpetrator is able to admit guilt can the process move forward.

The goal of the conversation at this point is to have the offending party focus on his or her behavior and to move the offender from shame to guilt, if necessary. If the offending party is overcome with shame, the peacemaker should remind the perpetrator that we are all flawed beings[401] and that, as Augustine said, "The confession of evil works is the first beginning of good works."

Once the offender is able to move from a focus on shame to one more of guilt, preparing the guilty party to apologize to the victim follows. The peacemaker helps the offender to muster the courage to apologize in the proper way: face-to-face, naming the wrong committed, taking responsibility without excuse or defense, expressing remorse for the damage done, and offering to make reparations if possible.

This verbal admission of wrongdoing may be spoken first to the peacemaker in private. If so, the peacemaker will need to prepare the offender to eventually make that same statement directly to the injured party. To help take some of the fear out of apologizing, the peacemaker may work with the other side to prepare the way for a gracious acceptance of the apology. This could involve speaking to the aggrieved party, letting that one know that an apology is in the works, and receiving assurances, if possible, that the apology will be received without attack.

Overall Summary

Confession of sin to God naturally flows from a repentant heart and mind. The sinner acknowledges and agrees with God that he or she has sinned against him. In the same way, on a social level, once parties on one side of the divide come to the realization that their words or actions have contributed to the conflict at hand, the sincerity of their new understanding is reflected in their willingness to verbally say so. At this stage, the most critical role for the peacemaker is to provide a safe environment to discuss these most sensitive issues. The process may begin with a private conversation between the offender and the peacemaker. Eventually, the words of apology will be spoken directly to the injured party. In the same way a person's confession of sin to God is expected after repentance, so the peacemaker encourages the offending party to follow up the recognition of wrongdoing with a verbal apology to the injured party.

Stage 8: Making Reparations

The Peacemaker Encourages the Offending Party to Make the Injured Party Materially Whole Again

What Is the Scriptural Basis for This Stage?
Premise
The Old Testament
The New Testament
  Zacchaeus
  Jesus
  The Apostle Paul
Summary

Like Father, Like Son

Stage 8: Making Reparations
The Cathleen Crowell Webb Story
Restoration
The Relationship Between Apology and Repair
  A Continuum
  Sam E. Antar
What If It Is Not Possible to Make the Injured Party Whole Again?
  Financial Reparations
  Symbolic Reparations

What Should the Peacemaker Do?

Overall Summary

In Stage 7, the offending party offers genuine words of apology that demonstrate changed thinking on the offender's part (Stage 6). This process continues here in Stage 8, in that the words are demonstrated by actions. This stage involves making the injured party as materially whole again as possible.

What is the Scriptural Basis for this Stage?

Premise

When people commit evil deeds against other people, the victims suffer material loss. By contrast, when people sin against God, who is beyond the reach of man's evil deeds, he suffers no such loss. Nevertheless, because the association between sinning against God and hurting others are so closely linked,[402] God requires that perpetrators make their victims whole through reparations.

The Old Testament

One of the words that is associated with the Hebrew word for peace, *shalom*[403] is the word *shalem*.[404] *Shalem* means to "make whole or good, restore,"[405] "to repay or compensate,"[406] and "to restore the balance."[407] In other words, closely related to the concept of shalomic peace is the concept of restoration. Establishing justice where there was injustice and bringing restoration where there has been loss is a significant component of what shalomic peace is all about. Consequently, there are many scenarios outlined in the Old Testament that require the offender to make restitution for losses caused to another.[408]

Exodus 21:33-34
33 "When a man opens a pit, or when a man digs a pit and does not cover it, and an ox or a donkey falls into it, 34 the owner of the pit shall make restoration. He shall give money to its owner, and the dead beast shall be his."

Exodus 22:5-6

5 "If a man causes a field or vineyard to be grazed over, or lets his beast loose and it feeds in another man's field, he shall make restitution from the best in his own field and in his own vineyard. 6 If fire breaks out and catches in thorns so that the sacked grain or the standing grain or the field is consumed, he who started the fire shall make full restitution."

Exodus 22:9 NIV

9 "In all cases of illegal possession of an ox, a donkey, a sheep, a garment, or any other lost property about which somebody says, 'This is mine,' both parties are to bring their cases before the judges. The one whom the judges declare guilty must pay back double to his neighbor."

Leviticus 24:18 NIV

18 "Anyone who takes the life of someone's animal must make restitution—life for life.

The New Testament

Zacchaeus

The concept of restoration and reparations continues in the New Testament. Consider the case of Zacchaeus and Jesus's assessment of Zacchaeus's mind-set.

Luke 19:1-10

1 He [Jesus] entered Jericho and was passing through. 2 And there was a man named Zacchaeus. He was a chief tax collector and was rich. 3 And he was seeking to see who Jesus was, but on account of the crowd he could not, because he was small of stature. 4 So he ran on ahead and climbed up into a sycamore tree to see him, for he was about to pass that way. 5 And when Jesus came to the place, he looked up

and said to him, "Zacchaeus, hurry and come down, for I must stay at your house today." 6 So he hurried and came down and received him joyfully. 7 And when they saw it, they all grumbled, "He has gone in to be the guest of a man who is a sinner." 8 And Zacchaeus stood and said to the Lord, "Behold, Lord, the half of my goods I give to the poor. And if [409] I have defrauded anyone of anything, I restore[410] it fourfold." 9 And Jesus said to him, "Today salvation has come to this house, since he also is a son of Abraham. 10 For the Son of Man came to seek and to save the lost."

Evidence of Zacchaeus's change of heart is reflected in his actions. "After recognizing his failures, he not only confesses them publicly but seeks to make appropriate restitution for the wrongs he has done."[411] Evidence of Zacchaeus's genuine change of mind and heart (repentance) is seen in his commitment to provide restitution at a level greater than the amount required by Israelite law (see Lev. 5:16). Having seen the error of his ways, it was his sincere desire to fully repair the wrongs he committed.

Jesus

At different times, Jesus spoke of the need to restore to the original possessor what was rightfully his. Jesus used the same word, "restore," that Zacchaeus used in Luke 19:8 to indicate that if you owed a debt to someone, you were obligated to pay it in full (see Matt. 5:26; 18:25-34; Luke 7:42; 10:35; 12:59). In Jesus's parable of the Good Samaritan, for example (Luke 10), Jesus presumed that the innkeeper would be repaid any debt he was owed. The thought that the Good Samaritan would have the innkeeper draw upon his resources without paying him back was not even contemplated. There is moral order upon which communities and societies are built. When that balance is broken, Jesus expected it to be repaired and made right. Reparations for actions that wrongly took away from the resources of another would fall into this category.

198

The Apostle Paul

We see this same pattern of reparations in the ministry of the apostle Paul. Paul intervened in a situation between Philemon, a Greek slave owner, and his runaway slave, Onesimus. To make a successful getaway, it appears that Onesimus stole money or property from Philemon (Philem. 18). Philemon traveled to Rome where he crossed paths with Paul. Paul led Onesimus to faith in Jesus (v. 10). Onesimus became useful to Paul and his ministry (vv. 11, 13). As time went on, "Paul realized that Onesimus had a responsibility to Philemon and should make restitution for his thievery. Thus Paul deemed it right to return Onesimus to Philemon."[412] Paul wrote a short letter to Philemon, saying in part,

> 17 So if you consider me your partner, receive him as you would receive me. 18 If he has wronged you at all, or owes you anything, charge that to my account. 19 I, Paul, write this with my own hand: I will repay[413] it....

In order to restore harmony between Onesimus and Philemon, the apostle Paul steps into the gap. He makes it clear that he will personally restore to Philemon whatever Onesimus had stolen.

Summary

The point to be made from the above texts is that there is an expectation that those who sincerely repent and confess their sins to God will follow through with appropriate actions. The process starts with speaking to God. It concludes by making things right with others by restoring to the aggrieved party what was lost. The attempt to make the other person whole is clear evidence that an offender means it when he or she says, "I am sorry for the wrong I committed." Indeed, this comprised the core of the apostle Paul's preaching. He regularly told his audiences that "they should repent and turn to God, performing deeds in keeping with their repentance" (Acts 26:20).*

Like Father, Like Son

In the same way God expects those who sinned against him and hurt others to make reparations to those harmed, so the peacemaker encourages the offending party to make the injured party materially whole again.

Stage 8: Making Reparations

The Cathleen Crowell Webb Story

A major turning point in the criminal justice system quietly took place in 1989. It was the first time in the U.S. that DNA evidence was used to exonerate a man who was wrongly convicted.[414] The inmate's name was Gary Dotson. He had been accused and convicted for a rape he did not commit and had already spent eight years in prison out of a scheduled twenty-five to fifty. The primary cause of his release from prison was not the DNA evidence, however. It was something else entirely, something unexpected, something that, for the longest time, was not believed by those in authority. Here's the story.

In 1977, Cathleen Crowell was a troubled sixteen-year-old girl in Illinois who claimed that she was raped. She did so because she believed she might have become pregnant as a result of having sex with her boyfriend.[415] Afraid that the foster family she was living with would throw her out if they knew the truth, she devised an alternative explanation. In a park, one evening after dark, she dirtied, disheveled, and cut herself before returning home with a

---

* John the Baptist preached the same thing to the people, "Bear fruits in keeping with repentance" (Luke 3:8, see also Matt. 3:8).

concocted story of being raped. But before she made it home, the police came upon her. Scared and not wanting the real story to come out, she told the police she was raped. She even included a general description of the man she alleged was the rapist. The more she lied, the more impossible it was for her to tell the truth.

Unfortunately, a man who resembled the description of the rapist was eventually picked up. Not wanting to be caught in a lie, this frightened teenager identified him in a lineup. At the trial two years later, in 1979, Gary Dotson was sentenced to twenty-five to fifty years behind bars. Cathleen, in her immaturity, was so utterly focused on not being caught in a lie that she was unable to fully appreciate the damage she was causing to another person and his family. When she heard the guilty verdict, she told herself, "It's going to be all right. He'll appeal. He'll get out. Something will turn up. I won't worry about it. I won't think about it. I won't."[416]

Fast-forward two years to 1981. Two important events had transpired since the trial. First, Cathy married David Webb and moved to New Hampshire. Then, months later, through the influence of a local pastor's wife, she became a Christian, making peace with God through Jesus Christ.[417]

Over the next couple of years, two children were born to Cathy and her husband. During this time, she explained that God was working on her, bringing things to her consciousness that up to that point in time were buried and too difficult to process.[418] But as the months rolled on, there was an increasing realization that she needed to make things right. Cathy posed a general question to the pastor's wife. "Don't you think that some things are better left alone? I mean, if a person has done something wrong and the Lord forgives him, don't you think that it could create unnecessary problems to go back, and drag a bad situation up again?"[419] In reply the pastor's wife asked whether going back would restore something that needed to be made whole again.[420]

Cathy was afraid. How would her husband react? Would he still love her? He knew about the rape but not the lie. No one did. What about her new life, her new extended family, and her new friends at church? What would they think? She prayed for strength to do what was right.[421] Eventually she shared her darkest secret with the pastor's wife and shortly thereafter with her husband. Their love for Cathy was affirmed, as it would later be by extended family and friends. Cathy also knew that she already had started down a path that would take her into unexplored territory. In the weeks and months to follow, an attorney was contacted, and the case was reopened. Cathy was determined to do all she could to free Gary Dotson, who at this point in time had served six years in prison.

Her recantation not only made local Chicago news but national news as well. Cathy had no idea that her private decision in rural New Hampshire would meet with such attention. But she was strengthened by her understanding of the Scriptures and God's will for justice to prevail. "I remembered how in the Bible Zacchaeus restored what he had stolen. I thought about what God had said about restoration in the Book of Leviticus. I realized that no matter what it cost me, I'd have to do all I could to free this innocent man."[422]

Cathy traveled to New York City to appear on NBC's *Today Show* and on ABC's *Good Morning America*. On the *Today Show*, Gary Dotson's mother, who was in Chicago, was also a guest via split screen. Crying Cathy apologized. "I'm so sorry for what I did to you and your family, especially to Gary."[423] Mrs. Dotson forgave Cathy and thanked her for courageously coming forward to tell the truth and set the record straight.

On April 4, 1985, a hearing was held. The case was presided over by the same judge who presided over the original case. During the hearing, Cathy recanted her original testimony and confessed that she had made up the entire rape story. The judge recessed the hearing for one week to decide whether or not Dotson's conviction should be overturned.

On April 11, more testimony was heard and then the judge rendered his decision. "The petitioner has failed to sustain his burden (of proof) and I cannot find that perjury was committed."[424] He cited Illinois case law, which treats recantation testimony as "very unreliable."[425] He said that he thought the original jury's decision to convict was the correct one.[426] Upon hearing that he had to return to prison, Dotson "slammed his hand on a courtroom table and burst into tears."[427] His mother also cried. Bewildered, she asked, "What happened?"[428]

The greatest outburst, however, came from Cathy. The Associated Press reported that after the decision, in the hallway as she clutched her husband's arm, she screamed, "He's innocent! ... He's innocent! I told the truth!"[429] She said, "I lied in 1979 and I'm telling the truth now. (The judge) is wrong. Gary Dotson is innocent."[430]

Given all the media attention surrounding the case, the governor of Illinois became involved. On May 12, 1985, the governor granted Gary Dotson not a pardon, but a commutation of his sentence. Though this freed him, he was still a convicted felon. And this conviction was the basis for Dotson's subsequent experiences in and out of prison. A failed telephone call to his parole officer, for example, landed him back behind bars.[431] Finally, in August 1989, with the development of forensic science, Dotson became the first person in American history to be fully exonerated due to DNA testing.

Proof of Gary Dotson's innocence did not begin with DNA evidence. It began when Cathy not only realized she had done wrong but also verbally confessed it. She chose to experience ridicule and shame in order for the truth to be told. Once the decision was made to go public, she became determined to do her best to return to

203

Gary Dotson what should not have been taken away, his freedom. In addition, Webb directed that all royalties from the sale of her 1985 book, entitled *Forgive Me*, go into a fund for Gary Dotson. She would not profit one cent from the book. Even though her own family was behind in their bills (exacerbated by the time and expense of trying to free Gary), she felt obliged to do what she could to restore to Gary a small portion of what she took away.

Restoration

The Relationship Between Apology and Repair

A Continuum. Making reparations to the injured party, whenever possible, is evidence of a true apology. It also reflects the need by the injured party to reestablish justice. (See Stage 3). In many cases, it is easy to conceive how a person can be made whole again. The next-door neighbor's child hits a baseball through a kitchen window. The parents agree to install a new one. Items stolen from a church are returned by the thief. If one is truly sorry, one should be willing to repair the imbalance or damage his or her actions caused.

A wrongdoer's confession alone is not sufficient to heal a relational breach if the injustice continues. What would we say about the person who apologizes for stealing tickets to a Broadway play yet still goes to the show using those tickets?* Bishop Tutu well said, "If someone steals my pen and then asks me to forgive him, unless he returns my pen the sincerity of his contrition and confession will be

---

* This is similar to the attitude the HBO cable network displayed to the Mormon Church regarding its television program, *Big Love*. The drama about a polygamous family in Utah was going to air an episode that depicted a sacred ceremony in the Mormon temple. Church leaders objected. HBO said it was not attempting to be offensive. "Obviously, it was not our intention to do anything disrespectful to the church, but to those who may be offended, we offer our sincere apology" (Associated Press, 2009, para. 4). Nonetheless, HBO went ahead and aired the episode. A sincere apology this was not, otherwise HBO executives would have changed their mind about airing the program. (See Stage 7). HBO's response would have been more appropriate if they did not couch it in the form of an apology.

considered nil."[432] Repentance, confession, and repair, whenever possible, are part of a continuum. At the core, they represent a change of mind and attitude from self-concern to concern for those whom one has hurt. If one is sincere at the beginning of the continuum, it should be evident at the end of it.

Repentance, confession, and repair, whenever possible, are part of a continuum.

Sam E. Antar. To illustrate the kind of attitude that is involved, consider the following statement from Sam E. Antar.

> My name is Sam E. Antar. I am a former CPA and former Chief Financial Officer of Crazy Eddie, Inc. During the 1980s, I helped mastermind with my cousin and uncle (co-founders of the company) one of the largest securities frauds of its time. This securities fraud cost investors hundreds of millions of dollars, cost many people their life savings, cost many people their jobs and careers, cost creditors hundreds of millions of dollars, and many people's suffering that cannot be measured. I was the government's key witness in both the criminal and civil prosecutions. I also fully cooperated with all civil plaintiffs in the prosecution of their claims. I make no excuses for my criminal conduct. Nor should I receive any praise for my cooperation.
>
> I take full and complete responsibility for my actions and apologize to all the victims of my crimes. ... However, my apologies, acceptance of responsibility, and the punishment imposed upon me by the court is not enough. I believe that acceptance of one's personal responsibility for past actions must be accompanied by corrective action and not include exploitation for personal gain. I believe that former criminals like me must do more than just express regret for our crimes and pay whatever punishment society imposes upon us. I believe that it is our obligation and responsibility to educate society, so that society can avoid future perils

caused by new generations of criminals. I also believe that any person's true test of character comes from overcoming past misdeeds and wrongdoing and trying to do something positive out of it without any personal gain or recognition.

I will make myself available to speak to any individual or group for no compensation or cost. I will pay for all travel and lodging costs out of my own pocket. Any individual is welcome to ask me questions personally. I will make myself available by phone or e-mail. ... I hope that by publicly exposing my own past criminal misdeeds that others will learn positively from them and use them as an example of how to avoid future frauds. ... I will not accept anything in return for any help I provide anyone–no thank you letters, nothing. [433]

Although Sam E. Antar doesn't make a direct contribution to those he committed fraud against, his statement does demonstrate the attitude of a man who is willing to do what he can to make up for the wrongs he has done by helping to prevent others from becoming victims themselves. Toward this end, he has spoken all over the country at his own expense.[434] Antar's attitude is key. Although he fulfilled all his legal obligations according to the criminal justice system as a convicted felon, he has chosen to do what he can to continue to pay society back for his crimes.

What If It Is Not Possible to Make the Injured Party Whole Again?

Financial Reparations. In those instances where it is not possible to restore what has been lost, money is a common means by which offenders demonstrate genuine contrition and compensate for the damage done. For example, on September 27, 1951, Konrad Adenauer, the first chancellor of the Federal Republic of Germany, spoke about the Jewish Holocaust perpetrated by the Nazi regime in Germany. He stated, "In our name, unspeakable crimes have been committed and they demand restitution, both moral and material, for the persons and properties of the Jews who have been so seriously harmed."[435] Actions followed the chancellor's words. Since that time, tens of billions of dollars have been paid out to victims and their families by the German government. They continue to this day. Nevertheless, it is still acknowledged that "no matter how large the sum, no amount of money will ever suffice to compensate for National Socialist [Nazi] persecution."[436] The willingness of the German government to make such payments for more than half a century, however, does demonstrate the sincerity of their confession. It is also significant to note that since Israel's birth as a nation, Germany has been one of the Jewish state's strongest allies.[437]

Symbolic Reparations. What about those cases when the offender lacks sufficient sums of money to provide to the aggrieved party? Such was the case in South Africa when the era of apartheid came to an end.* South Africa's Truth and Reconciliation Commission acknowledged that it was not possible for the nation to repair all the abuse and brutality that had taken place under apartheid over the course of decades, even if it had unlimited resources, which it did not.[438] The commission soberly stated, "Part of the task for healing in South Africa lies in accepting what cannot be done."[439] Notwithstanding this fact, the commission firmly asserted, "While the recommended reparations are not and cannot ever be proportionate to the harm suffered, reparations may be understood at least as an act of good faith and a serious attempt to alleviate some of the material and psychological trauma that victims endured."[440] Bishop Desmond Tutu, the chairman of the commission, readily admitted that the reparations of R30,000 ($4,000 to $4,600) to each of about 22,000 people,[441] were more symbolic than substantial. What these payments were intended to represent was a government formally apologizing to a large portion of its citizenry. The reparations were meant to be a soothing balm that would aid in the healing process.[442]

---

* Apartheid refers to the former system of racial segregation, discrimination, and gross human rights violations in South Africa by white South Africans against black South Africans.

207

Such an approach is inherent in the culture of the Navajo Indians. When it is impossible to make full material reparations, either because the loss was too great or the resources of the offender too small, or both, the Navajos turn to symbolic reparations in the form of livestock. What, for example, is the price tag for rape? There is none. On the other hand, "the act of delivering cattle as compensation is visible in a rural community. Members of that community will most likely know about the event. The public act of delivering cattle or horses shows the woman's innocence. It reinforces her dignity and tells the community she was wronged."[443] Such acts provide some monetary value, but, more importantly, such symbolic reparations provide a mechanism by which to restore individual dignity and maintain the peace of the community.[444]

What Should the Peacemaker Do?

The emphasis of this stage represents an increasingly popular concept and practice known as "restorative justice."[445] The focus is not on punishment but on repairing the social injustices caused by a person's wrongful acts. According to one restorative justice expert, "The first goal of justice, then, ought to be restitution and healing for victims."[446] The first question that should be asked and answered is, "What can be done to make things right?"[447] This has a broad application. Restorative justice "aims at the healing and the restoration of all concerned—of victims in the first place, but also of offenders, their families and the larger community."[448]

This stage is the applicational side of Stage 3, envisioning justice. In Stage 3, the peacemaker learns from the aggrieved party what justice looks like to them. In this stage, the perpetrators not only put forth what they believe they should and can do to make things right, but they will also consider the aggrieved party's perspective. Initially, there likely may be a gap between the two sides in terms of what justice looks like. "One person's justice is another person's barbarity."[449] The peacemaker is going to have to work with both sides toward creating consensus between the parties. "Agreement on justice is needed."[450] The form of reparations that will be enough to satisfy the victims' needs and bring healing will need to be worked out with the help of the peacemaker.

Overall Summary

The close relationship between the Hebrew word peace (*shalom*) and the verb meaning "to make whole, restore, repay" (*shalem*) is indicative of the fact that achieving shalomic peace includes restoring one's property. When people are deprived of something that is rightfully theirs, things remain out of balance, and justice is not established until the victims are made as whole again as possible.

A genuine verbal confession of sin to God is evidenced by a change in one's behavior and a willingness to make things right with the injured party. Likewise, on a social level, once disputants come to realize that their words or actions have contributed to the injury of another, the sincerity of their new awareness is reflected in their willingness not only to apologize, but also to do what is necessary to restore to the injured party what was lost, to the greatest extent possible. Reparations often will include financial restitution (as God required in the Old Testament and exemplified in the New Testament). If that is not possible, other forms of reparations can be offered. The peacemaker will work with both sides to achieve a meeting of the minds on this matter. In the same way God expects those who sinned against him and hurt others to make reparations to those harmed, so the peacemaker encourages the offending party to make the injured party materially whole again.

Stage 9: Exercising Faith

The Disputants Trust the Peacemaker to Make Peace Between Them

What Is the Scriptural Basis for This Stage?

Faith in Jesus the Mediator

Like Father, Like Son

Stage 9: Exercising Faith

Differences in the Outcomes of Faith in the Divine and Human Peacemaking Processes
  Timing of the Process
  Terms of Peace
  The Work of the Mediator
  The Trusted Dr. Ralph Bunche

Overall Summary

This stage examines the subject of faith. Faith in Jesus, the mediator between heaven and earth, is required for people to make peace with God. Faith is also needed in human mediators if the peacemaking process is going to be successful. After examining the differences between the outcome of faith in Jesus and all other mediators, this section culminates with a look at the work of Dr. Ralph Bunche, a world-renowned peacemaker.

What Is the Scriptural Basis for This Stage?

Faith in Jesus the Mediator

In the New Testament faith means: (1) "to consider something to be true and therefore worthy of one's trust, believe," and (2) "to entrust oneself to an entity in complete confidence, *believe (in), trust,* with implication of total commitment to the one who is trusted. … God and Christ are objects of this type of faith."[451] The New Testament teaches that the pathway back to God requires placing one's faith in Jesus. Consider the following passages.

John 1:11-12
11 He came to his own, and his own people did not receive him. 12 But to all who did receive him, who believed in his name, he gave the right to become children of God.

John 3:16-17
16 "For God so loved the world, that he gave his only Son, that whoever believes in him should not perish but have eternal life. 17 For God did not send his Son into the world to condemn the world, but in order that the world might be saved through him."

John 20:30-31
30 Now Jesus did many other signs in the presence of the disciples, which are not written in this book; 31 but these are

written so that you may believe that Jesus is the Christ, the Son of God, and that by believing you may have life in his name.

Acts 10:43
"To him all the prophets bear witness that everyone who believes in him receives forgiveness of sins through his name."

Acts 16:30-31
30 Then he brought them out and said, "Sirs, what must I do to be saved?" 31 And they said, "Believe in the Lord Jesus, and you will be saved, you and your household."

1 Timothy 1:15-16
15 The saying is trustworthy and deserving of full acceptance, that Christ Jesus came into the world to save sinners, of whom I am the foremost. 16 But I received mercy for this reason, that in me, as the foremost, Jesus Christ might display his perfect patience as an example to those who were to believe in him for eternal life.

As can be seen in the passages above (and many others), faith in Jesus is central. As mediator, "He has a share in the sinful corrupted world and He has a share in the divine eternal world of perfection. He is the Bridge between both. The Bridge, however is there to be crossed."[452] That crossing occurs when faith is exercised. It is a momentous occasion. "When the Mediator's person and work are appropriated by a sinner in trustful self-commitment, a new God-relationship is established."[453] Peace with God becomes the new reality.

Like Father, Like Son

In the same way people place their trust in Jesus as the mediator to make peace between them and God, so the parties in dispute place their trust in their mediator to make peace between them.

Stage 9: Exercising Faith

Faith in the peacemaker is essential because those in ongoing conflict often have little to no faith in each other. It is as if the disputants are standing on opposite banks of a river. The space between them represents the absence of trust.[454] Crossing a bridge back and forth, the mediator interacts separately with each party on their respective riverbank. Over time, the mediator builds up a strong enough relationship with each that each side comes to believe that the peacemaker has their best interests at heart. Slowly, each side is willing to meet with the mediator in the middle of the bridge and thus meet each other.

> *Faith in the peacemaker is essential because those in ongoing conflict often have little to no faith in each other.*

This is what made President Jimmy Carter so effective as a peacemaker in the negotiations with President Anwar Sadat of Egypt and Israel's Prime Minister Menachem Begin, resulting in the Camp David Accords. The process was not an easy one. Sadat and Begin were personally incompatible. Face-to-face negotiations proved to be futile. Consequently, Carter had to count "on his personal rapport with each man to bridge the gap."[455] In the end, the trust these two Middle East leaders had in President Carter carried the process far enough along that Sadat and Begin were able to agree to the terms of peace and later shake hands in front of cameras for the whole world to see.

Differences in the Outcomes of Faith in the Divine and Human Peacemaking Processes

There are differences between placing one's trust in Jesus as mediator and the trust people put in human mediators. When a person places his or her faith in Jesus, the peace process with God is "fast-tracked." The apostle Paul declared, "Therefore, if anyone is in Christ, he is a new creation. The old has passed away; behold, the new has come" (2 Cor. 5:17). Chafer, for example, listed thirty-three new realities that "instantaneously" and "simultaneously" occur in transforming the sinner's relationship to God the instant a person puts his or her faith in Jesus.[456] Other theologians have recognized the same thing in terms of the multidimensional yet immediate aspect of making peace with God.[457] Forgiveness from and reconciliation with God are among the immediate consequences. However, at least three differences between the work of Jesus as mediator and the work of all other mediators need to be pointed out. The differences relate to the timing of the process, the terms of the agreement, and the work of the mediator.

Timing of the Process

One of the chief differences between a person making peace with God and making peace with others is the time frame involved. As noted, making peace with God through faith is instantaneous. People often recall it as one of the most dramatic moments in their lives. Making peace with others, by contrast, can be a lengthy process. It is like the difference between making an operator-assisted telephone call to a remote region on the other side of the globe, which is virtually instantaneous, and sending a letter by courier, which can take days if not weeks. The effort of the courier, moreover, is fraught with uncertainties every step of the way.

The same can be said with respect to the faith that is placed in the mediator. Whereas the commitment to place one's faith in Jesus occurs at a specific point in time, placing faith in a human mediator is a process that develops more slowly over time. It begins with developing rapport (see Stage 2). It progresses until each party is willing to allow the mediator to present their perspective to their opponent. It culminates when each side gives free reign to the peacemaker to do what he or she believes is best to reach agreement.

215

Terms of Peace

A second difference between making peace with God and
making peace with others is the absence of negotiations with God.
As noted in chapter 3, the conflict between God and mankind is
clear-cut in terms of right and wrong. Sinful man has offended the
holy and righteous God. The "finger of blame" points in only one
direction: at man. Consequently, the "terms" of what needs to occur
for peace to emerge between heaven and earth have already been
established by God (e.g., repentance, confession, faith). When a
person, through faith, accepts God's terms, peace is guaranteed. The
outcome is not in doubt. However, this is not the situation when it
comes to making peace between people. In human conflicts, people
almost always point the finger of blame at each other. The terms of
peace offered by one side may be rejected by the other, in whole
or in part. Negotiations are an inevitable part of the process. They
may be successful, or they may break down, but the terms of peace
first have to be hammered out before they can be agreed upon.

The Work of the Mediator

There is a difference between the work that human mediators
do and the work that Jesus did as mediator. In the first case, every
situation requires fresh efforts by the mediator to work through the
maze of difficulties associated with the conflict. In practical terms
the mediator may engage in numerous activities. He or she may
become a conduit of communication between the parties and/or
provide a neutral location for the adversaries or their representatives to meet, transmit accurate, undistorted information about
reality and/or clear up misperceptions, help adversaries begin the
negotiation process, work to overcome the emotional and relational
barriers to peace each side may have, help forestall a deterioration
in relations, allow parties to save face, change meeting arrange-
ments and procedures as needed, assist in inventing new possibilities for agreement, represent persons not otherwise represented in
the negotiations, help work out the specific details of a mutually

acceptable agreement, add or find needed resources to facilitate agreement, bring to bear motivating factors and pressures for reaching agreement, and rally backing for the agreement.[458]

By contrast, in the case of Jesus, the work has already been accomplished on the cross. Jesus's work as mediator has already removed the barrier to peace between God and mankind. His *finished* work needs only to be accepted by faith. (More will be said about this in Stage 10.)

In terms of the outcome of faith in one's mediator, differences exist between the work of Jesus and all others. Differences in the divine and human peacemaking processes exist with regard to the timing of the process, the terms of peace, and the work of the mediator. That said, their essential similarity is that their presence and involvement in resolving conflict is indispensable.

The Trusted Dr. Ralph Bunche

In modern history, an outstanding example of a peacemaker who garnered the respect and trust of the warring sides is Dr. Ralph Bunche. In 1934 he became the first black American to graduate from Harvard with a Ph.D. in government and international relations. His skills were especially needed a decade and a half later as a peacemaker. On November 29, 1947, the United Nations adopted a resolution calling for the establishment of a Jewish state in the historic land of Israel. Israel declared its independence on May 14, 1948. Almost immediately, war broke out between the fledgling nation and surrounding Arab countries (Egypt, Jordan, Syria, and Lebanon).

On January 7, a cease-fire between Israel and Egypt was agreed upon. This was followed by armistice negotiations on the Greek island of Rhodes beginning on January 12. (Dr. Bunche chose to set up separate negotiations between Israel and each Arab state.) Dr. Bunche carried out a significant portion of his work by means of "shuttle diplomacy," that is, going back and forth between the parties in order to narrow the differences on a given area of the negotiations. Bunche noted, "Neither side [is] anxious to meet the other but both want me to persuade the other."[459] On other occasions, Dr. Bunche would bring the Israeli and Egyptian negotiating teams together for face-to-face discussions to review agreements already made in private, as well as to delve into areas that still needed resolution. This was physically easy to do as the two delegations were housed in the same hotel.

The negotiations, however, were grueling. In a letter to his wife, Ruth, Ralph wrote, "I talk, argue, coax, and threaten these stubborn people day and night, in the effort to reach agreement. I make a bit of progress here and another bit there, but it is so slow and so arduous. Sometimes I feel that I should just tell them to go home and forget about an armistice. … This is killing work. I haven't been out of the hotel for two weeks now."[460] About a week later, he wrote to Ruth again, saying, "One day we are all certain that there is no possibility of agreement and that the conference will break up in failure, and the next day one side or the other will make a concession, and we lift our hopes again and get back to work."[461]

It was just at times like these that the only thing keeping the parties together was the bond of trust and respect each side developed, not with each other, but with Dr. Bunche. For example, Dr. Bunche at one point noted, "Neither side will wish to take responsibility for terminating the negotiations and so [both] will try to shift that responsibility to me." His willingness to stay the course, as grueling as it was, was indispensable for the talks to continue.

Although he had no power to dictate solutions to the representatives of each country, he did have influence. For example, when the Israeli and Arab delegations would reach an impasse, Dr. Bunche would take the initiative to draft new proposals for each side to consider as a way of keeping the discussions alive. He had a gift of coming up with new ideas.[462] What is significant is that these proposals never would have been initiated by either party. Had they been, they would have been rejected out of hand by the other side.[463] But Dr. Bunche had an ability to keep bringing the parties closer and closer together until an agreement was reached that each side could live with.[464] Dr. Bunche was trusted by both sides. Therefore, he had the freedom to be innovative in moving the process forward.

Critical to the success of his work was the fact that Dr. Bunche fully understood the perspectives of each side. He was aware of the Jewish tragedy of the Holocaust. He was sympathetic with Arab nationalism.[465] Early on, he earned their trust. How? Said one, he had "an extraordinary capacity to understand the problems of other people, and to put himself in their shoes and understand them."[466] He explored each side's anxieties and fears for the purpose of proposing solutions that would relieve them. "The result was that he enjoyed the complete confidence of the people he dealt with."[467]

Here is a brief story that well illustrates the bonds of trust Dr. Bunche developed with the Israelis and the Egyptians. One evening, he invited both sides to dinner at the hotel. On the table were ornate pottery plates. He said to both delegations in a lighthearted manner, "You see these plates? If you negotiate a successful treaty, I'm gonna give you each a set of these plates. If you don't negotiate a treaty, I'm gonna break these plates over your head."[468]

From beginning to end, the negotiations between the Israelis and Egyptians lasted some seven weeks. With full agreement on a myriad of issues, Israel and Egypt signed an armistice agreement on February 23, 1949. Congratulations to Dr. Bunche flowed from all over the world, including U.S. President Truman, who wrote, "I wish also to congratulate the United Nations Mediator, Dr. Ralph Bunche, whose untiring efforts have so greatly contributed to the success of these negotiations."[469] Dr. Bunche continued his peacemaking work between Israel and its others Arab neighbors. An armistice agreement between Israel and Lebanon was signed on March 23, between Israel and Jordan on April 3, and between Israel and Syria on July 20.

When Bunche returned to the United States in mid-April, 1949, he returned home to a hero's welcome. A ticker-tape parade was held for him in New York City. Los Angeles declared, "Ralph Bunche Day." In 1950, Dr. Bunche was awarded the Nobel Peace Prize. Over a three-year span, Dr. Bunche was awarded over thirty honorary degrees,[470] in recognition of his outstanding work, a work built on trust.

Overall Summary

Foundational to the work of a peacemaker is the trust that he or she is accorded by each side in a given conflict. Since the lines of communication are down and trust levels are low to nonexistent, it is essential to the peacemaking process that the mediator, the one in the middle, earns the confidence of each side. By earning their trust, the mediator is then free to engage in activities and initiate processes that will begin to move the parties in a direction that will eventually allow them to trust each other and establish peace. Faith in the person and work of the peacemaker is at the center of this stage. In the same way people place their faith in Jesus as the mediator to make peace between them and God, so the parties in dispute place their trust in their mediator to make peace between them.

Stage 10: Granting Forgiveness

The Aggrieved Party Forgives the Offending Party

What Is the Scriptural Basis for This Stage?

Introduction
Forgiveness Means Freedom
    Freedom from Divine Punishment
    Freedom from Feelings of Guilt with Respect to God
How Can God Forgive Sin and Still Be Holy?
    The Dilemma
    The Death of Christ
        How Fair Is This?
        Amazing Grace
    The Core of Divine Forgiveness
God Stands Ready and Is Willing to Forgive
Forgiveness Is Conditional upon Repentance

Like Father, Like Son

Stage 10: Granting Forgiveness

Being Willing to Forgive
    Our Natural Orientation to Love
Forgiveness Is Conditional upon Repentance
    The Confusion Surrounding Unconditional Forgiveness
    Forgiveness Is for the Sinner
    Biblical Confirmation
    The Kairos Document
    Forgiveness Without Repentance Is Not Love
    The Willis Family

Stage 10: Granting Forgiveness (continued)

The Core of Human Forgiveness
Forgiveness Described
Forgiveness Illustrated
The Beauty of Forgiveness

What Should the Peacemaker Do?

Establish a Forum Where Forgiveness Can Occur

Overall Summary

This stage represents the culmination of all the previous stages. Because of how critical it is to the reconciliation process, a good deal of time is spent on examining not only what is involved when God forgives us, but also what should be involved when we forgive each other.

What Is the Scriptural Basis for This Stage?

Introduction

The original meaning of the principal word for forgiveness in Greek is "to send off ... release ... let go."[471] In the New Testament the word is primarily used for "the act of freeing from an obligation, guilt, or punishment, *pardon, cancellation*."[472] Consider two uses of the word in the New Testament when it is not referring to the forgiveness of sins. In one instance it is used to proclaim freedom to those under oppression and in captivity (Luke 4:18). In a second instance the word is used for the canceling of the financial debt of a borrower by the lender (Matt. 18:27). In both scenarios there was a release from a heavy burden. Those who were released were able to continue their lives free from their former oppressive situation or obligation.

In general, this is what occurs when God forgives us of our burdensome sins. He frees us from sin's punishment and guilt. Here is a sampling of texts.

Luke 24:45-47

45 Then he opened their minds to understand the Scriptures, 46 and said to them, "Thus it is written, that the Christ should suffer and on the third day rise from the dead, 47 and that repentance and forgiveness of sins should be proclaimed in his name to all nations, beginning from Jerusalem.

Acts 2:38

And Peter said to them, "Repent and be baptized every one of you in the name of Jesus Christ for the forgiveness of your sins, and you will receive the gift of the Holy Spirit."

Acts 3:19

"Repent therefore, and turn again, that your sins may be blotted out."

Acts 10:43

"To him all the prophets bear witness that everyone who believes in him [Jesus] receives forgiveness of sins through his name."

Acts 13:38

"Let it be known to you therefore, brothers, that through this man [Jesus] forgiveness of sins is proclaimed to you."

Poetic depictions of divine forgiveness from the Old Testament provide vivid images of what God's forgiveness includes.

Psalm 103:12

As far as the east is from the west, so far does he remove our transgressions from us.

Isaiah 38:17
You have cast all my sins behind your back.

Jeremiah 31:34
"For I will forgive their iniquity, and I will remember their sin no more."

Micah 7:19
You will cast all our sins into the depths of the sea.

Forgiveness Means Freedom

Freedom from Divine Punishment

Divine forgiveness involves freedom from sin's "punishment."[473] It means the "noninfliction of penalty" or the "noninfliction of suffering upon the transgressor."[474] As will be discussed further below, the New Testament teaches that Christ suffered our punishment for us. Therefore, we are, in essence, "free to go" and enjoy an unhindered relationship with God. The charges against us are inadmissible, much like inadmissible remarks made during a courtroom trial. The judge instructs jury members not to consider those remarks in reaching their verdict. While the reality of certain remarks cannot be erased, they are not part of the official record over which jury members deliberate.[475] This is what the Scriptures teach with respect to how God treats our sins. They are not part of the official record that can be brought to mind and used against us. Hence, for the sinner, forgiveness involves "making of no account the sin which has been committed."[476] The following passages are particularly illustrative of this understanding of forgiveness.

Romans 4:7-8
7 "Blessed are those whose lawless deeds are forgiven,[477] and whose sins are covered; 8 blessed is the man against whom the Lord will not count his sin."

Colossians 2:13-14

13 And you, who were dead in your trespasses and the uncircumcision of your flesh, God made alive together with him, having forgiven[478] us all our trespasses, 14 by canceling the record of debt that stood against us with its legal demands. This he set aside, nailing it to the cross.

Romans 8:1

There is therefore now no condemnation[479] for those who are in Christ Jesus.

Freedom from Feelings of Guilt with Respect to God

The second aspect of divine forgiveness has to do with its psychological effect. God's forgiveness frees one not only from the punishment for sin, but also from its "guilt."[480] "The event of wrongdoing is not undone, but the guilt resulting from such an event is pardoned." [481] This means that the burdens of self-reproach and self-deprecation before God are removed (see Heb. 9:14; 10:22; 1 Pet. 3:21). As Matthew Henry aptly said centuries ago, "Nothing can pacify an offended conscience but that which satisfied an offended God."[482] When God's divine justice is satisfied with respect to an individual's sin, then that individual's conscience can be at rest as far as God is concerned. (As far as others are concerned, this peacemaking process still needs to play out.) If God does not bring the record of our sins to mind, then neither should we. Forgiveness "removes all of the guilt and cause of alienation from the past, it assures a state of grace for the present, and it promises divine mercy and aid for the future"[483] One French writer beautifully captured this truth when she wrote, "When the soul has laid down its faults at the feet of God, it feels as though it had wings."[484]

How Can God Forgive and Still Be Holy?

The Dilemma

The divine declaration of a sinner's forgiveness is like the tip of a large theological iceberg. To fully understand what is involved, we need to view the topic from its base up to the top. The starting point for this discussion is to make the initial observation that God's forgiveness seemingly involves two irreconcilable aspects of his character: his holiness and his love. If God is absolutely holy and acts with righteousness, how can he forgive? If every person who ever lived stands condemned because of sin, in what sense is God all-loving?

Jewish thinkers have struggled with this subject.[485] One ancient rabbi suggested that God argues with himself over this dilemma and even prays the following to himself: "May it be My will that My mercy may suppress My anger and My mercy may prevail over My other attributes, so that I may deal with My children according to the attribute of mercy."[486] This speculation, of course, does not accord with the teaching of the Old and New Testaments, which contain an entirely different line of Jewish thought.

Reflecting on the idea that God would withhold judgment for sin in order to forgive, one Christian theologian asserted, "The soul might be saved, [but] God, in turn, would be lost."[487] That is to say, if God, who is holy, were compromised by the acceptance of sin, he would no longer be holy and therefore no longer be God. Said another theologian, "God can't suspend justice any more than God can cease being God."[488]

The tension of the dilemma between God's justice and love was graphically illustrated in the 1967 movie *Camelot*. King Arthur of England is intent on establishing a kingdom based on justice and the rule of law. Near the end of the film, an unexpected turn of events takes place. Guinevere, Arthur's beloved wife, is found

226

guilty of having engaged in an adulterous relationship with Sir Lancelot. While Sir Lancelot escapes capture, a jury sentences the queen to death by fire. The day and time of the execution arrives. The queen is tied to the stake. The signal to set fire to the stake is awaited, but no gesture is given by the king. Eventually, a friend of the king states the obvious, "Arthur, the executioner is waiting for your signal." King Arthur is speechless, filled with irreconcilable emotions.

One reviewer of the film wrote, "The fact that Arthur was Guinevere's husband, and at the same time her King, created the dilemma. If he carried out the sentence, he upheld the law and validates himself as a just and impartial king. Yet, in doing so, he calls into question his love. ... His heart tells him to set her free. If he did, it certainly would verify his great love for her. But by bending justice, and showing partiality, he would call into question his right to rule.[489]

Just then Sir Lancelot, with his mounted band of knights, rides into the public square and rescues Guinevere. King Arthur was spared from making an impossible decision, but such was not the case for God. The reviewer of the film, a Catholic priest, reflected, "Another time. Another place. Another King. The setting: A world lies estranged from the God who loves it. Like Guinevere, an unfaithful humanity stands guilty and in bondage, awaiting judgment's torch. Could God turn away from the righteous demands of justice? Or could he just turn away from those he love[s]?"[490]

The Death of Christ

How can God's love and justice be reconciled? We need to go deeper. The New Testament asserts that Jesus, the Messiah of Israel and Son of God, died to bear the judgment and penalty for the sins of the world in order to provide sinners a way of escape from God's righteous judgment. Jesus did not die for angels but on behalf of sinners, upon those whom God's righteous judgment was due to fall.

227

The Scriptures are replete with statements that affirm this truth.[491]

Matthew 20:28
"The Son of Man came not to be served but to serve, and to give his life as a ransom for many."

John 10:11
"I am the good shepherd. The good shepherd lays down his life for the sheep."

Matthew 26:27-28
27 And he took a cup, and when he had given thanks he gave it to them, saying, "Drink of it, all of you, 28 for this is my blood of the covenant, which is poured out for many for the forgiveness of sins."

Romans 5:8
But God shows his love for us in that while we were still sinners, Christ died for us.

1 Corinthians 15:3
For I delivered to you as of first importance what I also received: that Christ died for our sins in accordance with the Scriptures

1 Peter 3:18
For Christ also suffered once for sins, the righteous for the unrighteous, that he might bring us to God.

In light of the many biblical texts, theologians throughout the centuries have been quick to acknowledge that Jesus's death on the cross was substitutionary. In 1535, Martin Luther described Jesus's death this way. Jesus, he said, became "the greatest transgressor, murderer, adulterer, thief, blasphemer that ever was or ever could be on earth. When He took the sins of the whole world upon Himself, Christ was no longer an innocent person. He was a sinner burdened with the sins of a Paul who was a blasphemer; burdened with the sins of a Peter who denied Christ; burdened with the sins of a David who committed adultery and murder, and gave the heathen occasion to laugh at the Lord. In short, Christ was charged with the sins of all men."[492]

All evangelical theologians agree.[493] Jesus's death on the cross was substitutionary, that is, "He took the place of sinners … their guilt was imputed, and the punishment transferred, to Him."[494] As a result of Jesus's crucifixion, God is "satisfied" that his righteous judgment against sin and evil has been fulfilled.[495]

How Fair Is This? How fair is it that Jesus suffered in the place of all humanity? One critic believed that it was unethical. "That the suffering of the innocent should be taken in itself in lieu of the suffering of the guilty is self-evidently immoral. … The human judge who so acted would rouse the indignation of any modern civilized community."[496] In this last point, the critic is correct. Today one need only go to the Web site of the Innocence Project[497] to learn about the numerous cases where innocent people have been charged, convicted, and imprisoned for crimes they did not commit. These individuals may sit for years, even decades until new DNA evidence exonerates them. (Just consider the case of Gary Dotson discussed in Stage 8.)

PBS journalist Bill Moyers interviewed author John Grisham, who, among his many books, wrote *The Innocent Man*. It is a true story about Ron Williamson, who was wrongly convicted of first-degree murder. He sat on death row and came within five days of execution. He was finally exonerated of the crime by DNA evidence and freed, after unjustly spending eleven years behind bars. During the Moyers interview, Grisham remarked, "But think if you're an innocent man. If you know you didn't do the crime. And the guy who did do the murder is still out there. You're serving his time, and nobody's listening to you. Nobody's listening to you."[498] Grisham similarly told *USA Today*, "When I researched and wrote the book, it was impossible not to become indignant and infuriated."[499] That an innocent man should suffer instead of the one guilty of the ghastly crime is an outrage. The innocent are imprisoned while the guilty go free. Grisham's feelings reflect the feelings of the man who so argued about Jesus's suffering. There is, however, one significant difference.

Amazing Grace. According to the Scriptures, it was God himself, the offended party, in the person of his Son, who died in our place.[500] Rather than overlooking sin, the sentence for sin was carried out. In response to the sentiment that it is unfair for an innocent party to suffer for a guilty one, one theologian replied, "In the process of salvation God is not transferring penalty from one man (guilty) to another man (innocent). He is bearing it Himself. ... When Christ substitutes for sinful man in His death that is God Himself bearing the consequences of our sin, God saving man at cost to Himself, not at cost to someone else."[501] Many others have said the same. "The One who was offended bears the burden of the offense."[502] Since the Bible teaches that Jesus was God in the flesh, God bore the punishment of mankind's sin. "The One who demanded the penalty (God) was the One who paid it."[503] Charles Wesley exclaimed in 1738, "Amazing love! how can it be That Thou, my God shouldst die for me?"[504]

The Core of Divine Forgiveness

The cross is where God's justice and love meet. "The pardon of sin is not merely an act of mercy, but also an act of justice."[505] "Do you wish to see God's wrath? Look to the cross."[506] Here sin is judged and punished. Justice is established. But there is more! "Do you wish to see God's love? Look to the cross."[507] It is where love triumphs over judgment.[508] How? "Not by trampling upon the claims of justice, but by vicariously satisfying them."[509] On the cross God condemned and punished the sin of all while also expressing his great love for all. God's forgiveness of man at

230

its irreducible core, therefore, is premised on his loving-kindness and willingness to absorb the demands of justice on behalf of the repentant sinner. God, in the person of his Son, willingly bore the pain of his own judgment on mankind that was required by his holiness.

George Buttrick told of a picture of Jesus's crucifixion that he once saw in an Italian church. Initially, there didn't seem to be anything unusual about the painting. However, upon closer examination, another image within the picture became apparent. Buttrick explained, "There's a vast and shadowy Figure behind the figure of Jesus. The nail that pierces the hand of Jesus goes through to the hand of God. The spear thrust into the side of Jesus goes through into God's."[510] Though no human being is able to carry the sins of the entire world, God is more than able. According to the Bible, that is precisely what God did.

God Stands Ready and Is Willing to Forgive

With justice satisfactorily addressed in the death of Christ, the basis for divine forgiveness has been established. An invitation to be reconciled with God is extended to all. God stands ready and is willing to forgive us. Consider the following texts.[511]

Matthew 23:37 (cf. Luke 19:41-42)
"O Jerusalem, Jerusalem, the city that kills the prophets and stones those who are sent to it! How often would I have gathered your children together as a hen gathers her brood under her wings, and you would not!

Acts 3:13, 19-20
13 "The God of Abraham, the God of Isaac, and the God of Jacob, the God of our fathers, glorified his servant Jesus, whom you delivered over and denied in the presence of Pilate, when he had decided to release him. ... 19 Repent therefore, and

turn again, that your sins may be blotted out, 20 that times of refreshing may come from the presence of the Lord."

2 Corinthians 5:19-20
19 in Christ God was reconciling the world to himself, not counting their trespasses against them, and entrusting to us the message of reconciliation. 20 Therefore, we are ambassadors for Christ, God making his appeal through us. We implore you on behalf of Christ, be reconciled to God.

2 Timothy 2:3b-4
3 …God our Savior, 4 who desires all people to be saved and to come to the knowledge of the truth.

2 Peter 3:9
The Lord is not slow to fulfill his promise as some count slowness, but is patient toward you, not wishing that any should perish, but that all should reach repentance.

The same theme is found in the Old Testament with respect to faith in the God of Israel.

Psalm 86:5 NKJV
For You, Lord, are good, and ready to forgive, and abundant in mercy to all those who call upon You.

Isaiah 55:7
Let the wicked forsake his way, and the unrighteous man his thoughts; let him return to the Lord, that he may have compassion on him, and to our God, for he will abundantly pardon.

Nehemiah 9:16-17
16 "But they and our fathers acted presumptuously and stiffened their neck and did not obey your commandments. 17 They refused to obey and were not mindful of the wonders that you performed among them, but they stiffened

their neck and appointed a leader to return to their slavery in Egypt. But you are a God ready to forgive, gracious and merciful, slow to anger and abounding in steadfast love, and did not forsake them."

The door of God's forgiveness is open wide to those who are willing to take the steps to enter in. Because of his love, God is willing to forgive. There is, however, one condition.

Forgiveness is Conditional upon Repentance

There is widespread agreement on the biblical teaching that God's forgiveness is conditional upon a sinner's repentance. Monsma, writing in the *Zondervan Pictorial Encyclopedia of the Bible* stated, "It is clear that repentance as a condition of forgiveness of sin has been, and is, widely recognized, and that it is well supported by Scripture." He added that for God "to forgive without requiring repentance would be like condoning sin or being indifferent to it."[512] Houston, writing in the *Baker Encyclopedia of the Bible*, likewise stated, "Forgiveness is rooted in the character of God, but his forgiveness is never indiscriminate, for man must also be penitent."[513] Morro and Harrison, writing in the *International Standard Bible Encyclopedia*, stated, "God does not forgive without repentance."[514] This facet of God doesn't make him less loving (or bitter). It only means that whereas his love is unconditional, his forgiveness is not. God offers forgiveness to all, but "forgiveness can be received only when man affirms God's judgment on himself."[515]

To preach otherwise is to promote what Bonhoeffer, over a half a century ago, called "cheap grace."[516] This is a grace that says no change on the part of the sinner is required for God's grace to be applied. Nothing could be further from the truth. Divine forgiveness is not automatic. Otherwise there would be no point for the prophets, evangelists, apostles, and Jesus to have beseeched people to repent of their sins. If repentance is not required to make peace with God, that would mean that everyone is heaven bound. But if this were the case, then "what does it take to serve in hell?" as one Holocaust survivor put it.[517] To preach that everyone's sin is forgiven even without repentance would be to undercut the holiness and justice of God. It is an idea the Scriptures do not support. (See Appendix 2, "Additional Passages on Forgiveness," for further discussion.)

Like Father, Like Son

In the same way God forgives repentant sinners, so the peacemaker encourages aggrieved parties to forgive those who express genuine sorrow for the wrong they committed against them.

Ephesians 4:32
Be kind to one another, tenderhearted, forgiving one another, as God in Christ forgave you.

Colossians 3:13
… as the Lord has forgiven you, so you also must forgive.

Stage 10: Granting Forgiveness

Being Willing to Forgive

Our Natural Orientation to Love

Because of God's love, he stands ready to forgive repentant sinners. We ought to take the same posture and attitude. Being willing to forgive as God is willing to forgive is a posture of love. It also signals that the breach in the relationship needs to be addressed and will not be swept under the rug. Being willing to forgive someone who has done us harm is the opposite of having an embittered, vengeful attitude. The apostle Paul wrote,

Romans 12:17-21

17 Repay no one evil for evil, but give thought to do what is honorable in the sight of all. 18 If possible, so far as it depends on you, live peaceably with all. 19 Beloved, never avenge yourselves, but leave it to the wrath of God, for it is written, "Vengeance is mine, I will repay, says the Lord."[518] 20 To the contrary, "if your enemy is hungry, feed him; if he is thirsty, give him something to drink; for by so doing you will heap burning coals on his head." 21 Do not be overcome by evil, but overcome evil with good.[519]

The point here is that rather than take on an attitude of hate when hurt by others, our posture should be one of love. One pastor rightly put it, "A Christian who loves and offers grace is not bitter."[520]

The orientation to love is not only built into our DNA (see Appendix 1), but it is evidenced in Jesus's instructions to his followers. As God's unconditional orientation to rebellious mankind is one of love, so our attitude toward our fellow human beings ought to be the same.

Matthew 5:43-48

43 "You have heard that it was said, 'You shall love your neighbor and hate your enemy.' 44 But I say to you, Love your enemies and pray for those who persecute you, 45 so that you may be sons of your Father who is in heaven. For he makes his sun rise on the evil and on the good, and sends rain on the just and on the unjust. 46 For if you love those who love you, what reward do you have? Do not even the tax collectors do the same? 47 And if you greet only your brothers, what more are you doing than others? Do not even the Gentiles do the same? 48 You therefore must be perfect, as your heavenly Father is perfect.[521]

Commenting on this passage, one scholar remarked, "By loving and praying for our enemies we show that we are God's sons because we do what He does."[522] Though we experience all kinds of emotions in the face of conflict, taking on an attitude of love is not conjuring up something that is foreign to who we are. Rather, it reflects who we are at the deepest level.

Forgiveness Is Conditional upon Repentance

The Confusion Surrounding Unconditional Forgiveness

People often confuse love with forgiveness, but the two are not the same. What is true of God is also true of us. An individual can be a loving person and yet withhold forgiveness from a person who is unrepentant. Christians do not always make this distinction. Large numbers of Christians believe that forgiveness is something that should be given automatically, irrespective of whether the offender repents or not. The big concern in popular literature on forgiveness is that we don't become consumed with bitterness and thereby cripple our own lives over what someone else did to us.

Consider this example. Mandisa Hundley not only was a contestant on the television show *American Idol* but also was a top-nine finalist during the program's fifth season. She obviously passed her initial audition in order to be invited to Hollywood. After she left the audition room, Simon Cowell, one of the show's judges, made cutting remarks about Mandisa's weight. She didn't know about those comments until she watched the program with Christian friends and heard the comments for the first time. She was hurt and upset by the remarks aired to tens of millions of people. Her friends immediately began to pray for her. One prayed that she would forgive Simon. Mandisa immediately felt that her tears and hurt feelings were not as important as being able to forgive—which she did. "I've said worse things about others than what Simon said about me—and God keeps forgiving me. Besides, I learned forgiving has more to do with the person forgiving than the person being forgiven. I found peace. I let go of the bitterness."[523] Things

236

worked out well in the end. When Mandisa next saw Simon, she told him that she was hurt by what he said but that she forgave him. He, in turn, apologized.

This is a warm story, and I cite it because it highlights the almost unconscious acceptance of the belief that Christians are obligated to forgive an offender almost as soon as the offense has occurred and even before a follow-up interaction takes place. Given that there is and can be no law against love (Gal. 5:22-23), there is no place to criticize anyone who expresses it as Mandisa did. Personally, I would place Mandisa's actions under the category of choosing to "overlook" an offense, as described in chapter 5.

However, there are other stories that don't end as well, and the offense is more than a snide remark. Cooper Anderson interviewed a twenty-four-year-old married woman from the Congo as part of a larger *60 Minutes* story about the war that had been raging in that country for more than a decade. Over five million people had been killed during this time, making it the most lethal conflict since World War II. One of the weapons of this war, used to terrorize people, was rape. The woman Anderson interviewed told a gruesome story. One night, a year after her parents were murdered, a band of six soldiers broke into her home. All six soldiers, one after the other, raped her. They had her brother hold a flashlight so he could see what they were doing. When they were finished, they ordered the brother to rape his sister. He refused. They then stabbed him to death in front of his sister. The woman was then kidnapped and taken to the soldiers' camp. She was raped every day for eight months. Predictably, she became pregnant. Somehow she escaped her captors and found her way back home. Upon learning about what had happened, her husband abandoned her. The shame was too great. This woman was now left with two young children from her marriage and one on the way in a world bereft of those closest to her and filled with memories of horror. Incredibly, this is only one story among hundreds of thousands. A medical doctor who treated these rape victims at one hospital noted that these women are not just damaged physically. Many have been severely damaged psychologically. "Here at the hospital, we've seen women who've stopped living," he said.[524]

The idea that Christianity teaches that such behavior deserves to be unconditionally forgiven without repentance by the perpetrator goes beyond the pale of anything that Jesus, the apostles, or the other writers of the Scriptures ever conceived. But that statement is actually not strong enough. Unconditional forgiveness to unrepentant murderers, rapists, and swindlers is contrary to and stands in opposition to the very character of God. Does God forgive the unrepentant? No! Should we attempt to "out-love" God by forgiving those he is unwilling to forgive? Absurd! We are to forgive as God forgives us, which is based on repentance.

Does God forgive the unrepentant? No! Should we attempt to "out-love" God by forgiving those he is unwilling to forgive? Absurd! We are to forgive as God forgives us, which is based on repentance.

Forgiveness Is for the Sinner

The act of forgiveness denotes an interactive relationship. Forgiveness is a social act, not a private one. It is not something the aggrieved keeps to themselves. It is to be given to the offender. "Forgiveness is an interpersonal transaction between two parties."[525] By way of analogy, God does not forgive us in secret. Rather, his forgiveness signifies the establishing of a new relationship (or the renewal of an existing one). It is the means by which the relationship is restored.[526] In the same way an apology is not effective if one is merely talking to oneself (see Stage 7), neither is forgiveness.

238

Our Western culture teaches that forgiveness is practiced in isolation, by oneself for oneself. "We need to forgive the unrepentant for our own sake," says a popular book on forgiveness entitled *Forgive and Forget.*[527] This book, unfortunately, "is both representative of, and responsible for on some level, a great deal of wrong Christian thinking about forgiveness."[528] True forgiveness does not simply involve the offended party unilaterally forgiving and forgetting. True forgiveness first must be preceded by the offending party's remembering and repenting.[529]

We must keep in mind that in terms of the usage and meaning of the word in the New Testament, the "object" of forgiveness is another person's sins, not the psychological mind-set of the one forgiving.

We must keep in mind that in terms of the usage and meaning of the word in the New Testament, the "object" of forgiveness is another person's sins,[530] not the psychological mind-set of the one forgiving. As defined in the Scriptures, forgiveness is first and foremost about the release that the guilty party experiences as a result of being forgiven. When Jesus said to a sinful woman, "Your sins are forgiven … Go in peace" (Luke 7:48, 50), the impact of this interaction was to release the woman, not Jesus, from the burden of sin. When God forgives us, it is not for his benefit but for ours.

This is just the opposite of how many people practice forgiveness today. Consider these four lines from a poem I found on the Internet: "I forgive you for depriving me and for stealing my happiness. … I forgive you for accusing and rejecting me when I needed you most. … I forgive you for breaking my heart when all I did was to give you love. … I forgive you, not for you but for me to let go of this anger and find inner peace."[531] Could you ever imagine God forgiving on such a basis? Obviously not. Therefore, neither should we.

Biblical Confirmation

There are two passages in the New Testament that directly speak to this issue. The first example is from Jesus's own teaching on the subject. The second is based on the practice of the early church. First, Jesus taught,

> Luke 17:3-4
> 3 "Pay attention to yourselves! If your brother sins, rebuke him, and if he repents, forgive him, 4 and if he sins against you seven times in the day, and turns to you seven times, saying, 'I repent,' you must forgive him."[532]

Notice that forgiveness follows repentance. In the same way one would rebuke a brother only if that brother sins against you, you forgive him only if he repents. Or, stated in reverse, you don't rebuke those who don't sin against you. Likewise you don't forgive those who don't repent. British pastor and scholar John Stott wrote, "We are to rebuke a brother if he sins against us; we are to forgive him if he repents—and only if he repents. We must beware of cheapening forgiveness. ... God's forgiveness of us and our forgiveness of one another ... both are conditional upon repentance. If a brother who has sinned against us refuses to repent, we should not forgive him. Does this startle you? It is what Jesus taught. ... If we can restore to full and intimate fellowship with ourselves a sinning and unrepentant brother, we reveal not the depth of our love but its shallowness, for we are doing what is not for his highest good."[533] *

An example of the pattern Jesus spoke about is found in 2 Corinthians with reference to a repentant church member who had undergone church discipline. The apostle Paul wrote,

---

* Godet similarly stated, "The pardon to be granted to our brethren has no other limit than their repenting, and the confession by which it is expressed" (1889, vol. 2, p. 187).

2 Corinthians 2:5-8

5 Now if anyone has caused pain, he has caused it not to me, but in some measure—not to put it too severely—to all of you. 6 For such a one, this punishment by the majority is enough, 7 so you should rather turn to forgive and comfort him, or he may be overwhelmed by excessive sorrow. 8 So I beg you to reaffirm your love for him.

Here, we see that forgiveness is extended after this particular person repented of his ways. It is on the basis of repentance that forgiveness came. "Because the offender has shown genuine sorrow and repentance for his sin the punishment should be discontinued and he should be lovingly restored to their fellowship."[534] The observation not to be missed here is that forgiveness followed repentance.

Being willing to forgive unrepentant sinners in the same way God is willing to forgive unrepentant sinners means that our attitude should be one that emanates from love, not hate. Out of his love, God holds out the offer to forgive us while we are unforgiven (Rom. 5:8). We should follow suit. To do otherwise would be to abandon the biblical meaning of the word and God's pattern for us. To do otherwise in an attempt to make ourselves feel better is wrong and unnecessary. Emotionally, having a loving attitude of being willing to forgive frees the victim from self-destructive emotions of bitterness and vengeance. Thus, while we should be willing to forgive, we must withhold forgiveness until there is repentance. The practical difference is that in being willing to forgive, the offender is still being held accountable for his or her actions. By withholding forgiveness to the unrepentant, we do not become enablers of sin or injustice.

The Kairos Document

In 1985, when apartheid was in full flower in South Africa,* 156 theologians from over 20 South African denominations produced the "Kairos Document." These church leaders were emphatic on the point that there is no forgiveness without repentance. They wrote,

> There are conflicts where one side is a fully armed and violent oppressor while the other side is defenseless and oppressed. There are conflicts that can only be described as the struggle between justice and injustice, good and evil, God and the devil. To speak of reconciling these two is not only a mistaken application of the Christian idea of reconciliation, it is a total betrayal of all that Christian faith has ever meant. Nowhere in the Bible or in Christian tradition has it ever been suggested that we ought to try to reconcile good and evil, God and the devil. We are supposed to do away with evil, injustice, oppression and sin—not come to terms with it. We are supposed to oppose, confront and reject the devil and not try to sup with the devil.
>
> What this means in practice is that no reconciliation, no forgiveness and no negotiations are possible *without repentance.* The biblical teaching on reconciliation and forgiveness makes it quite clear that nobody can be forgiven and reconciled with God unless he or she repents of their sins. Nor are we expected to forgive the unrepentant sinner. When he or she repents we must be willing to forgive seventy times seven times but before that, we are expected to preach repentance to those who sin against us or against anyone."[535]

These 156 theologians further explained that any pressure to reconcile without acknowledgment of wrongdoing by those perpetuating injustice was untenable.

---

* Apartheid refers to the former system of racial segregation, discrimination, and gross human rights violations in South Africa by white South Africans against black South Africans.

242

In our situation in South Africa today it would be totally unChristian to plead for reconciliation and peace before the present injustices have been removed. Any such plea plays into the hands of the oppressor by trying to persuade those of us who are oppressed to accept our oppression and to become reconciled to the intolerable crimes that are committed against us. That is not Christian reconciliation, it is sin. It is asking us to become accomplices in our own oppression, to become servants of the devil.[536]

Morro and Harrison, writing in the *International Standard Bible Encyclopedia*, not only pointed out that "God does not forgive without repentance;" they also added, "nor is it required of mankind."[537] If shalomic peace is going to be achieved, repentance for wrongdoing cannot be deleted from the process required to achieve and sustain it.

Forgiveness Without Repentance Is Not Love

The book of Hebrews provides additional insight into the problem of unconditional forgiveness for sin. Such forgiveness doesn't demonstrate love. Paradoxically, it is evidence of a lack of love. Notice what the book of Hebrews says.

Hebrews 12:4-8
4 In your struggle against sin you have not yet resisted to the point of shedding your blood. 5 And have you forgotten the exhortation that addresses you as sons? "My son, do not regard lightly the discipline of the Lord, nor be weary when reproved by him. 6 For the Lord disciplines the one he loves, and chastises every son whom he receives." 7 It is for discipline that you have to endure. God is treating you as sons. For what son is there whom his father does not discipline? 8 If you are left without discipline, in which all have participated, then you are illegitimate children and not sons.

243

This passage teaches that those who are held accountable for their actions by God are loved by him.* By contrast, those who receive no correction when they do wrong are like unloved and unguided orphans. Today, our prisons are filled with young men who had no father figure to lovingly correct them along the way. The relevancy of this to our discussion of forgiveness is this: for any of us to turn a blind eye when a person hurts us or others, to remain silent when someone is doing wrong, to fail to confront and call upon such persons or groups to change their ways is not showing love. It is evidence of a lack of love and of indifference. In fact, it could be argued that silence represents tacit approval, even complicity in their behavior. As one blogger wrote on an online discussion board in response to one of my articles, "We are doing offenders a disservice if they are not held responsible for their actions. It is only through being held responsible that they are able to see the errors of their ways, change, and grow."[538] Can there really be true reconciliation and relational wholeness when unethical behavior goes unacknowledged, unaddressed, and uncorrected? Is this how God forgives? No! He calls us to repent.

Moreover, if we forgive someone without first conversing about the wrong we are forgiving, how can that broken relationship ever become fully reconciled? How can there be relational wholeness when injustice goes unacknowledged? If someone is truly forgiven, the aggrieved party cannot make accusations in the present or future about matters forgiven in the past. Unless a person wants to redefine the biblical meaning of forgiveness, when forgiveness occurs, the matter is closed. It means that the aggrieved party cannot later go back to the offender with a record of wrongs, for if the offender is still being held accountable, then in what sense has the person truly been forgiven? Once God forgives us of our past sins, we are free from them. If we forgive as God forgives, we must take the same approach.

---

* Revelation 3:19 similarly states, "Those whom I love, I reprove and discipline, so be zealous and repent."

It follows that to unconditionally forgive offenders is to enable them in their wrongdoing and sinful lifestyle. Accountability is removed, and if accountability is removed, there is no motive for offenders to change. To the contrary, silence represents tacit approval. The wrong seemingly becomes right, and justice is perverted.

This same line of reasoning stands behind the church discipline process outlined in Matthew 18:15-18.* If forgiveness were to unilaterally and immediately follow sin, what need would there be for such a process? But since forgiveness is conditional upon repentance, the church discipline process continues until repentance occurs or the unrepentant is removed from the fellowship of the church.

The Willis Family

By way of illustration, let's return to the apology statement made by ex-governor George Ryan and written in prison (see Stage 7). The governor said, in part,

> In addition to damaging the public's trust and confidence in government, I realize my mistakes had other implications and tangible effects on my constituents and the citizenry. I know that Reverend and Mrs. Willis suffered such effects—an unimaginable pain and loss—from mistakes made in my administration, both by me and others on my watch. My heart has and always will go out to the Willis family. They, like all of the people of Illinois, deserved far better than I gave them.

What is being referred to is the tragic and violent deaths of the six youngest of the Willises' nine children (Benjamin, 13; Joseph, 11; Samuel, 9; Hank, 6; Elizabeth, 3, and Peter, 6 weeks). They lost their lives in a fiery 1994 highway accident due to the negligence of the driver of an eighteen-wheel truck, a resident alien from Mexico who didn't speak English. He was unqualified to drive the eighteen-

---

* For a full discussion of Matthew 18:15-18, see chapter 6.

wheeler because he obtained his commercial license illegally. With the knowledge and approval of then Illinois Secretary of State Ryan, staffers had set up a program whereby commercial truck driver's licenses were sold to unqualified candidates, who not only had not passed the licensing test but in a number of instances didn't speak enough English to even take it. The money was used to fund Ryan's reelection campaign for secretary of state and later for governor.

Ryan was tried, and after a guilty verdict was rendered in April 2006 on all eighteen charges of corruption, Scott and Janet Willis each submitted a letter to the court, which the judge read to defendant Ryan and those present. Scott Willis (who at the time of the tragedy was a Baptist pastor on the south side of Chicago) wrote, in part,

> Almost 12 years have passed since Nov. 8, 1994. The heartache remains but has softened. Janet and I have prayed to not have a bitter or revengeful spirit. These feelings have only occasionally flared up but have not consumed or dominated our thoughts and are not the motive for this letter. Our thoughts are not on punishment. That is for the court to decide. The real tragedy is that no reconciliation has yet been attained between George Ryan and Janet and me. My wife and I have a strong desire to forgive Gov. Ryan but it must be on an honest basis: sorrow and admission. Even a 6-year-old boy knows when he's done wrong he needs to be truly sorry, and admit it. Then forgiveness and mercy can be graciously offered. That would be our joy.[539]

The Willises acknowledged that this ordeal had been hard on them and their family. Janet Willis revealed in her letter:

> In the years since, both my husband and I have struggled with depression. While my husband battled thoughts of suicide, I battled to keep my sanity. My parents have also had their battles. My mother taught the four boys piano

so we went to their house twice a week. She has battled depression ever since the accident. My husband and I have prayed and asked God to keep us from bitterness and to help us be faithful to him and he has. We tried to honor God by not complaining.[540]

The Willis case is incredibly tragic. Yet their stance was heroic as they stood firm on their understanding of what the Bible taught about forgiveness: their forgiveness was to be conditional upon the governor's acknowledgment of wrongdoing. They were willing to forgive. They were praying not to be bitter. And yet without an admission of guilt and responsibility by the governor, they could not forgive and he should not be forgiven.

Now, fast-forward two and a half years to December 2008, when Gov. Ryan did issue a public apology through his lawyer.[541] As apologies go, it was woefully inadequate (see Stage 7). The governor's remarks were not actually made directly to the Willises, nor did the governor specify what "mistakes" he was apologizing for. (The governor mentioned "mistakes" three times, not the fact that he was convicted of eighteen crimes.) Rather than helping the Willises, the "apology" actually put them in more of a bind. On the one hand, if they didn't positively respond to the governor's appeal, it would appear that they were not acting with Christian love but out of bitterness and anger. On the other hand, without any demonstrable repentance and confession for wrongdoing on the governor's part for which he accepted responsibility, how could they truly extend forgiveness–the very thing they wanted to do?

Scott Willis said he would like to sit down with the governor and go over the counts for which he was convicted, including "when he killed the investigation into the crash that took our children." Scott went on to say that he wasn't going to offer forgiveness if the governor didn't want to acknowledge his guilt. (Of course, if the governor didn't want to do that, what exactly was he apologizing for?) The reporter who filed this latest chapter of the story concluded his article with these remarks: "I'm glad there are people like the Willises to teach us, that there are people who believe that politicians like Ryan can change their hearts, that the door of forgiveness is always open, but that those who truly seek it must repent and accept the consequences that flow from what they've done."[542]

Just as asking for and receiving forgiveness is a relational activity between sinners and God, the same is true in our interactions with one another. As the Willises demonstrate, even under horrific circumstances, bitterness does not need to take center stage. Being willing to forgive while maintaining the need for justice and accountability are completely compatible. Why wouldn't they be? That's how God, who is perfect, acts toward us.

The Core of Human Forgiveness

Forgiveness Described

Theologian James Buswell wrote, "All forgiveness, human and divine, is in the very nature of the case vicarious, substitutional."[543] As noted above, the basis of peace between God and mankind is built upon God's loving-kindness and willingness to absorb the demands of justice on behalf of the repentant sinner. God, in the person of his Son, willingly bore the pain of his own judgment on mankind required by his holiness. In like manner, when one person says to the other, "I forgive you," that person is engaging in an act of love in which the aggrieved party is implicitly saying to the offender, "I am willing to bear the indignity, injury, and/or injustice of your acknowledged wrongs against me."

In the apology-forgiveness event, a unique social exchange takes place. On the one side of the equation, the offender, without defense, exposes his or her flawed humanity. Injustice is confessed, and a sincere apology is offered. On the other side of the equation, the innocent party says to the guilty, "I will bear the suffering you caused, including that which cannot be repaired and made right, and personally release you from any other obligation you might owe me for the wrong you committed."

When we forgive, we release the other person from the relational burden of his or her offense. This burden condemns the transgressor and obstructs the relationship with the person he or she injured. However, when forgiveness is granted, the condemnation and obstruction are removed. Human forgiveness parallels divine forgiveness in that it, too, is an act of triumphant love. It comes at the end of a process where apology and, if required, a commitment to making reparations, have been made. This expression of love, one patterned after God's own heart, ennobles the human experience for all involved.

Human forgiveness parallels divine forgiveness in that it, too, is an act of triumphant love. It comes at the end of a process where apology and, if required, a commitment to making reparations, have been made. This expression of love, one patterned after God's own heart, ennobles the human experience for all involved.

Forgiveness does not mean that justice is overlooked or ignored. Where human forgiveness is unlike divine forgiveness is that it does not include the victim suffering the judicial judgment of the offending party's sin as God in Christ did for us. Assault, for example, is still viewed by the government as a crime against the state. The offender is still obligated to undergo the consequences imposed by the criminal justice system. Nevertheless, human forgiveness mirrors divine forgiveness in that those who forgive repentant wrongdoers bear and, in love, transcend the impact of the wrong committed against them.

Forgiveness Illustrated

A man told about an event that occurred when he was a teenager. When no one was there, thieves broke into his family's home and went on a stealing spree. Only as the days wore on did the family begin to realize not just how many things were stolen but how many things that had sentimental value were gone. One such item was a special ring that belonged to the father. The ring had been given to him by his father the very day his father passed away. The man recalled, "I had never seen my dad cry, but he cried that day, and his tears were replaced by a deep anger. He vowed to kill the burglars, if he ever found them. Hearing my father, a peaceful man, speak those words scared my family."

About a week later, during suppertime, the doorbell rang. At the door was a woman with a shopping bag and her teenage son. After being invited inside, the mother began to explain why they were there. Days earlier she noticed her son wearing a new ring. She asked him where he got it. Finally, after some prodding, the teen said that he and some buddies had broken into a house and stole it, along with other items. The mother was aghast by what her son had done. The boy himself was having second thoughts and feeling remorseful. She told him to gather all the things he had stolen in a bag and return them to the owner. She would go with him.

As the details began to pour out, the narrator recalled, "With fear and uncertainty we watched my dad. We could see the angry glare in his eyes." After the story of what had happened was fully told, the teen said directly to the father, "Sir, I am sorry." The boy then started to cry. He admitted what he did was wrong and was willing to give the names and addresses of his accomplices to the police department.

At that very moment when he had confessed all, the young thief surrendered his immediate fate into the hands of the very

250

one he robbed. And it was at that moment that the father's demeanor dramatically changed. The accusatory glare in his eyes disappeared. The hard attitude he had been expressing due to the pain of his loss was replaced by a spirit of gentleness. Even though the sense of violation to the sanctity of the home was not restored, and even though there were many more items still out there likely lost forever, given the apology and the supporting evidence to demonstrate its sincerity, the father declared to the wayward teen, "I forgive you." Then, after giving him a fatherlike talk, the teen and his mother were asked to stay for dinner, which they did.*

The Beauty of Forgiveness

This story is just one of countless stories of forgiveness that occur every day on the planet. Without it, our world, which is populated by sinners, would be an intolerable place to live. "Without being forgiven, released from the consequences of what we have done, our capacity to act would, as it were, be confined to one single deed from which we could never recover; we would remain the victims of its consequences forever."[544] Forgiveness allows us to become free from the past and create a more loving future. The beauty of forgiveness is that it "is the only reaction which does not merely re-act but acts anew."[545] "Forgiveness re-creates."[546] It transforms our world "in a way that can only be described as miraculous."[547] Why? Because the apology by the guilty party reiterates the wrong that was committed, while the expression of love and forgiveness by the one who was hurt supersedes it!

---

* The teenager courageously kept his word and told the police about the incident and those involved. Things became so dangerous for him and his family that the family was forced to move away (which in retrospect, may have been the best outcome for the teen).

What Should the Peacemaker Do?

Isaiah 1:2-4, 16-18

2 Hear, O heavens, and give ear, O earth; for the LORD
has spoken: "Children have I reared and brought up, but
they have rebelled against me. 3 The ox knows its owner,
and the donkey its master's crib, but Israel does not know,
my people do not understand." 4 Ah, sinful nation, a
people laden with iniquity, offspring of evildoers, children
who deal corruptly! They have forsaken the Lord, they
have despised the Holy One of Israel, they are utterly
estranged. ...

16 Wash yourselves; make yourselves clean; remove the
evil of your deeds from before my eyes; cease to do evil,
17 learn to do good; seek justice, correct oppression; bring
justice to the fatherless, plead the widow's cause. 18 "Come
now, let us reason together, says the LORD: though your
sins are like scarlet, they shall be as white as snow; though
they are red like crimson, they shall become like wool."

Establish a Forum Where Forgiveness Can Occur

Before most people can grant forgiveness and move beyond a
past where they have suffered indignity, injury, and/or injustice at
the hands of another, they must be given the opportunity to declare
to the offender the nature of the offender's wrongdoing. (God
certainly speaks clearly when it comes to naming our sins as he did
with the nation of Israel in Isaiah 1 cited above.) Aggrieved parties
need to be able to bring to the light of day what happened to them
as a result of the untoward actions of the transgressor. They need
to be able to vent. It has been observed that "nothing obstructs the
effort to forgive another person as much as the experience of having
your own sense of the truth denied."[548]

252

Consider the case of Elizabeth Menkin whose sister was killed by a drunk driver. She revealed, "I decided I could stop hating her [the driver] if I felt she was really sorry. I wanted her to recognize that what she did was wrong, to feel remorse for the far-reaching terrible consequences of her crime, and to feel regret, shame, suffering, and humiliation."[549] In a mediation that was part of a victim-offender reconciliation program, Menkin and other family members who attended saw such apologetic remorse in a frail twenty-five-year-old woman. It was noteworthy that "she didn't contaminate the apology with defenses or excuses."[550] Moreover, and this was a significant portion of the process, "each of us had a chance to speak about what the crash and that loss of Elaine had meant to us and to ask all our questions."[551] Menkin shared that after the five-hour mediation session was over, "I could feel that a lot of the tension I had been carrying around had vanished. I had a sense of relief and realized it was because I had let go of feelings of vengeance and despair."[552]

The same is true on the international level when atrocities are committed by one side against the other. "A safe environment would have to be created by the third party in order for the low power group to articulate what happened to them and to have it acknowledged by the other that what happened to them was wrong and that no human being should have to suffer the way they did."[553]

Whether the peacemaker has been meeting privately with each disputant, with all the parties together, or in a combination of the two, he or she brings the parties together to provide a forum where stories by the injured can be told. As noted in Stage 7, behind the scenes and prior to this moment, the peacemaker should be using his or her skills, knowledge, and energy to effect a positive outcome. Charles Williams insightfully observed, "Many promising reconciliations have broken down because, while both parties came prepared to forgive, neither party came prepared to be forgiven."[554] The peacemaker should prepare offenders to apologize and the offended parties to accept.

While forgiveness is a free act that cannot be demanded or forced, the peacemaker can certainly encourage it. The offending party can be asked to reflect on the suffering they caused while the aggrieved party can be asked to reflect upon the frailties of their own human condition. They can be asked to be merciful in the same way he or she would want to be shown mercy by God[555] and by others. A genuine apology and a corresponding act of forgiveness brings the offender and offended to recognition of their common humanity.[556]

Overall Summary

At the deepest level, forgiveness has a way of "separating forgivable people from unforgivable actions."[557] Forgiveness is not about pretending things are other than they are. It is not about turning a blind eye to reality. It is not about sentimentality. True forgiveness exposes the harshness of people's actions and reveals the suffering those actions have caused. Yet, rather than seeking retaliation, the aggrieved party seeks a genuine apology, whereby reparations, if possible, are made and the offending party fully acknowledges and takes responsibility for the wrong that was committed. The peacemaker is instrumental in fitting the various pieces of the puzzle into a complete picture. Once an apology is offered, the aggrieved party, out of love, ideally, is willing to forgive. At that moment, the aggrieved party in essence says to the offender, "I am willing to bear the indignity, injury, and/or injustice of your acknowledged wrongs against me." This is the pattern that God has established for us. In the same way God forgives repentant sinners, so the peacemaker encourages aggrieved parties to forgive those who express genuine sorrow for the wrong they committed against them.

Stage 11

Building On the Spirit of Reconciliation

What Is the Scriptural Basis for This Stage?

Introduction
New Testament
    Meaning of the Word
    Timing
    Four Passages
Summary

Like Father, Like Son

Stage 11: Building on the Spirit of Reconciliation

Why Reconciliation Is So Important
When Forgiveness and Reconciliation Are
    Simultaneous Between People
        Eric Lomax and Nagase Takashi
When Forgiveness and Reconciliation Are Not
    Simultaneous Between People
The "Spirit" of Reconciliation Versus the "Reality" of
    Reconciliation

What Should the Peacemaker Do?

Overall Summary

If the parties exit Stage 10 with a positive result, their future relationship now becomes the focus. In this stage, we will compare divine and human reconciliation, their similarities and differences. If there is a desire to take the "spirit" of reconciliation, which emerged in Stage 10, and develop it into a "reality," then Stage 12 will be entered into by the parties to complete the peacemaking process. Stage 11 serves as a transitional stage between the two.

What Is the Scriptural Basis for This Stage?

Introduction

As discussed in chapter 2, reconciliation is viewed in the Scriptures as the apex of God's desire for a world that has ignored, rebelled against, and turned away from him. Despite this rebellion, "God was in Christ reconciling the world to himself" (2 Cor. 5:19 NASB). The ultimate role of Israel's Messiah was to bring God and humanity into harmony with each other. "It could be said that the whole work of Christ has to do with reconciliation."[558] Indeed, reconciliation has been considered "the central concept of Christianity."[559]

New Testament

Meaning of the Word

The original meaning of the word for reconciliation in classical Greek[560] was to "change" or "exchange." In the New Testament, when people are reconciled to God, they exchange a relationship of hostility for one of friendship.[561] Reconciliation, therefore, does not apply to relationships that are characterized by harmony but to those characterized by antagonism. It is "a term indicating the changed relationship for the better between persons or groups who formerly were at enmity with each other."[562] It is the "reestablishment of an interrupted or broken relationship."[563]

256

It differs in meaning from forgiveness. Whereas forgiveness speaks of "letting go," that is, releasing the obligation and guilt of sin, reconciliation speaks of "bringing together,"[564] whether it is among spouses (1 Cor. 7:11), among people of different ethnic backgrounds (Eph. 2:16), or with God (Rom. 6:10). Whereas forgiveness releases offenders from their injurious actions, removing those actions as obstacles between the parties, reconciliation brings the parties together into a right relationship with each other.

The history of the conflict will indicate whether the relationship prior to the hostility was a positive one or not. If it was positive, the entire reconciliation process looks like this: "(1) disruption of friendly relations because of (2) presumed or real provocation, (3) overt behavior designed to remove hostility, and (4) restoration of original friendly relations."[565]

Timing

Various terms are used to describe what it means to experience peace with God. As noted in Stage 9, when God bestows his forgiveness upon the repentant sinner, reconciliation instantaneously and simultaneously occurs.[566] No additional action needs to occur. Shalomic peace is the result.

Four Passages

There are four passages in the New Testament that refer to man being reconciled to God. Two of them are reproduced below. (The other two are Romans 5:6-11 and Eph. 2:14-19.)

2 Corinthians 5:17-21
17 Therefore, if anyone is in Christ, he is a new creation. The old has passed away; behold, the new has come. 18 All this is from God, who through Christ reconciled us to himself and gave us the ministry of reconciliation 19 that is, in Christ God was reconciling the world to himself, not counting their

trespasses against them, and entrusting to us the message of reconciliation. 20 Therefore, we are ambassadors for Christ, God making his appeal through us. We implore you on behalf of Christ, be reconciled to God. 21 For our sake he made him to be sin who knew no sin, so that in him we might become the righteousness of God.

Colossians 1:19-22
19 For in him [Christ] all the fullness of God was pleased to dwell, 20 and through him to reconcile to himself all things, whether on earth or in heaven, making peace by the blood of his cross. 21 And you, who once were alienated and hostile in mind, doing evil deeds, 22 he has now reconciled in his body of flesh by his death, in order to present you holy and blameless and above reproach before him.

Summary

"The history of the human race as presented in Scripture is primarily a history of man in a state of sin and rebellion against God and of God's plan of redemption to bring man back to himself."[567] When reconciliation between God and mankind occurs, the peace-making process is complete. The demarcation between offended and offending party vanishes. Though people everywhere are exhorted to be reconciled with God, the decision to be reconciled is not coerced. No matter how active Jesus has been as mediator to secure our peace with God, a person's decision to enter into that peace must be made voluntarily, of one's own free will. When that happens, shalomic peace characterizes the relationship. Apart from the majesty of God, the making of peace between God and man stands as the grandest theme of all Scripture.

Like Father, Like Son

In the same way God reconciles with those he has forgiven, so the peace-maker encourages the parties to build upon their spirit of reconciliation and work toward a future characterized by shalomic peace.

Stage 11: Building on the Spirit of Reconciliation

Why Reconciliation Is So Important

Even though reconciliation is most often thought of as being between two people, there is growing recognition that it is needed even on national and international levels. Psychologists Staub and Perlmann explained: "Reconciliation is more than the coexistence of formerly hostile groups living near each other. It is more even than formerly hostile groups interacting and working together ... Reconciliation means coming to accept one another and developing mutual trust."[568]

Today, reconciliation in international relations is receiving increased attention. The sense of insecurity and danger and the possibility of a relapse into fighting is greater when goodwill does not develop.[569] Even the signing of a peace agreement is, in and of itself, insufficient to end conflict. Such agreements commonly "fall far short of estab-lishing genuine peaceful relations between the former adversaries."[570] A peace agreement, though a noteworthy achievement, is far from the end of the matter. It only represents the end of one phase, namely, the fighting. The next phase, the implementation of the terms of the agreement and the adoption of new behaviors, remains to be seen. Consequently, the time frame right after signing a peace agreement is often fraught with uncertainties, difficulties, and pitfalls.[571] This is also true of smaller groups and interpersonal agreements.

The reason reconciliation is so important is because without it a standoff is the best scenario one can hope for. A new outbreak of the conflict can still occur at any time.[572] True reconciliation, by contrast, transforms a previously antagonistic relationship into a loving and secure one. It positively touches upon "the motivations, goals, beliefs, attitudes, and emotions" of those who have been in conflict.[573]

The reason reconciliation is so important is because without it a standoff is the best scenario one can hope for.

When Forgiveness and Reconciliation Are Simultaneous Between People

Eric Lomax and Nagase Takashi

There are times when forgiveness and reconciliation between people, as in the case between God and people, occur at the same time. Consider the case involving Eric Lomax. Lomax was a World War II prisoner of war held captive by the Japanese for over three years until the end of the war. While a POW, he assisted in building a radio to help the prisoners follow the events of the war. When the radio was discovered, as well as a map that Lomax drew of the region and its railway, he was interrogated, beaten, and tortured. Over time, he nearly starved to death.

In 1945 when the war was over, Lomax returned to England a psychologically changed man. He noted, "There is no statute of limitations on the effects of torture."[574] He was not able to share what happened to him with another person, including his new wife (his sweetheart before the war began). The only exceptions were with other former POW's whom Lomax saw infrequently. Nightmares of his time as a prisoner haunted him. Often, he would recall with anger the Japanese interpreter who was present at his interrogations. Ruminating on such memories, Lomax explained that since that time, his "capacity for enthusiasm and joy was replaced by surface coldness and docility."[575] His work provided a reprieve from the past. Yet, Lomax's unresolved emotional issues continued unabated over the decades and eventually contributed to the divorce from his wife in 1981.

After his retirement in 1982, Lomax's interest in what occurred during his time as a POW intensified. He had many unanswered questions. The idea of physical revenge was ever present, particularly against the interpreter. Unexpectedly, Lomax met and fell in love with a woman named Patti. They married. As she learned more about her new husband's war-related problems, she supported his search into the unanswered questions of his past.

Yet, it was Lomax's icy withdrawals over imagined insensitivities and the confrontational edge to his voice that became more and more difficult for his second wife to bear. Lomax wrote, "The ex-prisoner, even after several decades of 'forgetting', can puzzle and frighten others. It is impossible for others to help you come to terms with the past, if for you the past is a pile of wounded memories and angry humiliation, and the future is just a nursery of revenge."[576] Not wanting their relationship to break up, the couple decided to seek help, which at the age of nearly seventy changed Lomax's life. Over the course of the next four years, he started talking about his World War II trauma in full for the first time.

During that period, a fellow ex-POW gave Lomax an article to read about Mr. Nagase Takashi, the interpreter who was present during Lomax's interrogations. The article described how Takashi had devoted much of his life to making amends for the Japanese army's treatment of its prisoners of war and those who died in the labor camps. It even mentioned one particular POW who was singled out for a particular torture because he possessed a map of a railway the prisoners were building. Lomax realized that Takashi was referring to him.

In 1991, Lomax read a book Takashi wrote of his account of the war. In it, Takashi gives a detailed account of what Lomax experienced. Takashi concluded, "I still cannot stop shuddering every time I recall that horrible scene."[577] Takashi had left the war racked with guilt. After she also read the book, Lomax's wife, Patti, serving as an intermediary, wrote a letter to Nagase Takashi.

Lomax and Takashi met over a year later. Needless to say, a lot of groundwork was laid in advance. They met in Thailand at a museum near the River Kwae Bridge. Takashi, trembling and in tears, began his side of the conversation with the words, "I am very, very sorry."[578] He repeated his words over and over again. After he regained his composure, Takahsi said, "Fifty years is a long time, but for me it is a time of suffering. I never forgot you, I remember your face, especially your eyes."[579]

From this point forward, the interpersonal relationship that developed between these two men was as heartwarming as it was surprising. Yet, Lomax acknowledged as their time together in Thailand progressed that he needed to decide whether or not to forgive Takashi, a matter that was very important to Takashi. Lomax finally concluded, "I could no longer see the point of punishing Takashi by a refusal to reach out and forgive him. What mattered was our relations in the here and now, his obvious regret for what he had done and our mutual need to give our encounter some meaning beyond that of the emptiness of cruelty. It was surely worth salvaging as much as we could from the damage to both our lives."[580] For Lomax, it was all a matter of choosing the right moment.

From Thailand, Lomax, Takashi, and their wives flew to Japan, where they briefly visited Takashi's home and toured the sites. Lomax recalled with surprise that while he was in Japan he felt none of the anger toward Takashi that had so plagued his life. Shortly before his trip to Japan was over, Lomax asked Takashi to come to his hotel room. He had written out what he wanted to say. Among other things, Lomax told Takashi while forgetting what happened in

1943 was impossible, he could forgive him from his heart. Takashi, in return, was demonstrably moved and grateful.

When it was all over and they were back on a plane to England, Lomax turned to his wife and said, "Meeting Nagase has turned him from a hated enemy, with whom friendship would have been unthinkable, into a blood-brother."[581] In just the span of a few days, shalomic peace came to these two men whose lives had been inextricably linked over the course of their adult lives by haunting memories. Forgiveness and reconciliation were joined together in time and place. Now there would be a new relationship built on love and respect.

When Forgiveness and Reconciliation Are Not Simultaneous Between People

Forgiveness and reconciliation are distinguished by separate stages in the Judeo-Christian model, even though they are instantaneous and simultaneous when making peace with God, and sometimes between people, as with Lomax and Takashi. They are presented as separate stages for two reasons. First, as discussed above, the two concepts are sufficiently different. The second reason is that what occurs in an instant with God usually takes more time with us. Would that all enmity between people end in forgiveness and reconciliation, as in the case of Eric Lomax and Nagase Takashi, but this is simply not the norm. After a genuine apology is offered and forgiveness is granted, the parties are reconciled concerning the past. The future of that relationship, however, is yet to be determined.

In some instances, there was no relationship before the parties came into conflict and none is sought in its aftermath. Of the strangers who murdered her four sons, one mother said she had no relationship with them before they killed her children and she desired none with them afterward.[582] The same type of decision is made by

263

victims of rape. Even if there is a genuine apology and forgiveness and the past is addressed in a way that brings healthy closure, rape victims are unlikely to chart a course for the future that includes the rapist. In cases such as these, where strangers are involved and an apology is offered and forgiveness is granted, reconciliation can be said to be achieved only in the sense that the relationship returned to what it was prior to the crime (nonexistent).

The "Spirit" of Reconciliation Versus the "Reality" of Reconciliation

Where things can get sticky is in scenarios where (1) there was a positive past relationship (a family member, friend, or business associate) and/or (2) there will be a future relationship due to an existing social connection or physical proximity (a coworker, someone in the congregation, a next-door neighbor, or a next-door country). In most cases, even though the past conflict has been resolved, trust between the parties still needs to be rebuilt.

Consider the father and son who went into business together despite their history of conflict. After a decade of working together with flare-ups a continual part of their relationship, the son felt he could no longer work in the same environment with his father. However, they had built a very successful business together, and for the son to leave would mean to leave what he worked so long and hard to achieve. After more than a week away from the business, the son met with his father to see if they could work things out. The desire was there, and it was mutual. Unfortunately, other than their good intentions, there was no concrete plan to make their future relationship different from the past. Within days after the son returned to work, the same pattern of arguing emerged. The son realized it was a mistake to have come back and decided to leave for good.

Even though the "spirit" of reconciliation was present in the above scenario, its "reality" did not materialize. How can the parties move forward when, even though apologies and forgiveness have been offered and granted, there is still significant suspicion and mistrust about how the other side will act in the future? How can the spirit of reconciliation be transformed into reality?

What Should the Peacemaker Do?

At this stage, the most important thing for the peacemaker and parties to remember is that forgiveness is not the end of the process. Although it is possible that full reconciliation between the parties may occur at that time, in many instances this will not be the case.

The one thing the peacemaker must do is to learn from the parties if they are ready and willing to build on the present "spirit" of reconciliation reflected in their apology-forgiveness interchange. Are they ready to grow that spirit of reconciliation into a relationship characterized by goodwill and trust? Given that the goal of the Judeo-Christian model of peacemaking is reconciliation, the peacemaker would encourage the parties in this direction. It might be helpful for the peacemaker to remind the parties of their vision for shalomic peace (discussed in Stage 4) and explain that now is the time to begin to make that vision a reality. If the peacemaker learns that both sides want to move forward, the peacemaker must enter into a trust-building process with them, which is the focus of Stage 12.

Overall Summary

Apart from the majesty of God, the making of peace between God and mankind stands as the grandest theme of all Scripture. People everywhere are exhorted to be reconciled to God. The goal of reconciliation extends to people who have been in conflict with each other as well. Regardless of what has happened in the past, the parties have now interacted in such a way that healing has begun. They are now able to face the future with goodwill to make the experience of shalomic peace a reality. To the extent that there are remaining issues that still need to be resolved, the parties will enter Stage 12 with that spirit of reconciliation and the goal of making reconciliation a reality. In the same way God reconciles with those he has forgiven, so the peacemaker encourages the parties to build upon their spirit of reconciliation and work toward a future characterized by shalomic peace.

Stage 12

Problem Solving Follow-up

What Is the Scriptural Basis for This Stage?

Like Father, Like Son

Stage 12: Address Remaining Unresolved Issues

What Should the Peacemaker Do?
Nine Steps
1. Identify All Remaining Challenges and Problems
    A. Confirm Each Problem
    B. Clarify Each Identified Problem
    C. View Each Problem as It Relates to the Whole
2. Organize Issues by Category
3. Establish Criteria to Establish Potential Solutions
4. Reframe Positions into Questions Addressing Underlying Needs
5. Brainstorm Solutions
6. Evaluate Proposals
7. Decide upon the Solution for Each Problem
8. Work Out Details of Implementation and Follow-up
9. Record All Agreements
    Illustration: The End of World War II
Closing Illustration

Overall Summary

O nce past issues are successfully addressed by the parties, new, healthier patterns of interaction need to be developed. This represents the last phase of the peacemaking process. The parties should jointly answer such questions as: What must we do differently to insure that the past does not repeat itself? How can we work cooperatively to strengthen our relationship in the future? Such issues are the focus of this section.

What Is the Scriptural Basis for This Stage?

Philippians 2:12
Therefore, my beloved, as you have always obeyed, so now, not only as in my presence but much more in my absence, work out your own salvation with fear and trembling

This passage deals with a person's relationship with God after peace with God has been made. The point to be gleaned is that "salvation is not merely a gift received once for all; it expresses itself in an ongoing process in which the believer is strenuously involved."[583] Those who have made their peace with God are expected to build upon and "nurture their relationship with God."[584]

This work is not done alone. Jesus's role as mediator continues even after one has been reconciled to God. Indeed, when believers come to God in prayer, Jesus instructed them to come before God in his name (John 14:13-14; 15:16; 16:23-24). Jesus continues to intercede for them.

Romans 8:33-34
33 Who shall bring any charge against God's elect? It is God who justifies. 34 Who is to condemn? Christ Jesus is the one who died—more than that, who was raised—who is at the right hand of God, who indeed is interceding for us.

Hebrews 7:25
Consequently, he [Jesus] is able to save to the uttermost those who draw near to God through him, since he always lives to make intercession for them.

Hebrews 9:24
For Christ has entered, not into holy places made with hands, which are copies of the true things, but into heaven itself, now to appear in the presence of God on our behalf.

1 John 2:1
My little children, I am writing these things to you so that you may not sin. But if anyone does sin, we have an advocate with the Father, Jesus Christ the righteous.

Jesus's mediatorial role between God and mankind continues throughout a person's life even after the relationship with God has initially been restored. The difference is that Jesus's original mediatorial work was to reconcile enemies. Now it is done between friends. Through Jesus worshippers now have continual access to the presence of God, to confess sin, make requests, seek direction through his word, and generally nurture and develop their relationship with God.

Like Father, Like Son

In the same way Jesus continues to serve as mediator for believers even after they have made peace with God, so the parties rely upon the ongoing work of their peacemaker to help them resolve all remaining issues in order for reconciliation to be complete.

Stage 12: Address Remaining Unresolved Issues

It has been said that "reconciliation is a behavioral manifestation of forgiveness."[585] Given that the spirit of reconciliation was present in Stage 11, this next stage seeks to transform that spirit into reality. The processes outlined below help the parties to nurture their relationship and rebuild trust with one another.

What Should the Peacemaker Do?

Nine Steps

1. Identify All the Remaining Challenges and Problems

Before solutions can be considered, there needs to be confirmation of the problems and a full understanding of each. By way of definition, a problem can be said to exist when there is a gap between the present circumstance and a more desired one.

A. Confirm Each Problem. With input from the parties, the peacemaker should create a list of all the identified problems that need to be resolved. Is everyone in agreement that all the problems are valid ones? Distinguish between those problems that are agreed upon and those that are not. If possible and it makes sense, each problem should be broken down into its divisible components or subproblems. For example, the problem of "neglected grounds" can be divided into three areas: (1) landscaping, (2) mowing the grass, and (3) trash removal.

B. Clarify Each Identified Problem. Is each problem thoroughly understood? The peacemaker should ask questions that clarify each problem, such as: (1) Is the context and all components of the problem understood; that is, the who, what, when, why, where, how much, how long, how often? (2) Is the problem as described by one side understood in the same way by the other? (3) Is there agreement on the root and contributory causes? (4) Can everyone define what the problem is not? Utilizing research, surveys, interviews, outside experts, etc. to expand everyone's knowledge can serve a useful purpose in those situations that are particularly difficult to diagnose.

C. View Each Problem as It Relates to the Whole. The concept of the "hermeneutical circle" is helpful here. This is a concept that relates to the interplay between the whole and the parts. "We must understand the whole in terms of the detail and the detail in terms of the whole."[586] A sentence, for example, makes no sense unless the readers knows the meaning of the words. On the other hand, the meaning of individual words can be understood only by the larger context in which they are found.

Consider the following sentences using the word *line*.[587] "Hey, buddy, you need to go to the end of the *line*." "The Washington Redskins' offensive *line* is strong this year." "Did you seen him catch that *line* drive?" "Joe has always promoted the party *line*." "It looks like the storm blew the telephone *line* down." "Without a ruler, I can't draw a straight *line*." "A *line* of communication has been opened between the two countries." "Would you be so kind as to *line* up an appointment for me?"

Each sentence makes sense only by understanding the particular use and meaning of the word *line*. At the same time, the meaning of the word *line* is determined by its larger context. Hence, we see the "circular relationship."[588] There needs to be a dual vision "between the most local of local detail and the most global of global structure in such a way as to bring both into view simultaneously."[589] Problems should be analyzed in the same way.

271

2. Organize Issues by Category

After all the problems have been identified, it may be useful for the peacemaker to organize related areas under one category. Then the parties select the category they would like to address first. Under most circumstances, the peacemaker should encourage the parties to order the categories going from the easiest to resolve to the most difficult. Success in resolving easier issues will establish a good pattern for tackling more difficult ones. If there is more than one item in each category, select the order of the items to be discussed, again starting with the easiest item to resolve within the category.

3. Establish Criteria to Evaluate Potential Solutions

How can poor, fair, good, and excellent solutions be distinguished? What qualities would a widely accepted solution have? These questions should be answered before potential solutions are evaluated. As has been said, "If you can't reach consensus on criteria, it's not likely that you'll reach agreement on an acceptable alternative. On the other hand, if you can reach consensus on criteria, future decisions concerning this problem should be greatly simplified."[590] The peacemaker should ask the parties to complete this sentence: "A workable solution would meet the following criteria..."

Criteria may include: the Golden Rule, evidence, independent tests, opinions from specialists, recommendations from a mutually trusted third party, market value, industry standards, legal precedent, cultural and religious traditions, and even a random process (e.g., flipping a coin). The general guideline here is that the more independent these sources of authority, standards of practice, etc. are from the parties themselves, the more likely they will be accepted by both sides.[591] Other criteria could be relationship oriented. For example, "an acceptable solution must (1) build trust and improve our relationship, and (2) meet the needs of both sides, or at least, meet the needs of one party while not being incompatible with the needs of the other."

4. Reframe Positions into Questions Addressing Underlying Needs

In 1967, war broke out between Israel and her Arab neighbors. That conflict has become known as the "Six-Day War." When it was over, Israel had captured areas that improved its security against future invasions. One of the areas captured was the Sinai desert. After the war, Egypt's "position" was that there would be no peace with Israel unless Israel returned all of the Sinai. Israel's "position," on the other hand, was that it was not going to return to its militarily insecure pre-war borders. Israel wanted to keep a buffer zone between the two countries. Underlying Egypt's position was its "need" for sovereignty over centuries-old borders and, hence, national identity and dignity. Underlying Israel's position was its "need" for security. The agreement that was reached over the Sinai desert between Egypt's president, Anwar Sadat, and Israel's prime minister, Menachem Begin, mediated by President Jimmy Carter, met the underlying needs of both sides. Egyptian flags could fly everywhere in the Sinai. Egypt would thus regain its land, dignity, and prestige. Egyptian tanks and other military armaments, however, would be found nowhere. Israel would thus preserve its security. This change of focus from positions to underlying needs was instrumental in producing agreement between these two nations.

The peacemaker should have the parties reframe (reclassify) each identifiable problem into a broadly worded question that: (1) begins with the word "how," (2) identifies the need underlying the problem, and (3) does not contain the answer to the question in the question itself. For example: "There are more children in the church nursery than can be properly cared for." Reframe this, not as, "How can we get more staff in the nursery?" but as "How can we make the ratio between staff and children more manageable?" The first phrase contains the solution in the question itself, i.e., "get more staff." It may turn out, however, that the best solution in this particular situation is to ask mothers to keep their newborn infants with them in the service.

273

Peacemakers must uncover the reasons and motives behind the positions of the parties. Ask the question, "Why?" "Why is this your position?" Similarly, ask, "Why not?" "Why not accept their solution?" Define problems, not by parties' positions, but by their underlying needs and concerns.

5. Brainstorm Solutions

The goal here is to find ways to remove the obstacles that stand between the disputing parties. It may be helpful to change the environment to make it more informal and the seating so that everyone, side-by-side, is facing the list of needs together. What is involved here is a shift in thinking from an "I-versus-you" to a "we-versus-the-problem" mind-set. Brainstorming has been referred to as rough-draft thinking. It brings to light ideas that are not yet precisely formed.

At this stage, all the peacemaker wants to accomplish is to gather a host of ideas. The peacemaker should insure that there is no negative evaluation or criticism of any suggestion. Time for discussing and judging the ideas happens later. As ideas are listed, the recorder should not attribute a given idea to the person who suggested it. The peacemaker should explain, "Don't censor yourself. Be creative in your thinking. Way out ideas are welcome. Become like popping corn kernels just popping with ideas. The more ideas there are, the more options and wider the range of possible solutions there will be."[592]

6. Evaluate Proposals

The first part of this step involves engaging in the process of elimination. The peacemaker should facilitate a discussion whereby the parties agree to eliminate ideas that are (1) impractical, (2) clearly inadequate, or (3) do not meet the selected criteria. As the number of potential solutions narrow, a discussion should follow that (1) lists the advantages and disadvantages of each remaining proposal, (2) identifies those ideas that have the fewest problems, and (3) suggests ways an idea can be improved or disadvantages can be reduced. The biblical principle, "As iron sharpens iron, so one man sharpens another" (Prov. 27:17 niv), is applicable here.

7. Decide upon the Solution for Each Problem

Here, the peacemaker will encourage the parties to make decisions in terms of what they can mutually agree upon regarding each problem. It is important to keep in mind that not every solution requires wild enthusiasm for its acceptance. That is to say, there are different levels of support for a proposal, listed here from most to least. (1) Complete support: "I am 100 percent enthusiastic about the proposal"; (2) support with reservations: (a) "I agree with the major aspects of the proposal and have only minor concern on some detail"; (b) "Though I see some not-so-minor problems, I can live with the proposal"; (3) no opinion: "Since I do not have an opinion one way or the other, I will readily go along with the majority"; (4) reservations but willing to go along with the majority: (a) "I do not like the proposal, but I will not attempt to thwart the majority"; (b) "I will not oppose the majority, but I want my concerns formally noted"; (5) opposed: "I am opposed to the proposal and will vote against it."[593]

8. Work Out Details of Implementation and Follow-up

The following grid, known as the RASCI model,[594] can be used to aid in the implementation of each solution. To help insure that each solution is actually implemented, the following questions should be answered. (1) Who is *R*esponsible to carry this particular project to completion? There should be only one person ultimately responsible for a given project. (2) To whom is the responsible party *A*ccountable? To put it another way, who must *A*pprove (sign-off) on the work before it can begin? At different points in the project, a different person might fulfill this role.[595] (3) Who can or will play a *S*upport role in terms of providing resources and helping in the implementation of the project? (4) Who needs to be Consulted about the project at any given point in the implementation process? (5) Who needs to be Informed of the results?

9. Record All Agreements

The peacemaker or assigned recorder will write out all solutions that are agreed upon in a document called a "memorandum of agreement." This document incorporates the joint decisions reached during the discussions. It will be reviewed by all the parties for accuracy and needed modifications. It will continue to be revised until it reflects everyone's sentiment and is agreed upon. All the participants will sign the final document as a testimony to their collaborative work and their commitment to the implementation of future actions that need to be carried out.[596] A copy of the signed memorandum should be given to each participant.

Illustration: The End of World War II. The formal Japanese surrender to the U.S. took place on September 2, 1945, aboard the U.S.S. Missouri. Japanese diplomat Toshikazu Kase expected the signing ceremony to involve the worst of humiliations. To his great surprise, it did not. General MacArthur set the tone in the first sentence of his opening remarks, "We are gathered here, representatives of the major warring powers, to conclude a solemn agreement whereby peace may be restored."[597] According to UP war correspondent and witness of the surrender, Frank Tremaine, "MacArthur conducted that ceremony with extreme dignity, with carefully chosen words, but at no point said anything that could be interpreted as gloating, interpreted as baiting a beaten enemy. I thought it was the most dramatic, most moving ceremony I've ever witnessed."[598] According to Japanese diplomat Kase, "This narrow quarter-deck was now transformed into an altar of peace."[599] Admittedly, this was a formal surrender at the close of a war. However, the tenor of signing the terms of surrender exemplifies what the peacemaker should aim for when creating signed agreements between parties that have had strained relations in the past. Today, Japan is one of America's strongest allies.

Closing Illustration

Their golden wedding anniversary in the 1960s was a time of joy for Bob and Jane Johnson (not their real names). But only two years into their marriage when both were in their twenties, it was almost over. Bob had been unfaithful. Jane learned about it from the other woman, a young widow who lived on a nearby farm. But that was not the worst of it. The widow was pregnant with Bob's child. "My world collapsed," Jane revealed. "I wanted to die. I fought an urge to kill her. And him." Both Bob and the widow were repentant and ashamed for what had happened. Jane, after praying for the strength to forgive, was able to do so. But what about the unborn child? The young widow, in particular, was terrified over her circumstance. The spirit of reconciliation was present, but how would matters play out?

The three of them came up with an idea to resolve the problem. The baby would be born in the Johnsons' home, and Jane would raise the child as her own. (Neighbors thought that the widow was helping Jane throughout the pregnancy when the opposite was the case.) The plan worked without a hitch. A little boy was born to and raised by the Johnsons, their only child it turned out, as Jane was unable to bear any children of her own. Their son was never told the truth. The young widow eventually remarried and had three more children.

This story about forgiveness and full reconciliation originally was written by Jane in a "Dear Abby" letter. The last three lines say it all. "I have never mentioned this incident to my husband. It has been a closed chapter in our lives for fifty years. But I've read the love and gratitude in his eyes a thousand times."[600]

Overall Summary

In the same way Jesus continues to serve as mediator for believers even after they have made peace with God, so the parties rely upon the ongoing work of their peacemaker to help them resolve all remaining issues in order for reconciliation to be complete. If past issues have been successfully dealt with (Stages 1-11), the parties will be in the best possible position to resolve other outstanding issues relating to their future relationship. .

When reconciliation occurs, the peace-making process has come full circle. Indeed, if people are fully reconciled, an outside observer should not be able to tell there was a problem in the past. It would be similar to looking at the waters of a lake that had returned to calm after a storm. Such is the goal in the Judeo-Christian model of peace-making. The peacemaker assists the parties to achieve the goal of living in shalomic peace with one another.

If people are fully reconciled, an outside observer should not be able to tell there was a problem in the past.

Postscript

The South Africa Experience

The Historical Background

Truth and Reconciliation Commission

Its Peacemaking Role
The Innocent Told Their Stories
The Guilty Told Their Stories
Reparations
The Transformation

The Triumph of Love in South Africa

T his postscript not only highlights many of the stages of the Judeo-Christian model of peacemaking, but it captures the three major characteristics of the model as well (see chapter 2). That is to say, what happened in South Africa illustrates how love, not justice, is the first foundation of peace. It illustrates that reconciliation is the goal. And it illustrates the value of third party mediation as the means.

The Historical Background

One official summary of South Africa's past policy and practice of apartheid reads as follows:

During the period under review [1960-1994], the majority of South Africans were denied their fundamental rights, including the right to vote and the right to access to appropriate education, adequate housing, accessible health care and proper sanitation. Those who opposed apartheid were subjected to various forms of repression. Many organisations and individuals in opposition to the former state were banned and banished, protest marches were dispersed, freedom of speech was curtailed, and thousands were detained and imprisoned. This gave rise to tremendous frustration and anger amongst the disenfranchised. Soon, each act of repression by the state gave rise to a reciprocal act of resistance. The South African conflict spiralled out of control, resulting in horrific acts of violence and human rights abuses on all sides of the conflict. No section of society escaped these acts and abuses.[601]

Truth and Reconciliation Commission

Its Peacemaking Role

The importance of having the opportunity to tell one's story of injustice and injury was made abundantly clear in South Africa.

Toward this end, the Truth and Reconciliation Commission (TRC) was formed in 1995 with seventeen commissioners, chaired by Bishop Desmond Tutu. The commission served as a neutral third party to promote national unity and bring reconciliation to a country that had been deeply divided by race and the inhumane treatment of blacks by whites. "The Commission was conceived as part of the bridge-building process designed to help lead the nation away from a deeply divided past to a future founded on the recognition of human rights and democracy."[602] The proceedings of the commission were publicized through print, radio, and television. By radio, the South African Broadcasting Corporation communicated the proceedings in every official language of the country to every part of the country so that even the illiterate could hear.[603]

The hearings were set up by the commissioners so that perpetrators of gross human rights violations who openly confessed their activities would receive amnesty and not be subject to criminal prosecution.[604] In essence, the arrangement was amnesty for disclosure, freedom for truth. The commission was insistent that what was being offered was "accountable amnesty," not "impunity."[605] It was only for those who acknowledged their culpability before the world. Such acknowledgment, it should be noted, was not offered privately but was aired for all to see and hear. Public exposure was the cost of immunity against prosecution. "Perpetrators were not able to take refuge in anonymity or hide behind national amnesia."[606] Accordingly, an applicant's family and community would likely be shocked to learn that their beloved husband, father, and friend "was, for instance, a callous torturer or a member of a ruthless death squad that assassinated many opponents of the previous regime."[607] Those who did not admit to their crimes and were later found out were not protected from criminal prosecution.

281

The Innocent Told Their Stories·

The TRC's hearings clearly demonstrated that human beings have a fundamental need to tell their story. Pumla Gobodo-Madikizela, a South African psychologist, who served on the commission, noted that many victims of atrocity actually conceived of justice being achieved simply in terms of stating the truth about what happened to them.[608] It gave victims of atrocities a public voice to officials who were really listening for the first time. The impact of the hearings was palpable on various levels. Anglican Bishop David Beetge positively reflected that the commission "has given the opportunity for people to tell their story, stories which [could] never be told before ... There were so many unhealed wounds before the [TRC] began its work. The evidence of those who have given witness [is] that, by telling their story, they have shared a burden and found a new sense of peace."[609]

The TRC's hearings clearly demonstrated that human beings have a fundamental need to tell their story.

Consider just one example, that of Lucas Baba Sikwepere. He told how he was blinded by the police on December 31, 1985, outside the city of Cape Town. The police started shooting at people who had gathered around a police vehicle. Sikwepere tried to get away. He recounted, "I decided to walk, because I knew that if you run, you were going to be shot ... When I arrived at the place—when I thought, now I am safe, I felt something hitting my cheek ... I felt my eyes itching ... I was scratching my eyes, I wasn't quite sure what happened to my eyes."[610] It turned out that Mr. Sikwepere had been shot in the face and permanently lost his sight. He went on to describe to the commission how, two years later, "the police beat him with electric ropes, suffocated him, forced him to lie in an empty grave and tortured him in other ways."[611]

After his testimony was complete, a commissioner asked Mr. Sikwepere how he felt. He replied, "I feel that what has been making me sick all the time is the fact that I couldn't tell my story. But now it feels like I got my sight back by coming here and telling you the story."[612] Reflecting on the many emotionally charged reports of suffering shared during the hearings, one observer of the proceedings remarked, "Tears in public will not be the last tears, but knowing that one's tears are seen may grant a sense of acknowledgement that makes grief less lonely and terrifying."[613]

In the end, more than 21,000 people gave statements to the commission, over 19,000 of which were for gross violations of human rights. These included murder of family members, abduction, and torture.[614] In 2002, the TRC compiled and published over 900 pages of summary paragraphs describing tens of thousands of cases. Here is a typical entry: "ACKERMAN, Marita (45), was shot and killed when APLA operatives threw hand grenades at and opened fire on the congregation of St James' Church, Kenilworth, Cape Town, on 25 July 1993. Eleven people were killed and 58 wounded in the attack. See APLA ATTACKS. Three of four APLA members were granted amnesty for the attack. The fourth had his application struck off the roll for failing to attend the amnesty hearing (AC/1998/0018).[615]

The Guilty Told Their Stories

Although those applying for amnesty were required to make a full disclosure pertaining to the offense for which they were seeking amnesty, a demonstration of remorse was not required. Nevertheless, many were remorseful. This included Colonel Schobesberger of the Ciskei Defence Force, whose soldiers opened fired upon and killed over two dozen peaceful protesters in the city of Bisho. Before the commission Colonel Schobesberger stated, "We were forced in a position by our political leaders to stop the marchers. ... We followed orders and we regret it deeply. ... From my point of view and for the soldiers of the

Ciskei Defence Force I can speak, I say we are sorry. I say the burden of the Bisho massacre will be on our shoulders for the rest of our lives. We cannot wish it away, it happened. ... I ask the victims not to forget ... but to forgive us, to get the soldiers back into the community, to accept them fully, to try to understand also ... the pressure they were then [under]. This is all I can do. I'm sorry, this I can say and I'm sorry...[616]

Other officers followed suit. Bishop Tutu, who presided over this session, reported a dramatic change in the mood of the gathered crowd. It was very hostile prior to the colonel's testimony. It was preceded by the testimony of a major general who came across as a hard and uncaring man. However, after Colonel Schobesberger and his colleagues finished speaking, the people did something totally unexpected. They broke out in loud applause. Upon seeing and hearing the honest confession and contrition of these men, the anger in the room melted.[617]

A reporter reflected upon what was taking place in South Africa. He asserted that the hearings testified to the deep-seated need "to create a public realm where truth is truth and lies are lies, where actions are held accountable, where the state is held to certain standards. In South Africa, that is perhaps the deepest yearning of all, after decades of infamy."[618] Indeed, as painful as these public testimonies were to tell and hear, they represented the beginning of the moral reconstruction and reconciliation of the country.

Reparations

As part of the reconciliation process, the TRC recommended that reparations be made to those who suffered under apartheid. The commission report readily acknowledged that "no amount of reparations could ever make up for the losses suffered by individuals, families, and communities because of gross human rights violations."[619] Indeed, the country could not reverse the massive wrongs.

It simply did not have the resources. And money, of course, does not bring back lost loved ones.

Nevertheless, the government could, at the very least, make symbolic reparations. This would not only counterbalance amnesty for the perpetrators, but it also would provide tangible relief to those who, as a result of apartheid policies and practices, suffered real economic hardship.[620]   It was also believed that "without adequate reparation and rehabilitation measures, there can be no healing or reconciliation."[621] It was delayed in coming, but in November, 2003, the government started making payments of R30,000, approximately $4,000 to $4,600 to each apartheid victim.[622]

The Transformation

People who visited South Africa after Nelson Mandela was elected as the country's first black president in 1994, and after the TRC began its work, stood amazed. "The world could not quite believe what it was seeing," said Richard von Weizsacker, former president of the Federal Republic of Germany, in 1999.[623] Jewish author Solomon Schimmel spent three weeks in South Africa in 2001 for the specific purpose of seeing the country firsthand, speaking to people from every walk of life, and learning of their perspective. He said, "I have expected to see and hear blatant and intense manifestations of hatred and revenge against whites." But this he did not find. Instead, what he discovered was a "remarkable lack of overt rancor and hatred between blacks and whites, and the concerted effort to create a society in which racial harmony and economic justice will prevail."[624]

In 1997, award-winning journalist and African-American, Charlayne Hunter-Gault, moved to South Africa. She left the NewsHour with Jim Lehrer after working there as a correspondent for almost twenty years. In 2003, she was an invited guest speaker at Harvard University. She gave her assessment about the young

285

democracy in South Africa. She noted that she arrived at a time when the world was "still marveling, not only at the speed with which the deeply entrenched system of racial oppression known as apartheid had ended, but also at the mostly peaceful manner of the transition. That white South Africa had given up without a fight, that there had been no widespread civil conflict between blacks and whites was truly a miracle."[625]

The Triumph of Love in South Africa

How is it that South Africa was able to transition from apartheid into a democracy that included all its citizens without a widespread bloodbath? How did this nation of people "who should by right be consumed by bitterness and a lust for revenge"[626] act otherwise? The answer in large measure is that the commissioners, the corporate group of peacemakers, followed the Judeo-Christian path of forgiveness and reconciliation in carrying out their work.[627] In this process of confession, apology, and symbolic reparations for that which could never be restored, the victims were asked to bear the difference, and they did! They demonstrated "a remarkable generosity of spirit, an almost unprecedented magnanimity in their willingness to forgive those who had tormented them so."[628]

Having received, to a sufficient degree and on a national level, verbal acknowledgment that what was done to them was terribly wrong, the black victims of apartheid willingly bore the sins of their nation. They paid a "high price"[629] for the peace that followed. They did not rise up in military or political retribution. Civil war did not ensue, as it has in so many other countries. The bloodbath the world anticipated did not materialize.[630] When they forgave (and, incredibly, those who were not willing to forgive were the exception, not the *In this process of reconciliation, it was not justice but love that prevailed.*

286

rule),[631] they simultaneously agreed to bear the results of the physical, emotional, economic, educational, spiritual, and psychological evils that their fellow citizens perpetrated against them. In this process of reconciliation, it was not justice but love that prevailed.

Part 4
Other Approaches

Chapter 5

Selecting the Most Appropriate Approach to Your Conflict

Five Other Approaches

Accepting Annoyances
Overlooking Offenses
Matthew 18:15-18
Civil Law
The Criminal Justice System
　　When Grace in the Courtroom Backfired

Five Other Approaches

There are at least five different ways that conflict can be approached other than through the Judeo-Christian model of peacemaking. They are (1) to accept life's annoyances for what they are, (2) to overlook offenses, (3) for Christians in churches to utilize the process outlined in Matthew 18:15-18, (4) to take advantage of the civil court system, and (5) to depend on the government through the criminal justice system to arrest and charge a person with breaking the law. To distinguish the Judeo-Christian model from these other approaches, it is helpful to consider them.

Accepting Annoyances

There are times when the best approach to dealing with life's annoyances is to accept them as just that, annoyances that everyone has to put up with. These are matters that are not important in the overall scheme of things. For example, on the original *The People's Court* television program with Judge Wapner, there was a case about a man who lost 65 cents when he tried to buy a can of apple juice in a vending machine. The man then spent $25.20 on long-distance calls attempting to contact the machine's owner but was unable to do so. The customer filed court papers and sued the owner. The suit was for $25.85—65 cents for the apple juice and $25.20 for long-distance telephone calls. The defendant, the owner of the vending machine, said that he didn't owe the 65 cents because his records indicated that there was no overage in the machine compared to the products sold. He then filed a countersuit for $200 for lost wages. He reported that it cost him that much to take off from work to defend against the lawsuit.

After Judge Wapner heard the case, he made his ruling. The defendant couldn't sue for lost wages for appearing in court. The plaintiff couldn't sue for the $25.20 for the long distance calls. The judge recognized that the customer was suing on principle that one has a right to receive the goods one pays for. He also commented that there were many stubborn people in the world. The verdict was in favor of the plaintiff for 65 cents. The plaintiff won his case, but given all the time and expense involved in "righting this wrong," was it really worth it? To most people, the answer is no. There are many occasions when the wisest thing to do with regard to irritating, inconsiderate, or offensive words, actions, or, as in this case, non-actions, is to do nothing. They simply reflect life's unavoidable annoyances, which we would do well to accept as such and move on.

Overlooking Offenses

Proverbs 19:11 reads, "Good sense makes one slow to anger, and it is his glory to overlook an offense." What is the "offense" that is overlooked here? The Hebrew word is used to indicate "a willful, knowledgeable violation of a norm or standard."[632] It involves the idea of sin. Sometimes the two words, *sin* and *offense*, are used synonymously in the Old Testament.[633] Under the Mosaic law, an "offense" would allow the aggrieved party to take his case before Israel's judges.[634] The point is, the "offense" that one may consider overlooking goes beyond mere annoyance. It involves a real crossing of the line into immoral and hurtful behavior.[635]

As to what specific misbehavior one should consider overlooking, the text does not say. Ultimately, it is up to each person's discretion and understanding of the situation to decide what is "actionable" and what is better passed over and left alone. This verse teaches that a person is not required to demand justice, even in those cases where that person has every right to seek it.[636] One must rely on his or her own judgment to determine the best course of action.

Matthew 18:15-18

When a person overlooks the offense, there is nothing else to be done. On the other hand, when a person is unable to let matters go *within the church*, there are two paths one can pursue. One can either follow the outline provided in Matthew 18:15-18 or utilize the Judeo-Christian model of peacemaking. If the Matthew 18 process can be properly pursued, it should be, but the fact is that Matthew 18 will be applicable in only a minority of cases. (An in-depth discussion of this passage is found in chapter 6.)

Civil Law

Unlike the criminal justice system, breaches in civil law are viewed as being directly between the parties themselves. "In civil law there is the attempt to right a wrong, honor an agreement, or settle a dispute. If there is a victim, they get compensation, and the person who is the cause of the wrong pays, this being a civilized form of, or legal alternative to, revenge."[637]

Reimbursement, not incarceration, distinguishes civil justice from criminal justice. Nevertheless, civil law shares the same characteristic with criminal law in that shalomic peacemaking is not part of these win/lose proceedings. One disputant being ordered by the judge to pay the other may resolve a material issue, but this does not touch upon matters of mutual goodwill. The fact that one side is forced to do something that it was not willing to do voluntarily often results in just the opposite: a hardening of attitudes between the parties.

By contrast, the kinds of activities that tend to produce goodwill, such as the acknowledgment of wrongdoing, are discouraged in civil law. Why? Such admissions increase the likelihood of a defendant being held liable for damages.[638] They also may increase the amount awarded to the plaintiff. To take responsibility and apologize leaves oneself open to subsequent attack. Fearing the outcome, there is a strong history of lawyers advising their clients not to admit guilt (see Stage 7). Shalomic peace is not achieved through civil court proceedings.

The Criminal Justice System

Those attempting to reestablish shalomic peace will not find a pathway for this through the courts and penal system. Why not? In the penal system, attention is focused on the lawbreaker, not on the injured victim. The reason for this is that in the criminal justice system, offenses are considered first and foremost as crimes against the state, not the person against whom the crime was perpetrated.[639] Consequently, people convicted of breaking the law are punished through fines paid to the government, incarceration, and/ or execution. "Justice by the state determines blame and administers pain in a contest between the offender and the state directed by systematic rules."[640]

Since shalomic peacemaking between the offender and aggrieved party is not part of the criminal justice process, it is not part of the outcome. In fact, just the opposite sentiment is often generated. "I hope he rots in prison for the rest of his miserable life for what he did" is a common sentiment expressed by the injured or their families. Sue Molhan, whose son was senselessly murdered in his car during a robbery for what turned out to be $25 worth of jewelry, confirmed this. She observed that in the current system, victims are marginalized from the process. They become bystanders with little to no voice. She felt "cheated, powerless, and even more embittered by the way the court handled the case,"[641] which included allowing the offender to plea bargain to a lesser charge and avoid a trial. Offenders are not accountable to the victim or victim's family in any way. No direct questions are allowed, and no answers are forthcoming. As a result, according to Molhan, "Most victims want offenders to be held accountable through harsher punishment and stiffer sentencing."[642]

Our current judicial system, by its very structure, is not intended to bring emotional closure for victims or assist in their recovery. Fulfilling the interests of the state is its main objective. Hence, "The very vocabularies of healing and restoration are foreign to the legal language underpinning prosecution."[643]

When Grace in the Courtroom Backfired

Shalomic peace is not available in the criminal court system, even when there is a desire and an attempt by the victim to make it happen. Some years ago, a particularly brutal rape took place in New York City.[644] The victim was not only a nun, one whose chastity was her gift to God, but the assailants, using a nail file, carved twenty-seven crosses in her body in apparent mockery of her faith. The public outcry was great. After a massive manhunt by police, two suspects were arrested.

At the trial, events took an unexpected turn. The nun refused to testify against her torturers. The nun indicated that she had no desire for revenge. She hoped, rather, that her attackers would come to understand the great harm they had caused and change their ways. The prosecutor had no choice but to allow the two men to plead to lesser charges with less jail time.

Peace was attempted, but it came at the expense of justice. And without justice there can be no peace. The nun's motives, while personally laudable, are problematic on a societal level. Dangerous men, who gave no indication of remorse or reform, would be out on the streets of the city far sooner than otherwise would have been the case had the nun simply testified in court to what happened to her. In the court system, there is no room for vigilante justice—whether taking the law into one's own hands or taking the application of the law out of the hands of the officers of the court. Failing to hold people accountable for their criminal acts does not create a greater sense of community safety and love. It threatens it. A court of law is not the place to create shalomic peace. It was never designed to be such. It was designed to punish those found guilty as charged. For the guilty, the criminal justice system as practiced in this country is a pain delivery system. Shalomic peace is to be found elsewhere.[645] Given what has been presented in this book, that "elsewhere" is found through the Judeo-Christian model of peacemaking.

Chapter 6

Matthew 18:15-18: The Most Misapplied Passage on Church Conflict

An Examination of Matthew 18:15-18

Introduction

In looking for a way out of conflict, many Christians and churches, with the best intentions, misuse and misapply Matthew 18. They confuse this judicial disciplinary process that occurs on an interpersonal level ("If your brother sins against you..." [v. 15]) with an all-inclusive model of peacemaking. This is a mistake. This passage on church discipline is specifically limited to cases of sin within a congregation of believers that is serious enough to remove a member from its fellowship (v. 17).* Jesus's words here were not intended and should not be used as a general model for all conflict resolution. If Matthew 18 is wrongly applied in this more general way, it will cause an intensification of the conflict instead of its resolution. The right procedure used in the wrong circumstances is the wrong procedure. Let us now consider what Matthew 18 says and when it should be called into play.

The right procedure used in the wrong circumstances is the wrong procedure.

Matthew 18:15-18

15 "If your brother sins against you, go and tell him his fault,[646] between you and him alone. If he listens to you, you have gained your brother. 16 But if he does not listen, take one or two others along with you, that *every charge may be established by the evidence of two or three witnesses.*** 17 If he refuses to

---

* Jesus said of the unrepentant member, "Let him be to you as a Gentile [or, pagan, as in the NIV] and a tax collector" (Matt. 18:17). To the Jewish audience to whom Jesus was speaking, this meant to have nothing to do with him.

** I have italicized these words because they represent a quotation from Deut. 19:15. The New King James Version encloses the words in quotation marks. The New American Standard version uses capitalization to indicate the quoted words.

listen to them, tell it to the church. And if he refuses to listen even to the church, let him be to you as a Gentile and a tax collector. 18 Truly, I say to you, whatever you bind on earth shall be bound in heaven, and whatever you loose on earth shall be loosed in heaven."

The Text Applies Only when Two Conditions Exist

A Charge of Sin

First, Matthew 18 applies only when unrepentant sin is involved. The passage begins with the conditional statement, "If your brother sins against you." In the Greek, this is a third-class conditional sentence.[647] What this means is that for the second part of the sentence to be fulfilled ("Go and tell him his fault"), the first part of the sentence must occur ("your brother sins against you"). Jesus outlines the steps one is to take "if" your brother sins against you. But if your brother does not sin against you—if that condition is not fulfilled—then the subsequent steps are not to be fulfilled either.* If there is no charge of identifiable sin, the imposition of this passage for any other condition would be to misapply it.

The Presence of Eyewitnesses

Second, Matthew 18 applies only when there are at least two or three witnesses to the sin, not to a subsequent a conversation between the two disputants (see further below). The word *witness* is used in Matthew 18:16 in its "legal" sense.[648] That is, the witness is "one who testifies in legal matters."[649] In "legal proceedings," of which Matthew 18:16 is one,[650] this person is a "witness to facts," who can speak about those facts "from his own direct knowledge."[651] This means that when a sufficient number of witnesses to the sin do not

---

* Indeed, each step of the entire process is conditional. Even if the process is started, only when additional conditions are fulfilled does a green light appear to proceed to the next step.

exist, the process cannot move forward. Note the Old Testament text from which Jesus quoted.

Deuteronomy 19:15
A single witness shall not suffice against a person for any crime or for any wrong in connection with any offense that he has committed. *Only on the evidence of two witnesses or of three witnesses shall a charge be established.*[652]

In Jesus's day and prior throughout the history of Israel, a single eyewitness, even to murder, was not sufficient evidence or testimony to convict a person of a crime.

Numbers 35:30 (see also Deuteronomy 17:6)
If anyone kills a person, the murderer shall be put to death on the evidence of witnesses. But no person shall be put to death on the testimony of one witness.

In the Jewish culture of both the Old and New Testament eras, stringent guidelines were set forth to insure that false accusations and convictions did not occur. "In the judicial procedure outlined in the OT one witness was not adequate for personal testimony against anyone, but two or three witnesses were required (Dt. 17:6, 19:15). This principle was ingrained in Jewish law and is reiterated in the NT (cf. Mat. 18:16, 2 Cor. 13:1)."[653] Indeed, this principle was so thoroughly established that we find it reiterated in the first century by Jews of the Qumran community (those who produced the Dead Sea Scrolls),[654] among the writings of the Jewish historian Josephus,[655] and among the rabbis.

The rabbis in Jesus's day were particularly conscientious when it came to credible and reliable witness testimony. Certain occupations disqualified one from even being a witness.[656] If one was a close relative to the accused, that person was disqualified.[657] One who was either a friend or enemy of the accused was disqualified.[658] Moreover, the degree of certainty required by a witness was very high. The witness had to accurately recall the year, month, week, day, time of day, and place where the infraction occurred.[659] If there were significant discrepancies among the witnesses over such details, the case would be thrown out.[660] Such rules were intended to confirm the accuracy of one's memory and screen out testimony that could lead to the conviction of an innocent defendant based on tainted testimony. Though some of the rules may have made the bar for evidence to be considered too high, keep in mind that the prohibition against false testimony was incorporated in the Ten Commandments: "You shall not bear false witness against your neighbor" (Exod. 20:16; see also Mark 10:19). Undergirding the rabbinic traditions was their strong desire to conform to the ninth commandment.

Jesus, a Jewish theologian[661] who was well aware of rabbinic practices (e.g., Matt. 5:20-48), reaffirmed Old Testament law in Matthew 18:16 and felt no need to modify it. Rather, "the use of witnesses shows the link between the Messianic kingdom and the Israelite community of the Old Testament period."[662] The guidelines for the church carry the clear message that unless there are two or three witnesses to the act or event in question, a given case cannot move forward.

It is also important to keep in mind the possibility that the aggrieved party may be wrong in his or her accusation. Without witnesses, the evidence upon which the church as a whole is able to make a binding judgment against the alleged wayward member would be absent. As it was in the Old Testament, so it is in the New Testament. "The biblical requirement of additional witnesses safeguards the judicial process against false accusation, slander, and wrongful incrimination."[663] The witnesses must agree if called upon to confirm the charge of sin. Without such evidence, the process Jesus instituted would, by design, have to stop. "Strict judicial procedures are being followed at this point because a judicial action is about to take place."[664]

Here is a statement in the bylaws of one church that has it right: "It is important to understand who qualifies as a witness and what their function is in the disciplinary process. Biblically, a witness is a person who bears testimony of another's wrongdoing based on firsthand knowledge. A person is not constituted a witness who bears testimony based on hearsay, gossip, or secondhand knowledge (Deuteronomy 19:15-19). The Bible condemns false witnesses (Exodus 20:13). Accusations not substantiated by two or three witnesses must be left to the One who knows all things and judges righteously (Numbers 35:30; Psalm 51:3-4)."

Although reconciliation is the ultimate goal of Matthew 18, if there is no repentance for sin, believers "must gather evidence in the proper order in case they later need proof of what transpired."[665] The final disposition would be removal from the fellowship of the church (vv. 17-18). "The community is authorized to determine whether a sinning disciple continues with the community or is excluded. ... Repentance leads to loosing or forgiveness, and continued fellowship. The lack of repentance leads to binding, or retention of sin, and exclusion from the community."[666]

How Matthew 18 Is Misinterpreted and Misapplied

The improper use or application of Matthew 18 centers on the word *sin* and the word *witness.* The misinterpretations associated with these words are discussed below.

"If Your Brother Sins Against You"–Common Misinterpretation

The first misinterpretation sees Matthew 18 as providing an outline for resolving every form of conflict. That is to say, all conflict, regardless of whether or not sin is involved, is crammed into a process that was intended to have a very narrow application.

An article about church conflict endorsed by one evangelical denomination began by discussing church conflict of various kinds, stating, "People become dissatisfied with the way church leadership spends money, with a youth program which doesn't meet the needs of their children, with the style of worship or preaching," etc.[667] The article ended by saying that such church problems should be funneled through Matthew 18 for resolution. This conclusion, however, is unsupportable. Having a difference over how leadership prioritizes spending is not a matter of sin anymore than Paul and Barnabas's major conflict over whether or not to take Mark on their second missionary journey was a matter of sin (Acts 15:36-41).[668] Matthew 18 is triggered only when one person is being charged with doing wrong against another.

"Two or Three Witnesses"–Common Misinterpretation

There are those who identify the two or three witnesses, not as eyewitnesses of the sinful act being charged, but only as witnesses of the conversation the aggrieved party has with the one he or she is charging with sin. One commentator wrote, "These are not witnesses of the original wrong-doing but of the wronged person's attempts at reconciliation, and of the response the wrong-doer makes to them. They will be able to certify that the one has honestly tried to bring the other to a better mind, and that the other has or has not yielded to his efforts. If this fails, the wronged person is to 'tell it to the Church.'"[669]

In terms of uncovering the truth, such an interpretation of the text will not get you there. For example, if John charges Lyle with sin and Lyle denies the allegation, what good are witnesses to the conversation? Such witnesses do nothing to establish the truth. Moreover, how can someone be protected against false accusation if all that is needed to establish the charge as true are witnesses at the time the accusation is made? What if the one bringing the allegation is himself mistaken or even dishonest? As a third-class conditional statement (in the Greek), there is an element of uncertainty inherent in the statement, "if your brother sins against you."[670] It is not certain that he has. Yet under the above interpretation, the one

305

who accuses the other first wins. If John charges Lyle with sin first privately and then in front of "witnesses" and Lyle denies it privately to John and then later in front of others, his denial would be seen as clear evidence of an unrepentant heart. If the matter is taken to the church, then Lyle's continued denials of the charge will serve only to further demonstrate his obstinacy. This will then lead to his removal from fellowship. Ironically, witnesses of the conversation are actually instrumental in causing a new conflict. The original charge becomes irrelevant. It now becomes all about the response the alleged wrongdoer makes in front of the witnesses. This interpretation of Matthew 18:16 leads to its misapplication, and rather than finding resolution to the problem, it will make it worse.

"Two or Three Witnesses"–Drastic Misinterpretation

There is another, even more drastic, misinterpretation of the text. Popularized by Peacemaker Ministries, the very meaning of the word *witness* is changed into something entirely different, as the word is made to mean "mediator." In reference to Matthew 18:16, we read, "The role that these 'one or two others' are fulfilling is sometimes referred to as 'mediation.'... a mediator works with both sides to help them move toward a voluntary agreement."[671] The concept of mediator, inserted into Matthew 18:16, is then expanded to include fifteen additional roles these one or two others can play.[672] They are: (1) intercessor, (2) convener, (3) facilitator of communication and understanding, (4) model, (5) referee and protector, (6) trust builder, (7) resource expander, (8) generator of alternatives, (9) reality tester, (10) teacher and counselor, (11) encourager and coach, (12) confronter and exhorter, (13) proclaimer of forgiveness, (14) closer, (15) witness (in the sense described in the section above). Arbitrator and reconciler are additional roles this person can be asked to play, according to this understanding of Matthew 18:16.[673]

The extent to which a single word with a clearly defined

meaning has been commandeered to mean so many different things is stunning. It is also misleading. On what basis can the clear meaning of a single word be transformed into a multitude of textually unsupportable ones? If Jesus wanted to use a different word than *witness* in Matthew 18:16, he could have. He did not have to quote from Deuteronomy 19:15 to make his point, but he did. To later come along and alter the very essence of what he intended, without a shred of textual basis to do so, eviscerates the process Jesus established. It results in a misuse and misapplication of this important passage.

Getting a Clearer Understanding

Lest there be any doubt about the meaning of the word *witness*, let us see how Matthew used it elsewhere in his book and how the apostle Paul used it in 1 Timothy 5. Charges of wrongdoing are the subject in both instances.

Matthew 26:59-66

59 Now the chief priests and the whole Council were seeking false testimony[674] against Jesus that they might put him to death, 60 but they found none, though many false witnesses[675] came forward 61 and said, "This man said, 'I am able to destroy the temple of God, and to rebuild it in three days.'" 62 And the high priest stood up and said, "Have you no answer to make? What is it that these men testify against you?" 63 But Jesus remained silent. And the high priest said to him, "I adjure you by the living God, tell us if you are the Christ, the Son of God." 64 Jesus said to him, "You have said so. But I tell you, from now on you will see the Son of Man seated at the right hand of Power and coming on the clouds of heaven." 65 Then the high priest tore his robes and said, "He has uttered blasphemy. What further witnesses[676] do we need? You have now heard his blasphemy. 66 What is your judgment?" They answered, "He deserves death."

At Jesus's trial, false witnesses were offering false testimony in an attempt to manufacture grounds to put Jesus to death. That failed because too many details among them were not in agreement (see Mark 15:54). What sealed the verdict against Jesus were the words he spoke in front of his accusers. They now no longer needed witnesses. They became the witnesses. They had proof positive, because they knew from their own firsthand knowledge what Jesus said and who he claimed to be.

Now let us turn to the writings of the apostle Paul.

1 Timothy 5:19-20.
19 Do not admit a charge against an elder except on the evidence of two or three witnesses. 20 As for those who persist in sin, rebuke them in the presence of all, so that the rest may stand in fear.

This is an important passage because it parallels Matthew 18. The word translated "rebuke" in 1 Timothy 5:20 is the exact same word Jesus used in Matthew 18:15 that is translated "show him his fault." (The word also could be translated in Matt. 18:15, "rebuke him."[677]) In other words, if the common (mis)interpretation for Matthew 18:15-16 were applied to 1 Timothy 5, its lack of viability becomes even more apparent. Should one uncorroborated charge against an elder or pastor be allowed to stand simply because it was leveled in the presence of witnesses? Pastors, in particular, need every protection against false accusations. One minister observed, "Many a pastor has had his ministry destroyed over accusations that could not be proven false, though they were."[678] The apostle Paul states that a charge should not be admitted or entertained unless there are witnesses, that is, witnesses of the sin, not witnesses of the charge! "It was of utmost importance to safeguard innocent men from false accusations, and as Jewish law required the agreement of two witnesses before a man might be called upon to answer a charge (cf. Dt. 19:15), so it must be in the church (cf. Mt. 18:16, 2 Cor. 13:2), especially when an elder is implicated."[679] The idea that these witnesses are mediators and the like (see "drastic misinterpretation" above) requires no further discussion since there is no basis upon which to even consider it.

Other passages in the New Testament that use the word *witness* in a judicial sense[680] include the following.

Acts 6:11-13
11 Then they secretly instigated men who said, "We have heard him speak blasphemous words against Moses and God." 12 And they stirred up the people and the elders and the scribes, and they came upon him and seized him and brought him before the council, 13 and they set up false witnesses who said, "This man never ceases to speak words against this holy place and the law.

Acts 7:58
Then they cast him [Stephen] out of the city and stoned him. And the witnesses laid down their garments at the feet of a young man named Saul.

2 Corinthians 13:1
This is the third time I am coming to you. Every charge must be established by the evidence of two or three witnesses.

Hebrews 10:28
Anyone who has set aside the law of Moses dies without mercy on the evidence of two or three witnesses.

Summary

Matthew 18 is a critically important passage that instructs the church on how to deal with sin on an interpersonal level that is serious enough to remove an unrepentant member from fellowship. The passage outlines the formal process for church discipline, using the word *witness* in its legal sense.[681] Two or three eyewitnesses of past wrongdoing are required when sin is being charged. Without such witnesses, the judicial process as outlined in Matthew 18 cannot proceed. Before someone can be expelled from a church, evidence for the basis of that expulsion from multiple sources must be secured. If all the conditions of the passage can be met, it should by all means be used.

Matthew 18 is not applicable for resolving differences of opinion and other kinds of problems. When this judicial, church discipline process is inappropriately applied, for example, for differences of opinion over church goals, policies, allocation of resources, building projects, etc., expect an escalation of the conflict, even a church split. Using Matthew 18 for the majority of conflicts that typically emerge in a church is like trying to fit a square peg into a round hole. It is the wrong process.

The Judeo-Christian model of peacemaking should be utilized for all situations when Matthew 18 cannot or should not be used. This model of peacemaking is based on the process that God established to make peace with all of humanity. It can and should be used both inside and outside the church.

Appendixes

Appendix 1

When Love Fails

When Love Fails
Introduction
A Brief Journey into the Loveless Extremities of
Human Existence
    Infancy
    Childhood
    Troubled Teenage Boys
    Adult Children of Divorce
    Adults in General
    Old Age
Summary

Relevance to Peacemaking

When Love Fails

Introduction

What follows is a brief journey into the loveless extremities of human existence. What is life like when love fails, that is, when it is seriously disrupted or withheld? What is life like when love, the glue that holds people together, loses its adhering power? This excursion is presented to bolster the premise that love, not justice, is the first foundation of peace.

A Brief Journey into the Loveless Extremities of Human Existence

Infancy

In the thirteenth century, the German king, Frederick II, was curious to learn what language babies would speak if no one spoke to them. The king wondered whether they would come to speak Greek, Latin, Hebrew, Arabic, or perhaps the dialect of their biological parents if the infants were left on their own. To find out, a select group of infants were chosen. The king ordered the foster mother and nurses who were to care for these tots to be absolutely silent. "Nurse them, clean them, bath them, but don't coo or speak to them," was his command. In the end, the experiment was a dismal failure. Not only did these children fail to develop any language skills. They all died. A contemporary of the king, a man named Salimbene, offered this succinct analysis of what happened: "They could not live without the petting and the joyful faces and loving words of their foster mothers."[682]

Now jump forward to the early twentieth century. *Uncontrollable* was a word used to describe the death rate among infants and toddlers in orphanages all across America. Hear the voices of three medical doctors from that era. Dr. Hamill,

314

of Philadelphia: "I had the honor [sarcastically speaking] to be connected with an institution in Philadelphia in which the mortality among all infants under 1 year when admitted to the institution and retained there until death, was 100 percent. That is, no infant admitted under 1 year of age lived to be 2 years old." Dr. Southworth from New York City: "I can give an instance of this difficulty from an institution that no longer exists, in which on account of the very considerable mortality among the infants admitted it was customary to enter the condition of every infant on its admission card as hopeless." Dr. Knox of Baltimore: "I can give testimony from Baltimore of the same kind. A year or two ago I had occasion to investigate [orphaned] babies sent to the different institutions by the city supervisors ... None of those that stayed continuously in the institutions lived to the end of the first year."[683]

What in the world was going on? The medical community diagnosed the problem as "marasmus," a wasting disease of unknown origin. But according to the dissenting voice of Dr. Henry Dwight Chapin, the fantastic death rate was due to the babies being emotionally forsaken in institutional settings. He argued that the absence of "mothering" was the problem.

Chapin minced no words at a gathering of physicians in Boston in 1914. The doctor asserted, "The best conditions for the infant thus require a home and a mother. The further we get away from these vital necessities of beginning life, the greater will be our failure to get adequate results in trying to help the needy infant. ... I believe the plan of collecting babies in institutions should be abandoned, as, on the whole, doing more harm than good. ... The high mortality is not so much due to lapses in care or details in management as to the system itself, which fails because it is wrong. ... rarely, if ever, is sufficient individual care given to infants in institutions."[684] Bringing his speech to a close, Dr. Chapin exclaimed, "If the present workers in this field will not improve their methods, then some future generation with wider vision, truer courage, and broader human feeling will accomplish this needed reform."[685] Chapin's call for reform was heeded.[686] Foster care spread throughout the U.S., and there was a dramatic lowering of the death rate among young orphans.

The sad truth is that when infants are physically provided for but emotionally starved, tragedy strikes. If babies are not spoken to, smiled at, touched, held, and given sustained, loving interaction, they will die prematurely. On a more positive note, in this same time frame, Dr. Fritz Talbot recalled cases with much happier endings. He related, "I remember that twenty-eight years ago [that is, in 1913] in Dusseldorf, Germany, I made a visit to a hospital, and there was a very fat old lady wandering around the ward with a baby on her hip, a very measly baby. I asked Schlossman what she was doing with the baby, and he said that whenever he had a baby for whom he and his associates had done everything they knew how to do medically and were unsuccessful, he gave the baby to Old Anna, and told her to take it in charge, and that Old Anna was always successful."[687] Tender, loving care was what these babies desperately needed to live.

Childhood

In the 1930s, Harold Skeels worked with twenty-five young children. All were living in an Iowa state institution. The children were divided into two groups. Skeels placed thirteen of the children, the experimental group, into a home for mentally retarded teenage girls and women. The average age of the children was nineteen months. The average IQ was 64. Of one of the boys Skeels said, he "was not only retarded, but showed perservative patterns of behavior,* particularly rocking back and forth incessantly."[688] The other twelve children, the control group, had an average age of seventeen months and an average IQ of 87.

The home for the mentally retarded teenage girls and women

---

* Perservative behavior is "repeating behavior which has lost its original function" (Webster, 1999, slide 30).

was divided into eight wards with approximately thirty girls to a ward. Each ward received one or two of the tots. These toddlers instantly became the center of attention. They were doted upon. They were taken on car rides and field trips. In addition to this general care, in almost every case, either an older girl or a hospital attendant became particularly attached to a given child, almost as if that child were adopted by that person. An "intense adult-child relationship" developed between the pair.[689]

The experience for the other group of toddlers, the control group, was significantly different. They were not separated out or distinguished from the larger population. They received the typical care that was representative of that era. This meant many children had far fewer caretakers. While the children received good physical and medical care, their social interactions were wanting. Contact with the adults or older child assistants focused on daily care issues such as eating, bathing, going to the bathroom, etc. The children went outside the nursery room only for short periods of time to take a walk and to get some fresh air. Of these children, Skeels noted, "The outstanding feature is the profound lack of mental stimulation or experiences usually associated with the life of a young child in the ordinary home."[690]

Over the next year and a half, Skeels watched the development of these two groups. At the end of nineteen months, he found that the "experimental" group of children had an average IQ of 92, a gain of 28 points. The IQ's of the control group of children, by contrast, dropped to an average of 61, a drop of 26 points. In addition, at the end of the experimental period, eleven of the thirteen children from the experimental group ended up in adoptive homes. None from the control group were adopted.[691]

More than two decades after completing his last post-experimental follow-up with the children in the 1940s, Skeels set out to find out what happened to these children. What he found was stunning.[692] All thirteen of the experimental children, now adults, were found to be self-supporting. Eleven of the thirteen had graduated high school. Four had at least one year of college. A fifth had a B.A. and was enrolled in graduate school. The children in the control group, on average, finished only the fourth grade. One had died in adolescence, and the rest remained institutionalized.

As this investigation makes abundantly clear, when secure bonds of attachment are not formed at this critical stage in a young child's life, the damage that is done lasts a lifetime. The sad truth is that when young children have their physical needs met but are emotionally neglected—if they don't receive sustained, loving interaction—they will be mentally handicapped for the rest of their lives.

Harold Skeels received the Joseph P. Kennedy International Award in 1968. This award is recognized by many as the "Nobel Prize" for significant contributions in the field of mental retardation. Just before Skeels accepted his award, he was introduced by a well-spoken young man, dressed in a tuxedo, who had recently earned his Master's degree. During his introductory words, the young man revealed to the audience that not only was he one of the children in the experimental group, but in particular, he was the one who "sat in the corner rocking."[693]

Troubled Teenage Boys

After twenty-five years of study and interaction, the central thesis of Dr. James Garbarino's descriptive and highly acclaimed book, *Lost Boys*, is that kids who kill are not connected by love. "Whether it is outright abandonment or psychological rejection, violent boys often leave infancy and early childhood with one of the biggest strikes against them that a child can have—disrupted attachment relationships."[694] They become emotionally retarded,[695] lack empathy,[696] have a diminished capacity to enjoy life,[697] and engage in violent and antisocial behavior. The sad truth is that when sustained, demonstrable love is withdrawn from

318

preadolescent boys, they will be emotionally stunted, unfeeling, cruel, and violent when they become teens.

On a more positive note, Garbarino revealed that for some boys a "compensatory relationship" can make all the difference in his development.[698] That is, when attachments in a boy's immediate family are minimal, other family members or someone outside the family can make the critical difference in the boy's life. Such was the case of Roger Tory Peterson. Raised in a house where an abusive and alcoholic father dominated, Roger was a troubled youth. To escape his intolerable family life, he took to the hills in and about his hometown of Jamestown, New York. He not only found peace in nature but also became fascinated by birds. Peterson's seventh-grade teacher encouraged her students to join a Junior Audubon Club. Roger did and became part of a healthy group setting where he was accepted. Making positive relational connections, he was "lost" no more. In 1934, in his mid-twenties, Peterson published, *A Field Guide to the Birds*, and it has never stopped selling. The publisher, the Houghton Mifflin Company, stated that the work is "the most successful series of nature guides ever published in the United States."[699] It has "received every major award for ornithology, natural science, and conservation, as well as numerous honorary degrees, medals, and citations, including the Presidential Medal of Freedom." And just to think, "as is often the case, it was an influential teacher who turned a young boy away from mischief and toward a new future."

Adult Children of Divorce

Wallerstein and Lewis published the findings of their work entitled, "The Unexpected Legacy of Divorce: Report of a 25-Year Study."[700] Unlike the boys Garbarino worked with, Wallestein's study was conducted with children who were "psychologically sturdy" and "had never been referred to counseling for emotional problems." Moreover, this group of children, ranging from ages 3 to 18, was particularly chosen because they came from white, middle-class homes, where issues of poverty and racial discrimination were not factors. The study was designed to look at divorce "under the best of circumstances."[701] This final follow-up study of the 131 children, now adults, was completed twenty-five years later. Their ages ranged between 28 and 43. What did the researchers discover? "The central finding of this study is that parental divorce impacts detrimentally the capacity to love and be loved within a lasting, committed relationship."[702] They found that "divorce begets fewer marriages, poorer marriages, and more divorces."[703] Children of divorce are hardest hit when they become adults. The sad truth is that when children experience the loss of trust and security through the divorce of their parents, they will be less able to emotionally bond in secure and trusting relationships with their future spouses.

Adults in General

Dean Ornish received his medical training, in part, at Harvard Medical School and has served as clinical professor of medicine at the University of California, San Francisco. His research has been widely published in medical journals, as well as in popular magazines such as *Newsweek, Time,* and *U.S. News and World Report.* In his book, *Love and Survival: The Scientific Basis for the Healing Power of Intimacy,* Ornish expressed his shock at learning from study after study the stunning difference loving relationships make upon one's physical health and the ability to forestall premature death and the onset of diseases of every kind.[704] In a *Newsweek* article, Dr. Ornish reiterated the scientific findings. Those who are rich in relationships and socially connected compared to those who are lonely fare much better when it comes to cardiovascular disease. Referring to strong, relational bonds, he stated, "I'm not aware of any other factor in medicine—not diet, not smoking, not exercise, not genetics, not drugs, not surgery—that has a greater impact on our quality of life, incidence of illness and premature death."[705] The sad truth is that when adults live detached lives they experience greater sickness and disease and have a shorter life span than those who are rich in love and emotional support.

Old Age

Comedian, actor, and writer Steve Martin wrote an autobiography of his eighteen-year career as a stand-up comedian. His memoir also included personal information about his family life growing up. He did not have a close relationship with his father. Hostility framed the relationship, and silence between the two characterized it. It wasn't until his father was in his eighties that he told Steve that he loved him for the very first time in his life. Near the end of his life, bedridden, and with his health in serious decline, the elder Martin confessed to his son that he wanted to cry. When Steve asked him why, his father poignantly replied, "For all the love I received and couldn't return."[706] A few more words were spoken between the father and son, and then father and son wept for the all their empty years.[707] This one story may not carry the same weight as the investigative studies presented in previous cases. Yet, there is no reason to believe that the self-recrimination Steve's father felt is not similar to other people's experience in old age. The sad truth is that when adults fail to demonstrate love to others during their lives, they will likely be filled with remorse at their death.

Summary

"People who need people are" not only "the luckiest people in the world," as the popular 1960s song put it. They are also the only people in the world. When people become disconnected from others, when the back-and-forth flow of love is cut off, there is premature physical, emotional, and/or psychological death. When there is relational failure, the fullness of the human experience is never realized.

The basic human need for love and social bonding is revealed in the first pages of the Bible. The very first "not good" recorded in the Scriptures occurred when God said of Adam, "It is not good that the man should be alone" (Gen. 2:18). This is significant. We discover that the first emotional ache experienced by man was not for God (because man's relationship with God had not yet been broken). The first emotional ache was for another person. Being relationally isolated from others was an undesirable state at the first moment of man's existence. Soon thereafter God created Eve, a wife and companion for Adam. Then things became "very good" (Gen. 1:27, 31). The very first life lesson from the Bible is that without love for others, life is incomplete. No wonder Jesus called it the second greatest commandment right after love for God (Matt. 22:34-40).

Relevance to Peacemaking

How does the above excursion into the loveless extremities of human existence relate to conflict? Ongoing conflict, by its very nature, produces a disassociative state between fellow humans. Unresolved conflict represents relational breakdown and disconnect. Unresolved conflict propels people toward social isolation. The paths of those who are minimally loved and those who have lost love through conflict begin to merge. We end up losing some of ourselves. Some instances may have little impact. In other instances, the impact will be significant. In all cases, however, conflict launches people in the opposite direction of the universal, visceral need to be emotionally attached to others. Without the orientation to love, there will be no reconciliation. And without reconciliation, there will be no peace.

Conflict launches people in the opposite direction of the universal, visceral need to be emotionally attached to others.

Appendix 2

Additional Passages on Forgiveness

Additional Passages on Forgiveness

Jesus's Words on the Cross
  Commentary
  Addendum
The Lord's Prayer
Jesus's Parable on Forgiveness
  Prior Passage
  The Parable Itself
  Corresponding Passage

Overall Summary

Additional Passages on Forgiveness

There are three passages that should be considered to complete the discussion on forgiveness (see Stage 10). They are Jesus's words on the cross, the Lord's Prayer, and Jesus's parable on forgiveness. They are sometimes cited to argue for unilateral and unconditional forgiveness. As we shall see, such teaching is not supported by these texts.

Jesus's Words on the Cross

When Jesus was on the cross, one of the statements he made was, "Father, forgive them, for they know not what they do." There are no conditions associated with these words. Let's look at this text in its full context, along with other relevant passages, to help us better understand what Jesus was saying.

> Luke 23:32-34, 39-43
> 32 Two others, who were criminals, were led away to be put to death with him. 33 And when they came to the place that is called The Skull, there they crucified him, and the criminals, one on his right and one on his left. 34 And Jesus said, "Father, forgive them, for they know not what they do."
>
> 39 One of the criminals who were hanged railed at him, saying, "Are you not the Christ? Save yourself and us!" 40 But the other rebuked him, saying, "Do you not fear God, since you are under the same sentence of condemnation? 41 And we indeed justly, for we are receiving the due reward of our deeds; but this man has done nothing wrong." 42 And he said, "Jesus, remember me when you come into your kingdom." 43 And he said to him, "Truly, I say to you, today you will be with me in Paradise."

Commentary

Before we begin, we need to note the fact that Luke wrote both the gospel of Luke and the book of Acts. Both were written decades after Jesus's resurrection, well into the birth and expansion of the early church and within a few years of each other.[709] By the time Luke put pen to paper, he would have had the perspective of seeing how some of what was recorded in his gospel played out in the early church. As one scholar put it, "In writing the Gospel, Luke antici-pated Acts, so that much in the Gospel has its fulfillment and clarity in Acts. To try to understand either without the other is a fruitless exercise in excessive rigidity."[710]

Returning to Jesus's words on the cross, we observe that Jesus did not unconditionally forgive those who crucified him. His statement did not reflect the same assurance that he gave to the criminal being crucified next to him (v. 43). What Jesus did was to pray for "them" (v. 34). Many scholars believe that "them" refers to the Jewish religious leaders.[711] They thought they were crucifying just another man. They did not realize they were crucifying the Son of God. The question that immediately follows, then, is this: Was Jesus's prayer for forgiveness fulfilled, and if so, when? The answer to these questions is given in the book of Acts. Let's take a closer look.

Notice that the "ignorance" motif in Luke 23:34 (i.e., "they know not what they do") specifically related to Jesus's crucifixion occurs again in the book of Acts.* Its recurrence helps us to properly interpret the meaning of Jesus's words on the cross. Here are those texts.

Acts 3:12-15, 17-29
12 Peter ... addressed the people: "Men of Israel, ... 13 The God of Abraham, the God of Isaac, and the God of Jacob, the God of our fathers, glorified his servant Jesus, whom you delivered

---

* If the "them" were to include the Roman soldiers, then Acts 17:30 should be added to the passages from Acts that refer to the "ignorance" motif for Gentiles. Acts 17:30 reads, "The times of ignorance God overlooked, but now he commands all people everywhere to repent."

over and denied in the presence of Pilate, when he had decided to release him. 14 But you denied the Holy and Righteous One, and asked for a murderer to be granted to you, 15 and you killed the Author of life, whom God raised from the dead. To this we are witnesses. … 17 And now, brothers, I know that you acted in ignorance, as did also your rulers. 18 But what God foretold by the mouth of all the prophets, that his Christ would suffer, he thus fulfilled. 19 Repent therefore, and turn again, that your sins may be blotted out, 20 that times of refreshing may come from the presence of the Lord, and that he may send the Christ appointed for you, Jesus."

Acts 13:16, 26-31, 38-39

16 So Paul stood up, and motioning with his hand said: "Men of Israel and you who fear God, listen. … 26 Brothers, sons of the family of Abraham, and those among you who fear God, to us has been sent the message of this salvation. 27 For those who live in Jerusalem and their rulers, because they did not recognize him [Jesus] nor understand the utterances of the prophets, which are read every Sabbath, fulfilled them by condemning him. 28 And though they found in him no guilt worthy of death, they asked Pilate to have him executed. 29 And when they had carried out all that was written of him, they took him down from the tree and laid him in a tomb. 30 But God raised him from the dead, 31 and for many days he appeared to those who had come up with him from Galilee to Jerusalem, who are now his witnesses to the people. … 38 Let it be known to you therefore, brothers, that through this man forgiveness of sins is proclaimed to you, 39 and by him everyone who believes is freed from everything from which you could not be freed by the law of Moses."

God provided opportunity for Jesus's prayer on the cross to be answered and forgiveness to be granted to those willing to accept the offer. But they first had to repent of their sins and put their faith in Jesus as their Messiah. "This forgiveness needed to be accepted in order for anyone to obtain salvation. And some would do so."[712] Jesus could have forgiven these people from the cross. He had the authority to do so.[713] But he did not because their heart was anything but right with God. If they were to be forgiven, they would have to come the way every other sinner comes, through repentance and faith. Jesus was willing to forgive them. He desired "that they change their thinking."[714] But they were not willing to acknowledge their own sins the day Jesus was put to death for their sins and those of all mankind.

Addendum

Much the same can be said about Stephen's prayer in Acts 7:60 as he was being stoned to death: "And falling to his knees he cried out with a loud voice, 'Lord, do not hold this sin against them.'" One of those present was a rabbi named Saul (Acts 7:58). Stephen's prayer was answered in Saul's life. Rabbi Saul, who later became the apostle Paul, also "acted ignorantly in unbelief" (1 Tim. 1:13) but repented of his sins and came to faith in Jesus. It was only then that he was forgiven by God (Acts 26:1-23; 1 Tim. 1:12-16) and Stephen's prayer was answered. There is no other way to find peace with God apart from such a change in the heart and mind of the sinner.

The Lord's Prayer

Matthew 6:9-15

9 "Pray then like this: 'Our Father in heaven, hallowed be your name. 10 Your kingdom come, your will be done, on earth as it is in heaven. 11 Give us this day our daily bread, 12 and forgive us our debts, as we also have forgiven our debtors. 13 And lead us not into temptation, but deliver us from evil. 14 For if you forgive others their trespasses, your heavenly Father will also forgive you, 15 but if you do not forgive others their trespasses, neither will your Father forgive your trespasses.'"

This is not a prayer for salvation but one of acknowledgment of God's sovereignty over one's life and a reconnection of our relationship with him that is daily disrupted by sin (v. 11).[715] The plural pronoun "our" in verse 9 indicates that this is "a prayer that is to be prayed in fellowship with other believers"[716] and that a relationship with God already has been established.[717]

In verse 12 this daily prayer for forgiveness is expressed in terms of a debt, "a metaphor for sins which need to be forgiven."[718] The one praying is aware of and repentant for his or her sins and is asking God to be released from that moral debt.[719] Acknowledging one's sins is a prerequisite for forgiveness.

As we turn to believers forgiving others, the "as" in the middle of verse 12 is instructive. The word in the original is "a conjunction marking a point of comparison."[720] In this case, the comparison is between God and believers as "human forgiveness is modeled after God's."[721] The verse pictures individuals who daily come back to their heavenly Father and, in essence, say, "Please forgive us again. We have reflected a spirit of forgiveness toward others in the same way you forgive us." Because God's forgiveness is predicated upon our recognition and repentance of sin, our forgiveness of others likewise should be predicated on their repentance.

Jesus's Parable on Forgiveness

Jesus illustrates his teaching in Matthew 6 by means of a parable on forgiveness he tells his disciples in Matthew 18.

Matthew 18:21-35
21 Then Peter came up and said to him, "Lord, how often will my brother sin against me, and I forgive him? As many as seven times?" 22 Jesus said to him, "I do not say to you seven times, but seventy times seven. 23 Therefore the kingdom of heaven may be compared to a king who wished to settle accounts with his

servants. 24 When he began to settle, one was brought to him who owed him ten thousand talents.* 25 And since he could not pay, his master ordered him to be sold, with his wife and children and all that he had, and payment to be made. 26 So the servant fell on his knees, imploring him, 'Have patience with me, and I will pay you everything.' 27 And out of pity for him, the master of that servant released him and forgave him the debt. 28 But when that same servant went out, he found one of his fellow servants who owed him a hundred denarii,** and seizing him, he began to choke him, saying, 'Pay what you owe.' 29 So his fellow servant fell down and pleaded with him, 'Have patience with me, and I will pay you.' 30 He refused and went and put him in prison until he should pay the debt. 31 When his fellow servants saw what had taken place, they were greatly distressed, and they went and reported to their master all that had taken place. 32 Then his master summoned him and said to him, 'You wicked servant! I forgave you all that debt because you pleaded with me. 33 And should not you have had mercy on your fellow servant, as I had mercy on you?' 34 And in anger his master delivered him to the jailers, until he should pay all his debt. 35 So also my heavenly Father will do to every one of you, if you do not forgive your brother from your heart."

Prior Passage

The passage immediately prior to this parable deals with church discipline (Matt. 18:15-20). In that passage, an opportunity for wayward believers to return to the fellowship of the church is offered on three different occasions. But to take advantage of any one of these opportunities the person who has sinned against another must repent. It is from this discussion that Peter then asks Jesus in verse 21, "How often will my brother sin against me, and I forgive him?" Though "repentance" is not mentioned in verses 21-22, it is understood, given the preceding context.

---

* A *talent* was a monetary unit worth about twenty years' wages for a laborer.

** A *denarius* was a day's wage for a laborer.

The Parable Itself

Jesus provides a parable on forgiveness in response to Peter's question to him in verse 21. Jesus frames his illustration by making a parallel between forgiving another's sin against you and forgiving another's debt to you. The same basic Greek words for "debt" and "debtors" mentioned in the Lord's Prayer (Matt. 6:12) are also used throughout this passage (vv. 24, 28, 30, 32, and 34). That forgiveness is what Jesus is actually speaking about is made abundantly clear in verse 35.

The servants in this parable each acknowledge their debt (sin). The servants recognize and confess that they are in debt (have sinned) and are obligated to make things right. The analogy for us is clear. As God has forgiven us for our sins, conditional upon our recognition and confession of our sinful behavior, so we must do the same for those who acknowledge their sin and come to us with a sincere apology.

Corresponding Passage

It should be noted that Matthew 18:21-22 corresponds to what Jesus taught in Luke 17:3-4 on a later occasion in his ministry. Notice the similarity.

Matthew 18:21-22
21 Then Peter came up and said to him, "Lord, how often will my brother sin against me, and I forgive him? As many as seven times?" 22 Jesus said to him, "I do not say to you seven times, but seventy times seven."

Luke 17:3-4
3 "Pay attention to yourselves! If your brother sins, rebuke him, and if he repents, forgive him, 4 and if he sins against you seven times in the day, and turns to you seven times, saying, 'I repent,' you must forgive him."

Though Jesus doesn't use the word for "repent" in the Matthew passage, he does in the passage in Luke. If one reviews Jesus's complete teaching with regard to how many times a person should forgive his brother and under what conditions, repentance as a condition for forgiveness is clearly part of the equation.[722]

Overall Summary

An examination of these additional texts concerning forgiveness makes it clear that divine forgiveness is based upon awareness, repentance, and admission of sin by the sinner. As God forgives us, we are to forgive others. Hence, human forgiveness also should be based upon awareness, repentance, and admission of wrongs by the wrongdoer. Nothing in these additional passages suggests otherwise.

Endnotes

1   Princeton University, 2006.
2   See Prager, 2004, para. 11.
3   Dudley, 2000, para. 4; Dudley, Zingery, Breeden, n.d., pp. 1-2.
4   Costantino and Merchant, 1996, p. ii.
5   UN Paper, 2002, last para.
6   La Guardia, 2003.
7   Spokesman to the Secretary General, 2003, section, Questions and Answers, para. 16.
8   BDAG, 2000, p. 1024.
9   Robinson, 1996, p. 1122.
10   Hare, 1993, p. 60; France, 1985, p. 111. The assumption of that day was that the son, for example, would adopt the vocation of his father and therefore be like him (Carson, 2000a, p, 31).
11   Young, 1995, p. 87; Carson, 2000a, p, 31.
12   Burtchaell, 1989, p. 229. More is said about this subject in Stage 3.
13   United Nations, 1945.
14   Note: The phrase "peace-loving," used one time, is about loving peace, not about loving others.
15   In light of the description given of the human condition in verse 3, the opening "But" of verse 4 is significant. "Precisely at the point where God has every right to express His judgment of us, He chooses instead to meet us with kindness and love" (Demarest, 1984, p. 335). Another scholar remarked that Jesus came to tell people "not of the justice which would pursue them forever until it caught up with them, but of the love which would never let them go" (William Barclay Estate, 2003, p. 293).
16   The Scriptures also teach that, "God is light" (1 John 1:5). Metaphorically speaking, we are not to understand that God is partially light, but all-encompassing light. In its entirety, the verse reads, "God is light, and in him is no darkness at all" (1 John 1:5). Similarly, when the Scriptures affirm that God is love, God is not partly love but entirely love.
17   Geisler, 2003, vol. 2, p. 369.
18   Hoehner, 2001, p. 711.
19   Chafer, 1947, vol. 1, p. 206.
20   Carson, 2000, pp. 319-20.
21   Volf, 2001, p. 42.
22   Lederach, 2005, p. 42.
23   Volf, 2001, p. 40.
24   White, 1984, p. 917. See also Guthrie, 1981, p. 486.
25   BDAG, 2000, p. 521 (καταλλάσσω).

Endnotes

26 Lederach, 2001, p. 193. Reconciliation, said another, is "an embryonic concept" (Hermann, 2004, p. 41). Accordingly, it wasn't until Wilmot and Hocker's sixth edition of their text, *Interpersonal Conflict*, in 2001 that a discussion on reconciliation was first introduced (p. xii, chapter 10). Moore, in his highly acclaimed text, *The Mediation Process*, informed his readers in 2003 that considerations relating to reconciliation were "on the cutting edge of dispute resolution practice" (p. 345).

27 The transformative model of mediation, for example, explicitly states that "relationship enhancement" is not one of its aims (Senft, 2007, p. 21).

28 Ross, 2004, p. 197.

29 Bar-Siman-Tov, 2004, p. 41.

30 For example, see Lederach, 1997, pp. 23-35; Chapman, 2001, pp. 256-57; Botcharova, 2001, pp. 287-92; Kriesberg, 2007, pp. 320-22.

31 See Brunner, 1934, p. 40

32 Chafer, 1948, vol. 3, pp. 17-30; Shedd, 2003, pp. 681-82; Strong, 1907, pp. 710-76, Grudem, 1994, pp. 624-29.

33 I substituted the ESV translation of Hebrews 1:1, which Edwards cited, in place of an older translation which he used that reads, "in divers portions and divers manners.'

34 Edwards, 1956, p. 2025.

35 BDAG, 2000, p. 634. See also Robertson, 1997 on I Timothy 2:5; Becker, 1975, p. 372.

36 That is, in Classical Greek, approx. 700 to 300 BC (Palmer, 2002, para. 1-2).

37 Becker, 1975, 372-73.

38 Oepke, 1967, p. 599.

39 Oepke, 1967, p. 601.

40 BDAG, 2000, p. 634.

41 Louw and Nida, 1989, p. 502.

42 Oepke, 1967, p. 619.

43 See also Matt. 11:27; John 10:9; Acts 4:12; Rom. 5:1, 10-11; 2 Cor. 5:19-20; Heb. 2:14, 17-18; 4:14-16, 1 Pet. 3:18.

44 Oepke, 1967, p. 622.

45 Tenney, 1975, pp. 712-13.

46 Oftentimes, Moses interceded for the people after they had sinned against God. Passages include: Exod. 32:1-35; 33:1-23; Num. 13:25–14:39; 21:4-9. See also Exod. 5:1 and 8:8, where Moses served as mediator between God and Pharaoh.

47 The establishment of the office of prophet looks back to the time when Moses stood as mediator between God and the people, as described in Deut. 18:15, 19.

48 Referencing Deut. 17:18-20, one Old Testament scholar remarked, "The primary activity of the king is to study Torah [the Mosaic law], to submit to the demands and conditions of the Mosaic covenant" (Brueggemann, 2005, p. 607).

49 Oepke, 1967, p. 614.

50 Bush, 1999, para. 15.

51 Bush, 1999, para. 17.

52 Susskind, 2000, p. 131.

53 Chasin quoted in Bush and Folger, 2005, p. 121.

334

54 See Rubin quoted in Bush and Folger, 1994, p. xii. See also Senft, 2007, p. 21 cited above.

55 BDAG, 2000, p. 839, ποιέω

56 BDAG, 2000, p. 288, εἰρηνοποιός. See also p. 216.

57 The term *peacemaking mediator* is used in this work to distinguish the goal of this mediator from those whose goals are not to bring about reconciliation of the parties or even the resolution of the dispute (Senft, 2007, p. 19; Bush and Folger, 2005, 1994). Peacemakers and mediators in the Judeo-Christian model have the making of peace as their goal.

58 In this instance, the two components of the word *peacemaker* ("to make" and "peace") are used separately. In the context of Ephesians 2:15, to *make* means to "bring about, etc., make, establish peace" (BDAG, 2000, p. 839, ποιέω).

59 The compound verb form of the word *peacemaker* means, "to cause a right or harmonious relationship" (BDAG, 2000, p. 288, εἰρηνοποιέω).

60 Bruce, n.d, p. 100.

61 Turner, 1991, p. 13.

62 Turner, 1991, p. 13.

63 The underlying philosophy, however, remained the same. The 1973 Manifesto reads, "As in 1933, humanists still believe that traditional theism, especially faith in the prayer-hearing God, assumed to live and care for persons, to hear and understand their prayers, and to be able to do something about them, is an unproved and outmoded faith" (American Humanist Association, 1973, Preface).

64 American Humanist Association, 1973, Preface.

65 American Humanist Association, 1973, Introduction.

66 Baldoni, 1999, pp. 3-4.

67 Quoted in Cose, 2008, para. 6.

68 Tolle, 2005, pp. 11-12.

69 Gen. 1:4, 10, 12, 18, 21, 25, 31. In 1 Timothy 4:4, the apostle Paul explicitly stated, "For everything created by God is good."

70 Geisler, 2003, vol. 2, p. 316; Thiessen, 1949, p. 129; Strong, 1907, pp. 296f; Buswell, 1962, vol. 1, p. 62.

71 Kohler, 1918, p. 101. See Ryrie, 1999, p. 42.

72 Harrison, 1982, p. 725.

73 Kohler, 1918, p. 101.

74 Strong, 1907, p. 269.

75 Grudem, 1994, p. 203

76 See also Exod. 15:11; Deut. 32:4; 1 Sam. 2:2; Ps. 5:4; 92:15; 145:17; Hab. 1:13 (NASB); Heb. 6:18; James 1:14; 1 Pet. 1:14-15; 1 John 1:5.

77 The footnote to this text reads, "Or Let your name be kept holy, or Let your name be treated with reverence."

78 Gen. 1:27 reads, "God created man in his own image, in the image of God he created him; male and female he created them."

79 Augustine, 405, chapter 34.

80 Augustine, 426, Book 12, chapter 6.

81 Warner, 1995, p. 35.

82 Warner, 1995, p. 35.

83 Ryrie, 1999, p. 233

84 See Gen. 9:6 and James 3:9.

85 Tinder, 1989, p. 76.

86 Augustine's widely accepted understanding of evil is that, though evil is real, it does not have an essence of its own (388, chapter 5). Evil is the perversion of good. It does not exist in and of itself. If good is not present, evil cannot exist because evil is the subtraction of something other than itself. Evil is a parasite that is dependent on the presence of good. In fact, it can be spoken of only in relation to good. Evil brings decay to that which is pure, confusion to that which is orderly, and corruption to that which is intact. Because it represents an adulteration of good, evil is best understood in negative terms, such as unsanitary, unhealthy, unreliable, uncivilized, incurable, and inhumane. Such an understanding of evil is not limited to Christian thinkers. Many Jewish scholars have long come to the same conclusion, not ascribing any existence to evil in and of itself. "Evil to them is the negation of good, just as darkness is the negation of light, or poverty of riches" (Kohler, 1918, p. 178). When evil exists it always does so in the midst of a greater good. That is why I used the word *almost* in the sentence to which this note is attached.

87 Martin Luther King, quoted in Carson, 2000, p. 318.

88 Solzhenitsyn, 1973, 1974, p. 168. See also Martin Luther King in Carson, 2000, p. 318.

89 See also Gen. 8:21; Isa. 53:6; John 8:7,9; Rom. 3:19-20; 1 John 1:8.

90 Volf, 2005, p. 196; Ryrie, 1999, p. 243; Plantinga, 1995, p. 13; Cohen, 1995, p. 101.

91 United States Department of Justice, 2004, section "The Response to Crime," para. 5.

92 Wenham, 1988, p. 474.

93 See also Lev. 6:1-3; Acts 5:1-4

94 Psalm 51 is King David's private confession after Nathan the prophet confronted him for his double sin against Uriah (adultery and murder) in 2 Samuel 12.

95 Biblical texts include Prov. 15:3; Isa. 40:26-27; 46:9-10; Ps. 139:1-4, 15-16; Matt. 6:7-8; 10:29; 1 John 3:19-20.

96 Biblical texts include Ps. 90:8; Isa. 29:15; Jer. 16:17; Luke 16:15; Heb. 4:13. See also 1 Kings 8:38-39, 2 Kings 19:27, Ps. 44:20-21; 94:6-11; Isa. 29:10; Jer. 23:24; and 1 Cor. 4:5.

97 Thiessen, 1979, p. 80.

98 Morris, 1965a, p. 149.

99 Morris, 1965a, p. 150.

100 Elwell, 1988, vol. 2, p. 1784.

101 United States Institute of Peace, 2004, p. 29.

102 History Place, 1999, para.s 1, 8.

103 Volf, 2005, p. 139.

104 Carson, 2000, p. 67.

105 Geisler, 2004, vol. 3, p. 248.

106 Geisler, 2004, vol. 3, pp. 181-82.

107 Lightner, 1995, p. 191-92. See also Dever, 2008, p. 2501.

108 Rifkin, 1980, p. 6,

109 Many scientists believe that the universe as a whole is a closed system and that it will eventually burn out and turn cold.
110 Murningham, 2002, pp. 56, 58.
111 Profits would be donated to charity.
112 Murningham, 2002, p. 63.
113 Murningham, 2002, p. 63.
114 Ury, 1993, p. 121, and Augsburger, 1992.
115 Kriesberg, 2007, p. 232.
116 Volf, 1996, p. 215.
117 Shelley, 1985, p. 77.
118 This is the norm in victim/offender reconciliation programs, where victims initiate the mediatorial process (White, 2001, p. 14).
119 Moore, 2003, p. 87.
120 Burtchaell, 1987, p. 220.
121 Burtchaell, 1987, p. 221.
122 Volf, 1996, p. 80.
123 Plantinga, 1995, p. 57.
124 South Africa's Bishop Desmond Tutu, a Nobel Peace Prize winner, has graphically described this pattern. In 1994, he traveled to Rwanda, where approximately 800,000 people had been killed in fighting between the Hutus and Tutsis during a hundred-day period. In a speech to an audience that included many of the nation's leading politicians, Tutu illustrated the cycle of "top dog" and "underdog" that needed to be broken in that country. The underdogs remember all the pain and suffering the top dogs have inflicted on them until the time they are strong enough to topple the top dogs. As the new top dogs they unleash an "orgy of retribution" against the new underdogs. The new underdogs store up memories of this new wave of abuse until they eventually topple the top dogs, and the cycle begins again. Tutu told his audience that the Tutsis were now back in power after waiting some thirty years. If they unleash a wave of revenge against the Hutus for injustices of the past three decades, the Hutus are capable of waiting and doing the same. "If retributive justice is your last word in this country, you have had it. You can write off the possibility of ever having a stable Rwanda....Your history of the spiral of reprisal provoking a counter-reprisal provoking a counter-reprisal will remain this way. You need something to go beyond that spiral, to break through" (Tutu, 1998, para. 20).
125 Volkan, 1997, p. 34. This has been called the "transgenerational transmission of trauma" (pp. 44, 48).
126 Sadat, 1977a, p. 51.
127 Sadat, 1977b, para. 4 and 5.
128 Sadat, 1977b, final para.
129 With reference to this case of intense personal disagreement, ministry partners Paul and Barnabas, "separated" because of a strong difference of opinion (Acts 15:39). Interestingly, the same basic word that is used to describe this separation is also used in the New Testament for divorce (Mat. 19:6; 1 Cor. 7:10, 11, 15), except here in Acts 15:39, it is a strengthened form of the word. This strengthened form of the word occurs elsewhere in the New Testament

only in Rev. 6:14 where it refers to the sky splitting apart. Clearly, the break between these two spiritual leaders was dramatic and sharp.

130 For example, the apostle Paul wrote to the Corinthian church, "For I fear that perhaps when I come I may find you not as I wish, and that you may find me not as you wish – that perhaps there may be quarreling, jealousy, anger, hostility, slander, gossip, conceit, and disorder" (2 Cor. 12:20).

131 Leas, 1979, p. 1.

132 Bufford, quoted in Lowry and Meyers, 1991, p. 26.

133 Lowry and Meyers, 1991, p. 26

134 Rediger, 1997, p. 48.

135 Greenhouse, 1986, p. 106.

136 Decades ago, one scholar made the perceptive observation, "competition within a group which is in theory harmoniously united tends to become fiercer and more emotionally involved than in one where competition is accepted as normal" (Dore, 1959, p. 343). Conflict often creates greater damage in organizations of goodwill simply because it is not anticipated (Kriesberg, 1994, p. 7). This is true of the church!

137 Wilmot and Hocker, 2001, 6th ed., p. 3.

138 Wilmot and Hocker, 2007, 7th ed., p. 5.

139 Christianity Today International, 2004; Dudley and Roozen, 2001.

140 See Moore, 2003, pp. 454-56, for a list that originated with the Society of Professionals in Dispute Resolution.

141 See American Arbitration Association, American Bar Association, Association for Conflict Resolution, 2005, Standard IV.

142 A non-Christian mediator, for example, one who does not understand the theology or the culture of the church, would be less than an ideal candidate for that setting.

143 See Moore, 2003, pp. 454-56, for the standards that were developed in 1989 by the Society of Professionals in Dispute Resolution; see the Standards of Conduct for Mediators jointly developed in 2005 by the American Arbitration Association, American Bar Association, and Association for Conflict Resolution; see also the related Standards of Practice developed by the International Ombudsman Association, 2007.

144 CPP, 2008, p. 15.

145 CPP, 2008, p. 2.

146 Schellenberg and Parks-Savage, 2007, p. 476.

147 Amandus, 1997, section, "The Hammerblow," para. 12.

148 Center for Reformed Theology and Apologetics, 1996-2006, para. 1.

149 See also Matt. 1:18-25; Col. 1:15-19; Heb. 1:1-3.

150 Jesus used this title for himself more than any other in the NT. It highlights his humanity.

151 Elwell, 1988, "Priests and Levites," p. 1763

152 See Leviticus 16.

153 See also Heb. 2:17-18.

154 Calvin, 1845, vol. II, chapter xii, page 1.

155 Shaw, 1996, para. F.; see also Colosi, 1999, p. 421.

156 Moore, 2003, p. 93.

157 Groopman, 1997, p. 9.

158 Cohen, 2003, p. 14.

159 See Fisher and Ury, 1991, p. 23.

160 Bowling and Hoffman, 2003, p. 40.

161 Cloke, 2001, p. 13.

162 Benjamin, 2003, p. 111.

163 Not all conflict resolution practitioners take this approach. Bowling and Hoffman have observed that a widespread view in the mediation field in the U.S. is for mediators to stay rather detached from the parties they are working with (2003, pp. 22-24). This can be explained, in part, by the fact that most mediators do not pursue reconciliation as their goal.

164 Yardley, 2007, para. 5.

165 Griffin, 1977, p. 29.

166 Griffin, 1977, p. 172.

167 Brenner, 1995, p. 119.

168 Brenner, 1995, p. 96.

169 Brenner, 1995, p. 108.

170 Wiesel, 1960, p. 32.

171 Cohen, 1995, p. 370. See also Peli, 1984, p. 50, who wrote, "No sin goes without its retribution, whether it be meted out by a terrestrial or a celestial court. The belief in reward and punishment is fundamental to Jewish belief: 'A man who says that the Holy One, blessed be He, is lax in the execution of justice, shall be disemboweled for it is stated [in the Babylonian Talmud], He is the Rock, His work is perfect; for all His ways are judgment" (1984, p. 50).

172 Geisler, 2004, vol. 3, p. 160. In this vein, Chafer pointedly wrote, "The supposition that the creature is free from responsibility and accountability to his Creator is the worst of delusions – second only to that irrational notion that God is not cognizant of the creature's sin, or that sin can be hid from God" (1947, vol. 2, p. 257).

173 Grudem, 1994, p. 509.

174 The evangelical view of judgment corresponds to the traditional Jewish view. One rabbi wrote, "Sin and its punishment are born together. No sin goes without its retribution, whether it be meted out by a terrestrial or celestial court. The belief in reward and punishment is fundamental to Jewish belief" (Peli, 1984, p. 50).

175 See also Exod. 32:7-10, 23; Jos. 23:16; Isa. 1:28; 13:9-13; 66:24; Jer. 21:11; Zeph. 1:12.

176 See also Matt. 3:7-10; 16:27, 46; Rom. 2:5; 3:5, 1 Cor. 6:9-11; Eph. 5:6; Col. 3:25; Heb. 9:27; 10:26-27, 31; James 5:1-8; Rev. 21:22-27.

177 King, 1965, near end of speech.

178 Tutu, 2004, p. 2.

179 Strong, 1907, p. 766.

180 Zehr, 2005, p. 188.

181 Jacoby, 1983, p. 291.

182 Quoted in Cohen, 2002, p. 17.

183 Zehr, 2005, p. 188.

184 Eisenhower, 1957, para. 37.

Endnotes

185 Quoted in Petersen, 2001, p. 13.
186 News4jax.com, 2009, para. 20.
187 America's Most Wanted, 2009, para. 8.
188 Michaud, 2009, para. 1.
189 Cotts and Fortado, 2009, para. 10.
190 Portfolio Staff, 2009, p. 5.
191 Minow, 1998, p. 16.
192 See, for example, Rom. 8:4ff; Gal. 5:16, 18, 22-25.
193 McKeever, 2001, sec. "McKeever's Lincoln," para. 5.
194 BDAG, ἀδικέω, 2000, p. 20.
195 BDAG, ἀδικία, 2000, p. 20. See also Vine, 1996, "Unrighteousness."
196 In 1 John 5:17 NASB we read, "All unrighteousness is sin." In that context, the word *unrighteousness* includes, "unjust deeds and injustice amongst men" (Gunther, 1978, p. 575).
197 The Western Greek text of Acts 6:1 adds to the end of the verse "because it was being administered by Hebrews" (Bruce, 1988, p. 119). This addition, though not part of the original, nevertheless still provides an early reference to the cultural tensions that existed.
198 Longenecker, 1981, pp. 326-30; Bruce, 1988, pp. 119-20; Marshall, 1980, pp. 124-26.
199 Moo, 2000, p. 99.
200 Witherington, III, 1995, p. 241.
201 See 1 Cor. 1:13; 3:1-9; 11:18.
202 Burdick, 1979, vol. 1, p. 945.
203 BDAG, 2000, p. 1058.
204 Marshall, 1979, p. 91.
205 Booth, 2004, paragraphs 6-9.
206 The experience of being put out of the church without valid justification can be spiritually and emotionally devastating. Read, for example, one couple's story published in a Canadian newspaper (McLean, 2005).
207 In the OT, see such passages as Isa. 1:16-17; Jer. 22:3; Zech. 7:8-10.
208 Augustine, 426, City of God, Book 19, Chapter 12.
209 Often, words that had one meaning in classical Greek (prior to 300 BC) took on expanded meanings in Koine Greek (approx. 300 BC to AD 300). Koine Greek is the Greek of the New Testament. One reason is due to the translation of the Hebrew Old Testament into Koine Greek around 250-200 BC. This translation is known as the Septuagint. The meaning of various Hebrew words and concepts found in the Old Testament were being incorporated into Koine Greek. In time, due to the influence of the OT and its translation into Greek and its use in the NT, a fuller meaning of the word *peace* emerged. For further discussion, see Foulkes, 1996, p. 891; Beck and Brown, 1976, p. 780; and Gregory, 1976, p. 667.
210 Youngblood, 1986, p. 732.
211 Von Rad, 1964, p. 406; Stotts, 1973, p. 98.
212 It should be noted that although this relational meaning of peace is found in the New Testament, the concept of peace also is used to convey the additional sense of internal peace and serenity (e.g., John 14:27; Col. 3:5; Phil. 4:6-7).

213 Plantinga, 1995, p. 10.
214 Harris, Archer, and Waltke, 1980, p. 931.
215 Brueggemann , 2001, p. 51.
216 King, 1963, para. 23. King was specifically referring to "positive peace," which is synonymous with the concept of the Hebrew word *shalom.*
217 Stotts, 1973, p. 98.
218 Earl of Birkenhead, 1936, pp. 450-58.
219 See *The Reader's Digest,* December, 1939, pp. 73-75.
220 In 1998, when then Secretary-General Kofi Annan spoke before a special commemorative meeting of the General Assembly to honor fifty years of peacekeeping by the UN, he too affirmed that Isaiah's words in 2:4, though not yet realized, are a most worthy "ideal for humanity." He added, "If, in our service as United Nations peacekeepers, we can help make that ideal more true than false, more promising than distant, more able to protect the innocent than embolden the guilty, we will have done our part" (Annan, 1998, last para.). Though the UN has not and does not have the ability to make this vision of a divinely instituted shalomic peace throughout the earth a reality, it still embraces it.
221 Gottman, 2001, p. 209.
222 Cambodian Genocide Program, Yale University, 2009, para. 1.
223 Cambodian Genocide Program, Yale University, 2009, para. 1.
224 Lederach, 1999, p. 76.
225 *Xinhua,* 2006, para. 14-15.
226 Livni, 2007, second to last para.
227 Kriesberg, 2007, p. 276.
228 Boulding, 1998, p. 110.
229 Lederach, 2005, p. 182.
230 Lederach, 2005, pp. 5, 62.
231 See also 1 John 2:23.
232 Morris, 1995, p. 772.
233 To hear excepts of it, see Harris, 2008.
234 JLS1950B, 2008, Nov. 12, 4:09 pm.
235 Harris, et. al., 2009, p. 3.
236 Kantzer, 2006, page 2, no 3.
237 See further Lederach, 2005, p. 35; Bar-Tal and Bennick, 2004, p. 26.
238 PBS / WGBH, 1999-2000, begin with para. "Mikhail Gorbachev, General Secretary USSR."
239 Wikipedia Encyclopedia, 2009, para. 1
240 Brahm and Burgess, 2003, para. 3.
241 Young (1995, p. 88), for example, tells the AD 500 rabbinic story about Aaron, Moses' brother, who used shuttle diplomacy to make peace between two men.
242 Glaser, 1996-2005, para. 1.
243 Some Greek manuscripts read, "from one blood," and this is reflected in the New King James Version. The phrase "from one blood" even more dramatically highlights our shared humanity.
244 Robertson, 1997 on Acts 17:26.
245 Moses, 1983, pp. 12-17.
246 Arendt, 1964, p. 252.

247 Quoted in Milgram, 1974, p. 2. About Hitler's Third Reich, Snow added that it was obedience, not rebellion, that produced "the most wicked large-scale actions in the history of the world." The 1978 mass suicides of over 900 Americans at the People's Temple in Jonestown, Guyana exhibited a similar pattern. At the command of their cult leader, the Reverend Jim Jones, "the great majority of the 910 people who died did so in an orderly, willful fashion" (Cialdini, 2009, p. 128).

248 Ritzer, 2000, p. 575.

249 Hewitt, 1994, p. 15.

250 Psychologist Erik H. Erikson coined the term *pseudospeciation* to refer to "the tendency to portray one's own tribe or ethnic group as human while describing other groups as subhuman" (quoted in Volkan, 1997, p. 24).

251 Beaumont, 2005-2008, para. "The Road to Violence."

252 Witty, 2001, p. 1.

253 Columbia Encyclopedia, 2001-2007, "Ethnocentrism," para. 1.

254 Worchel, 1999, pp. xv, 13, 20, et. al.

255 The hostile actions of one's adversaries frequently become attributed to their *internal* character deficiencies. By contrast, the hostile behavior of one's own group is perceived as normal reactions to *external* circumstances.

256 Griffin, 2004, pp. 136-37.

257 North, 1998, p. 23.

258 Lewis, 1952, p. 104.

259 See Smedes, 1996, p. 6.

260 Butler, 1838, p. 86.

261 Diggs, 1996, p. 78.

262 NASA's Career Management Office, 2002, p. 4.

263 Enright, 1996, p. 110.

264 This quote was accessed at http://en.thinkexist.com/quotes/henry_wadsworth_longfellow/3.html.

265 See Stage 2 for additional information on Griffin's story.

266 Griffin, 1977, p. 104.

267 Wilmot and Hocker, 2001, p. 58.

268 Shelley, 1985 , pp. 37-41.

269 Haugk, 1988, pp. 27-30. It should be noted that Haugk has worked as both a pastor and clinical psychologist.

270 For example, see Rediger, 1997, chapter 9.

271 Vine, 1996, p. 281 (metanoeō, in contrast to pronoeō, to perceive beforehand).

272 Vine, 1996, p. 281.

273 μετανοέω (metanoia)

274 Robertson, 1997, on Matt. 3:2.

275 Louw and Nida, 1989, p. 509.

276 Goetzmann, 1975, p. 358.

277 Crowe, Jr., 1993, p. 297.

278 Crowe, Jr., 1993, p. 292.

279 Berkhof, 1958, p. 485.

280 Chafer, 1948, vol. 3, p. 372.

281 Grudem, 1994, p. 713.
282 See also Isa. 1:2-4, 16-20; Jer. 3:12-15; Mark 1:4; Luke 5:29-32; 13:1-5; 24:44-47; Acts 2:38-39; 8:22-23; 17:30-31; 20:17-21; 26:19-20; 2 Pet. 3:9.
283 The Babylonian Talmud, containing rabbinic writings codified around AD 500, contains the following entry: "Seven things were created before the world, viz., The Torah, repentance, the Garden of Eden, Gehenna, the Throne of Glory, the Temple, and the name of the Messiah. The Torah, for it is written, The Lord possessed me [sc. the Torah] in the beginning of his way, before his works of old. Repentance, for it is written, Before the mountains were brought forth, or ever thou hadst formed the earth and the world ... Thou turnest man to destruction, and sayest, Repent, ye sons of men" (section Nedarim 39b, in Epstein, 1952, para. 2).
284 Sawyer, 1992, p. 4.
285 Safer, 1994, p. 8.
286 Sawyer, 1992, p. 5.
287 Palfreman, 1993, p. 5.
288 Safer, 1994, p. 13.
289 Palfreman, 1993, p. 8.
290 Palfreman, 1993, p. 8.
291 Palfreman, 1993, p. 7.
292 Safer, 1994, p. 14.
293 Palfreman, 1993, p. 7.
294 American Psychological Association, 1994, section VI.
295 American Psychological Association, 2003, para. 4.
296 American Academy of Child and Adolescent Psychiatry, 2008, para. 1.
297 According to one analysis, the reason this occurred was because of (1) an unswerving commitment to the process, (2) the lack of knowledge about the complexities of the problem (autism), and (3) a passionate yet unfounded belief in what the outcome should be despite evidence to the contrary (Twachtman-Cullen, 1997, pp. 149-52).
298 Kriesberg, 2007, p. 222.
299 Budiansky, 1995, p. 52.
300 Ki-moon, 2008, para. 11ff.
301 Cohen, 2003, p. 7.
302 Cohen, 2003, pp. 4, 54.
303 Kriesberg, 2007, p. 222.
304 Rawls, 2005 (1971), pp. 136-42.
305 The veil of ignorance is really just another form of "reframing" discussed in Stage 5.
306 Lorenzini, 2002-2009, para. 16.
307 Walsh, 2003, para. 1.
308 King, 1963, para. 7. Less than half a year after he wrote this, members of the Ku Klux Klan planted dynamite with a time-delayed detonator in the basement of the 16th Street Baptist Church. The bomb went off during Sunday school, killing four youths ages 11 to 14 (an event memorialized by Spike Lee's 1997 film, *Four Little Girls*). More than twenty other people were wounded.
309 King Encyclopedia, n.d., para. 2

310 Carpenter et. al., 1963.

311 King, 1963, para. 3.

312 King, 1963, para. 14.

313 King, 1963, para. 15.

314 King, 1963, para. 20.

315 King, 1963, para. 23.

316 King, 1963, para. 29.

317 Metcalf and Metcalf, 2006, p. 182.

318 Goldstein, Martin, and Cialdini, 2008, p. 147.

319 Why did I say that to my friend? Around 600 BC, God declared through the prophet Jeremiah that only when the sun and the stars stop shining and the ocean's waters stir no more would the descendants of Israel cease to be (Jer. 31:35-37). The apostle Paul in Romans 11 likewise assumed the continued existence of the Jews until the return of the Messiah. Therefore, when the Jew stops existing, then I will have cause to give up my faith in the Bible as God's revelation to mankind. Until then, my underlying belief is that the survival of the Jewish people triumphantly testifies to the God of Israel's existence and providential hand. My friend now knew what it would take for me to admit that I was wrong about my faith. What makes the existence of the Jew all the more remarkable is that no other people have suffered as much and yet still survive. This is well documented. "Hatred of the Jew has been humanity's greatest hatred. While hatred of other groups has always existed, no hatred has been as universal, as deep, or as permanent as anti-semitism" (Prager and Telushkin, 1983, p. 17). Although they have been scattered throughout the world, and from AD 70 to 1948 were without a land of their own, the Jews have neither been eradicated through centuries of persecution nor culturally assimilated. This is unparalleled in the history of mankind. McDowell and Stewart (1980) write, "History has demonstrated that any people who leave their homeland will, after about five generations, lose their national identity by being absorbed into the new culture" (p. 32). But this was not so with the Jews. This unparalleled phenomenon of Jewish survival has not gone unnoticed by others. When King Frederick the Great (1712-1786) asked a clergyman for proof of the truths of Christianity, the pastor's reply was simply, "Your majesty ... the Jews!" (Rosenzweig, 1971, p. 415). Rousseau (1712-1778) was more specific in his observation. "The Jews afford an astonishing spectacle. The laws of Solon, Numa, and Lycurgus are dead; those of Moses, much more ancient, continue to live. Athens, Sparta, and Rome have perished and left no offspring on the earth. But Zion, destroyed, has not lost her children; they are preserved, they multiply, they spread throughout the world. ... They mingle with all peoples, yet are not confused with them; they have no rulers, yet they are always a people" (quoted in Durant, 1967, p. 619. See Twain, 1899, last para.). The survival of the Jews, including the rebirth of the nation of Israel, is for me a living monument testifying to the existence of the God of Abraham, Isaac, and Jacob, and the divine inspiration of Scriptures, which claim to be his revelation.

320 Moore, 2003, p. 385. See also Benjamin, 2003, p. 113.

321 Colosi, 1999, p. 425.

322 Krivis, 2006, p. 289.

323 Kriesberg, 2007, p. 232.
324 Fisher and Ury, 1991, p. 82.
325 Kaner, 1996, p. 21.
326 Lehrer, 2008, p. 40.
327 Lehrer, 2008, p. 40. In 1908, French mathematician Henri Poincare spoke of this same phenomenon (Poincare, 1908, p. 90).
328 Kounios quoted in Lehrer, 2008, p. 440.
329 Benjamin, 2009, para. 9.
330 Grudem, 2008, p. 1994.
331 See also Hebrews 12:11 (NASB).
332 See also Matt. 27:3-4 (NIV, NASB); Matt. 21:38-42 (NASB, NKJV). See also Matt. 14:6-10; Rom. 2:14-15.
333 ὁμολογέω, (homolegeō), BDAG, 2000, p. 708.
334 Vine, 1996, p. 224 ("homos, same, legō, to speak"). In classical Greek (the Greek spoken prior to the Koine Greek of the NT), the idea of verbally agreeing with another was inherent in the meaning of the word (Michel, 1967, p. 200).
335 An example of verse 8 is Proverbs 30:20. It reads, "This is the way of an adulteress: she eats and wipes her mouth and says, 'I have done no wrong.'"
336 This passage reflects the general Old Testament teaching. For example, Proverbs 28:13 reads, "Whoever conceals his transgressions will not prosper, but he who confesses and forsakes them will obtain mercy."
337 Constable, 2007, 1 John 1:9.
338 Harris, Archer, Walker, 1980, vol. 1, p. 845.
339 Interpreted, "When I refused to confess my sin" (NET Bible, 1996-2003); The New Living Translation, 1996).
340 Selah may be a liturgical notation. The exact meaning is not known.
341 ἐξομολογέω (exhomolegeō)
342 Zerwick, 1981, pp. 5, 100.
343 Michel, 1967, p. 205.
344 Furst, 1975, p. 346.
345 Michel, 1967, p. 205.
346 Mark 1:4-5 is a parallel passage.
347 Quoted in Robertson, 1997, vol. 1, Matt. 3:6.
348 Louw and Nida, 1989, p. 419. See also Acts 19:18-19 and James 5:16.
349 E.g., Lev. 5:5; Num. 5:7; Neh. 9:1-3.
350 Reuters, 1990, p. A7.
351 Protzman, 1990, p. 1.
352 Allen, 1989.
353 This true confession has been slightly edited for readability, including maintaining the first person throughout for consistency. All names are fictitious.
354 Neil, 2001.
355 Peli, 1984, p. 92.
356 O'Conner and Bush, 2006, p. 2, para. 5.
357 Robinson, 2007, para. 3, 5.
358 Fusco, et. al, 2007, para. 9.
359 Fitzgerald, 2008, p. 1.

360 Korecki, 2008, last para.
361 Durbin, 2008, p. 1.
362 Sun-Times Staff, 2008, para.s 1-3.
363 http://www.chicagobreakingnews.com/2008/12/ryan-to-give-public-apology.
html (retrieved May 19, 2009).
364 Clinton, 1998a, para. 11.
365 Clinton, 1998b, para.s 6, 8-10.
366 Clinton, 1998c, para. 13ff.
367 Thomasson, 1998, p. A16.
368 In his book, *My Life*, President Clinton revealed his thinking. "As a husband, I had done something wrong that I needed to apologize and atone for; as President, I was in a legal and political struggle with forces who had abused the criminal and civil laws and severely damaged innocent people in their attempt to destroy my presidency and cripple my ability to serve" (Clinton, 2004, p. 776). As you read through President Clinton's memoir, he makes it clear that while he was sorry for the sexual encounters he had with Monica Lewinsky, he rejected the idea that his testimony under oath (not the general misleading statements he made prior to his confession) rose to the level of perjury or obstruction of justice as charged in Congress's 1998 articles of impeachment against him. In other words, President Clinton argued that what he did was wrong, but he argued that he did not break the law (Clinton, H., 2003, p. 474). Therefore, he would fight that charge and attempts to impeach him from office. After he was out of office, President Clinton did call his actions "indefensible" and made many private and public unconditional apologies for his actions, particularly to his wife (Clinton, H. 2003, pp. 473, 469). In 2004, in a *60 Minutes'* interview, Clinton, offered this unprotected statement regarding the episode with Monica Lewinsky: "I think I did something for the worst possible reason – just because I could. I think that's just about the most morally indefensible reason that anybody could have for doing anything. There are lots of sophisticated explanations, more complicated psychological explanations, but none of them are an excuse" (Kurtz, 2004, para. 4).
369 Tavuchis, 1991, p. 22.
370 Tavuchis, 1991, p. 31.
371 Pettigrove, 2003, p. 10.
372 Tavuchis, 1991, p. 17.
373 Tavuchis, 1991, p. 3.
374 Alter, 1999, sec. IV., B., 4, para. 1.
375 Alter, 1999, sec. III, para. 9.
376 Tavuchis, 1991, p. 14.
377 Minow, 1998, p. 114.
378 Schimmel, 2002, p. 134. See also Tavuchis, 1991, p. 23.
379 Taft, 2000, pp. 1136-37.
380 Sack, 2008, para. 5.
381 Robbennolt, 2003, pp. 465-67.
382 Alter, 1999, p. sec. I, para. 2-3; see also Taft, 2000, p. 1151.
383 Sorry Works! Coalition, 2007, para. 1.
384 Gotbaum, 2007, para. 1.

Endnotes

385 Gotbaum, 2007, para. 1.
386 National Public Radio, 2007, audio beginning at the 2:56th minute/second.
387 National Public Radio, 2007, audio beginning at the 5:46th minute/second.
388 Helpline Reconciliation Agreement, cited in Alter, 1999, sec. II, para. 16
389 Alter, 1999, sec. I, para. 4.
390 Alter, 1999, sec. II, para. 16 (quoting the Helpline Reconciliation Agreement).
391 Alter, 1999, sec. I, para. 3-4
392 Peli, 1984, p. 93.
393 Tangney, et. al., 2005, 2002, 1998.
394 Tangney, Boone, and Dearing, 2005, p. 147.
395 See Tangney and Dearing, 2002, chapter 6.
396 Tavuchis, 1991, p. 41.
397 Lazare, 2004, pp. 160-62.
398 Minow, 1998, p. 115.
399 Lazare, 1995, p. 42.
400 Hicks, 2001, p. 147.
401 See chapter 3.
402 See Gen. 13:13; 39:6-9; Lev. 6:1-3; Ps. 51:4; Luke 15:17-18; Acts 5:1-4. See also Matt. 22:36-40, esp. v. 39a, on the close association between loving God and loving others.
403 שׁלוֹם , šālôm
404 שָׁלֵם, šālēm
405 Brown, Driver and Briggs, 1976, p. 1022.
406 μlev;, VanGemeren, 1997, vol. 4, p. 130.
407 Fensham, 1996, p. 244.
408 In a number of situations, the Mosaic law required the offender not only to give back the full value of what was lost but also to provide restitution that went over and above the initial loss. This, no doubt, served as a deterrent to would-be thieves and others who might be inclined to act against their neighbors. See Exod. 22:1, 4; Lev. 6:1-6 (cf. Num 5:5-7, where a different Hebrew word is used to convey the concept of restoration).
409 The Greek construction (a first-class conditional statement) indicates that Zacchaeus assumed that he had defrauded others. See Robertson, 1997, vol. 2, Luke 19:8. See also Wallace, 1996, pp. 690, 694.
410 ἀποδίδωμι, means "to restore to an original possessor, give back, return" (BDAG, 2000, p. 110).
411 Bock, 1996b, p. 480.
412 Deibler, 1985, p.769.
413 ἀποτίνω, means "to make compensation, *pay damages*" (BDAG, 2000, p. 124).
414 U.S. News and World Report, Feb. 16, 2003 (see under year 1989); Chicago Sun-Times, Jan. 10, 2003, p. 6.
415 It turned out that she was not pregnant.
416 Webb, 1985, p. 130.
417 Webb, 1985, p. 161.
418 Webb, 1985, p. 170.
419 Webb, 1985, p. 179.

347

420 Webb, 1985, p. 179.
421 It has been said, "The telling of the complete truth at all times is so fraught with danger, that it is possible only to the one who trusts completely in God" (Ellison, 1986, p. 1125). Such seems to be the case here.
422 Webb, 1985, p. 192.
423 Associated Press. Orlando Sentinel. April 5, 1985, p. A.1
424 Associated Press. Sun Sentinel. Apr 12, 1985, p. 1.A.
425 *San Diego Union*, April 12, 1985, p. A.2.
426 *San Diego Union*, April 12, 1985, p. A.2
427 UPI, *New York Times*, April 15, 1985, p. D.13.
428 *New York Times*, April 12, 1985, p. A.1.
429 Associated Press. Sun Sentinel. Apr 12, 1985, p. 1.A.
430 *San Diego Union*, April 12, 1985, p. A.2
431 This information along with other information about Dotson is contained on the Web site of the Center on Wrongful Convictions.
432 Tutu, 2004, p. 57.
433 Antar, 2005-2009a, para.s 1-4. Antar, 2005-2009b, para.s 1, 4, 6.
434 I was curious to learn how Mr. Antar could afford to make appearances all over the country at his own expense. I learned the answer from an interview he did that appeared in *Fortune* magazine. "He travels around the country entirely on his own nickel, he says, and can afford to not because of any pile of money he stashed from the Crazy Eddie era but because his wife, the daughter of a New York real estate developer, is wealthy" (Carbonara, 2007, para. 4).
435 German Embassy, Wash, D.C., 2005, para. 9.
436 German Embassy, Wash, D.C., 2005, para. 10.
437 In 2005, on the fortieth anniversary of the establishment of formal diplomatic relations between Israel and Germany, then German Chancellor Gerhard Schroder stated that the establishment of relations "paved the way for a development about which we Germans are very pleased and deeply grateful: the rapprochement and reconciliation between the people in Germany and Israel. ... There is hardly another country with which Israel maintains such close relations as with Germany—in science, business, and culture" (Schroder, 2005, para. 6).
438 Truth and Reconciliation Commission, 2003, vol. 6, section 2, chapter 7, p. 161.
439 Truth and Reconciliation Commission, 2003, vol. 6, section 2, chapter 7, p. 161.
440 Truth and Reconciliation Commission, 2003, vol. 6, section 2, chapter 7, p. 163.
441 Amnesty International, 2006, pp. 13-14; United States Department of State, 2008, section Government and Political Conditions: Challenges Ahead, para. 2.
442 Tutu, 1999a, p. 61; Amnesty International, 2006, pp. 13-14.
443 Yazzie and Zion, 1996, p. 168.
444 Yazzie and Zion, 1996, p. 169.
445 See Zehr, 1995, chapter 8; Truth and Reconciliation Commission, 1998, vol. 1, p. 126.
446 See Zehr, 2005, p. 186.
447 See Zehr, 2005, p. 186.
448 Truth and Reconciliation Commission, vol. 1, 1998, p. 126.
449 Volf, 1996, p. 195.

450 Volf, 1996, p. 196.
451 BDAG, 2000, pp. 816, 817, (πιστεύω,)
452 Brunner, 1934, p. 532.
453 Grounds, 1975, p. 587.
454 Colosi, 1999, p. 421.
455 Bourne, 1997, p. 405.
456 Chafer, 1948, vol. 3, pp. 234-66.
457 Geisler, 2004, vol. 3, pp. 222-30; Liefeld, 1988, p. 294; White, 1984, p. 968.
458 Kriesberg, 2007, pp. 229-36. See further in Stage 12. See page 27 as well.
459 Urquhart, 1993, p. 204.
460 Urquhart, 1993, p. 208.
461 Urquhart, 1993, p. 208.
462 PBS, 2001a, para. 1.
463 PBS, 2001a, para. 1
464 PBS, 2001b, para. 1.
465 PBS, 2001b, para. 2.
466 PBS, 2001b, para. 1.
467 Kreisler, 1996, para. 16.
468 Oren, 2007, para.s 34-35. See also Urquhart, 1993, p. 211.
469 Urquhart, 1993, p. 211.
470 Nobel Foundation, 1950, 2007, para. 9.
471 Bultmann, 1964, p. 509.
472 BDAG, 2000, pp. 155, 156. Greek: ἄφεσις, ἀφίημι: forgiveness, to forgive
473 BDAG, 2000, p. 155.
474 Shedd, 2003, pp. 698, 697 .
475 See Geisler, 2004, vol. 3, p. 227.
476 See Vorlander, 1975, p. 701.
477 The Greek work is ἀφίημι, the verb form of the word for forgiveness.
478 A different Greek word for forgiveness is used here, χαρίζομαι, a verb. It means, "to show oneself gracious by forgiving wrongdoing, *forgive, pardon* (BDAG, 2000, p. 1078).
479 Though the word for "forgiveness" is not used in this verse, the outcome of divine forgiveness is evident.
480 BDAG, 2000, p. 155. See also Louw and Nida, 1989, p. 502.
481 Louw and Nida, 1989, vol. 1. p. 502.
482 Quoted in Shedd, 2003, p. 708.
483 Morro and Harrison, 1982, p. 342.
484 Guerin, 1977, p. 564.
485 Auerbach, 2004, p. 153.
486 Newman, 1998, p. 25 (who cited the Babylonian Talmud, Berakot 7a).
487 Chafer, vol. 2, 1947, p. 256.
488 Volf, 2005, p. 143.
489 Hoare, 2001, The Execution Scene section, para. 4.
490 Hoare, 2001, Another Execution Scene section, para. 1.
491 See also Luke 22:19; Rom. 4:24-25; 1 Cor. 8:11; 2 Cor. 5:14-15, 21; Gal. 1:3b-4; 2:20; Eph. 5:2, 5; 1 Thess. 1:9-10; Heb. 2:9; 9:28; 1 Pet. 2:21, 24; 1 John 3:16.
492 Luther, 1949, chapter 3, verse 13. Crisp, a seventeenth-century theologian,

similarly stated, "Hast thou been an idolater, hast thou been a blasphemer, hast thou been a murderer, an adulterer, a thief, a liar, a drunkard? If thou hast part in the Lord, all these transgressions of thine become actually the transgressions of Christ" (quoted in Chafer, 1948, vol. 3, p. 70).

493 Here is a short list: Berkhof, 1958, p. 376; Chafer and Walvoord, 1974, p. 60; Thiessen, 1979, p. 235; Ryrie, 1999, p. 333; Geisler, 2004, vol. 3, p. 232.

494 Berkhof, 1958, p. 376.

495 The theological term for this "satisfaction" is *propitiated*. In 1 John 4:10 we read, "In this is love, not that we have loved God but that he loved us and sent his Son to be the propitiation [or, satisfaction] for our sins." (See also 1 John 2:2; Heb. 2:17; Rom. 3:21-25). The propitiation that is spoken of in these verses refers to the turning away of an offended party's anger. "Propitiation means placating or satisfying the wrath of God by the atoning sacrifice of Christ" (Ryrie, 1999, p. 339). The debt for sin has been paid in full by the death of Jesus, and God is satisfied. There is no need for any additional action against the sinner. (See further Morris, 1988, p. 1784, and Shedd, 2003, p. 698).

496 Quoted in Morris, 1965b, p. 409.

497 http://www.innocenceproject.org

498 Moyers, 2008, beginning at 9.5 minutes.

499 Memmott, 2006, Section: A Hard Look at the System, para. 4.

500 The divinity of Jesus is discussed in Stage 2.

501 Morris, 1965b, p. 410.

502 Volf, 2005, p. 145.

503 Geisler, 2004, vol. 3, p. 245. See also Thiessen, 1979, p. 236.

504 Logos Hymnal, 1995, "And Can It Be?" stanza 1.

505 Hopkins, quoted in Shedd, 2003, p. 698.

506 Carson, 2000a, p. 71.

507 Carson, 2000a, p. 70.

508 See Geisler, 2004, vol. 3, p. 246.

509 Strong, 1907, p. 266.

510 Quoted in Stott, 1986, p. 158.

511 See also Acts 2:22-23, 36-38; 3:13-15, 19-20; Isa. 55:7.

512 Monsma, 1976, p. 599.

513 See Houston, 1988, p. 811.

514 Morro and Harrison, 1982, p. 342.

515 Bultmann, 1964, p. 512.

516 Bonhoeffer, 2001, p. 44.

517 Shachnow, quoted in Wiesenthal, 1997, p. 243.

518 Paul did the very thing he wrote about. Later he states, "Alexander the coppersmith did me great harm; the Lord will repay him according to his deeds" (2 Tim. 4:14).

519 Paul quoted from Prov. 25:21-22. When it was first penned, the phrase, "burning coals on his head" was often understood to mean, "'burning pangs of shame' a person will feel when good is returned for evil, his shame producing remorse and contrition" (Waltke, 2005, p. 331). An Old Testament scholar explained, "The expression may reflect an Egyptian expiation ritual, in which a guilty person, as a sign of his repentance, carried a basin of glowing coals on his head. The meaning here, then, would be that in returning good for

evil–and so being kind to your enemy (see Ro. 12:20)–you may cause him to repent or change" (Barker, 2008, Prov. 25:22).

520 Brauns, 2008, p. 66.

521 Such admonitions to love echo what is found in the Old Testament. Exodus 23:4-5 reads, "If you meet your enemy's ox or his donkey going astray, you shall bring it back to him. If you see the donkey of one who hates you lying down under its burden, you shall refrain from leaving him with it; you shall rescue it with him." Leviticus 19:18 reads, "You shall not take vengeance or bear a grudge against the sons of your own people, but you shall love your neighbor as yourself: I am the Lord."

522 Constable, 2008, Matthew, pp. 92-93.

523 Hertz, 2007, para. 5.

524 CBS Interactive, 2008, p. 1.

525 Augsburger, 1992, p. 286. See also Tavuchis, 1991, p. 46.

526 Vorlander, 1975, p. 703.

527 Smedes, 1984, p. 95. This book is still in print and by its 2007 printing had sold over 400,000 copies.

528 Brauns, 2008, p. 64.

529 Frayling, 1999, para. 7.

530 Bultmann, 1964, p. 511.

531 Mantakana, 2008, para. 1-3, 5.

532 This passage is more detailed and explicit than a similar passage found in Matt. 18:21-22 in terms of what is involved in the process of forgiveness.

533 Stott, 1964, p. 35.

534 Barker, 2008, 2 Cor. 2:5-11.

535 Kairos Document, 1985, sec. 3.1 Reconciliation, para. 2, 4.

536 Kairos Document, 1985, sec. 3.1 Reconciliation, para. 3.

537 Morro and Harrison, 1982, p. 341.

538 The quote includes minor editorial changes.

539 Willis, S., 2006, para. 8-9.

540 Willis, J. 2006, para. 6-7.

541 Reproduced in Stage 7.

542 Kass, 2008, last para.

543 Buswell, 1962, vol. 2, p. 76.

544 Arendt, 1958, p. 237.

545 Arendt, 1958, p. 241.

546 Augsburger, 1992, p. 283.

547 Tavuchis, 1991, p. 8.

548 Wilmot and Hocker, 2007, 319.

549 Menkin, 1994, para. 17.

550 Menkin, 1994, para. 27.

551 Menkin, 1994, para. 28.

552 Menkin, 1994, para. 38.

553 Hicks, 2001, p. 147.

554 Quoted in Andrews, 1990, p. 114.

555 This sentiment reflects both Jewish and Christian perspectives. Newman asserted that the dominant rabbinic position is that it is a Jew's duty to forgive

when the offender repents of his or her wrongdoing. He concludes, "The Judaic view of forgiveness as a moral imperative has been shaped decisively by the beliefs in a compassionate God whom we have a duty to emulate" (1987, p. 155). In Matt. 18:23-35 Jesus provided an extended illustration for his followers, teaching them to forgive others in the same way they have been forgiven by God.

556 Minow 1998, p. 14; Thomas, 1999, para. 13.
557 Cloke, 2001, p. 94.
558 Guthrie, 1981, p. 486.
559 White, 1984, p. 917. See also Guthrie, 1981, p. 486.
560 Classical Greek was in vogue approx. 700 to 300 BC (Palmer, 2002, para. 1-2).
561 BDAG, 2000, p. 521. (καταλλάσσω). To reconcile, as noted above, is to "exchange... hostility for a friendly relationship," from the verb "to reconcile" (καταλλάσσω).
562 Matera, 1996, p. 856.
563 BDAG, 2000, p. 521, from the noun "reconciliation" (καταλλαγή).
564 Geisler, 2004, vol. 3, p. 226.
565 Louw and Nida, 1989, vol. 1, p. 301.
566 Chafer, 1948, vol. 3, pp. 234-66; Geisler, 2004, vol. 3, pp. 222-30; Liefeld, 1988, p. 294; White, 1984, p. 968.
567 Grudem, 1994, p. 490.
568 Staub and Perlman, 2001, pp. 206-7.
569 Staub and Perlman, 2001, p. 207.
570 Bar-Tal and Bennick, 2004, p. 12. See also Hermann, 2004, p. 40.
571 Stedman, 2002, p. 2. Bar-Siman-Tov noted that "reaching a political formula for resolving the conflict of interest is necessary but insufficient for surmounting the political and psychological barriers that may foil the normalization and stabilization of peace relations" (2004, p. 61).
572 Haus, 2003, para. 9-10.
573 Bar-Tal and Bennick, 2004, p. 12.
574 Lomax, 1995, p. 200.
575 Lomax, 1995, p. 213.
576 Lomax, 1995, p. 233.
577 Lomax, 1995, p. 249.
578 Lomax, 1995, p. 263.
579 Lomax, 1995, p. 263.
580 Lomax, 1995, p. 269.
581 Lomax, 1995, p. 276.
582 Lord, 1991, p. 903.
583 Barker, 2008, Philippians 2:12.
584 Dennis and Grudem, 2008, p. 2284.
585 Lewicki and Tomlinson, 2003, Section "Rebuilding Trust," para. 2.
586 Gadamer, 1993, p. 291.
587 Adapted from Murray, 1998, para. 8.
588 Gadamer, 1993, p. 291.
589 Geertz quoted in Bernstein, 1983, p. 133.

590 Doyle and Straus, 1976, p. 238.

591 Fisher and Ury, 1991, p. 82.

592 For additional ways to think creatively, see Stage 6.

593 See Kaner, 2007, pp. 278ff.

594 Value Based Management.net, 2009

595 Lindstrom, 2006, p. 6

596 Some mediators suggest that any significant impasses the parties experienced during mediation should be included in the memorandum. The statement might simply read, "These are areas where we have agreed to disagree." Such an explicit acknowledgment can serve as a clear reminder what areas need further discussion and resolution.

597 MacArthur, 1945, begin at 2 minutes and 42 seconds.

598 PBS, 2004-2006, para. 70.

599 PBS, 2004-2006, para. 71.

600 Quoted in Petersen, 1986, pp. 146-47. The original article appeared in *McCall's* magazine, January, 1963.

601 Truth and Reconciliation Commission, 1998, vol. 5, p. 170.

602 Truth and Reconciliation Commission, 1998, vol. 1, p. 48.

603 Truth and Reconciliation Commission, 1998, vol. 1, pp. 19-20, 104, 112, 357.

604 On the topic of amnesty, the TRC report states, "We have been concerned, too, that many consider only one aspect of justice. Certainly, amnesty cannot be viewed as justice if we think of justice only as retributive and punitive in nature. We believe, however, that there is another kind of justice—a restorative justice which is concerned not so much with punishment as with correcting imbalances, restoring broken relationships—with healing, harmony and recon- ciliation. Such justice focuses on the experience of victims; hence the impor- tance of reparation (1998, vol. 1, p. 9).

605 Truth and Reconciliation Commission, 1998, vol. 1, p. 118.

606 Truth and Reconciliation Commission, 1998, vol. 1, p. 120.

607 Truth and Reconciliation Commission, 1998, vol. 1, p. 9.

608 Minow, 1998, p. 60.

609 Truth and Reconciliation Commission, 1998, vol. 5, p. 351.

610 Truth and Reconciliation Commission, 1998, vol. 5, p. 352. The report goes on to acknowledge that not all storytelling heals or brings peace. But it certainly did for many.

611 Truth and Reconciliation Commission, 1998, vol. 5, p. 352.

612 Truth and Reconciliation Commission, 1998, vol. 5, p. 352.

613 Minow, 1998, p. 68. See also Tutu, 1999, p. 148.

614 Truth and Reconciliation Commission, 2002, vol. 7, p. 1.

615 Truth and Reconciliation Commission, 2002, vol. 7, p. 10.

616 Truth and Reconciliation Commission, 1996, section: Question and Answers: Col. Schobesberger, para. 13, 15, 16.

617 Tutu, 1999a, pp. 150-51.

618 Ignatieff, 1997, p. 93

619 Truth and Reconciliation Commission, 1998, vol. 1, p. 125.

620 Truth and Reconciliation Commission, 1998, vol. 1, p. 125.

621 Truth and Reconciliation Commission, 1998, vol. 5, p. 170.

622 Amnesty International, 2006, pp. 13-14; United States Department of State, 2008, section Government and Political Conditions: Challenges Ahead, para. 2.

623 Tutu, 1999a, p. 261.

624 Schimmel, 2002, p. 226.

625 Hunter-Gault, 2003, p. 15. See also Schimmel, 2002, p. 226.

626 Tutu, 1999b, p. 18.

627 Schimmel, 2002, p. 222; Chapman, 2001, p. 250; Tutu, 1999a, p. 82.

628 Tutu, 1999a, p. 144. See also the Truth and Reconciliation Commission, 1998, vol. 1, p. 116.

629 Tutu, 1999a, p. 55.

630 Tutu, 1999a, p. 260.

631 Tutu, 1999a, p. 271.

632 Carpenter and Grisanti, 1997, Vol. 3. p. 707.

633 See, for example, Exod. 34:7; Lev. 16:21; Job 13:23; Ps. 32:5; Isa. 59:12; Ezek. 21:24; Dan. 9:24.

634 Exod. 22:9 NASB, niv, nkjv.

635 For example, Joseph was asked by his brothers to forgive them for the transgression (and evil) they perpetrated against him (which he did). See Gen. 50:15-17, 20.

636 Other considerations may come into play. For example, "love covers all offenses" (Prov. 10:12), "love covers a multitude of sins" (1 Pet. 4:8), and love "keeps no record of wrongs" (1 Cor. 13:5 niv) may be applicable.

637 Wikipedia, 2008, para. 3.

638 Robbennolt, 2003, pp. 465-67.

639 United States Department of Justice, 2004, section "The Response to Crime," para. 5. The concept parallels the biblical concept discussed earlier, that all sin, including that committed on a social level against others, is ultimately sin against God.

640 Zehr, 2005, p. 181.

641 Janusz, 1992, p. 102.

642 Molhan, 1992, p. 109.

643 Minow, 1998, p. 63.

644 Jacoby, 1983, pp. 302-5.

645 It is beyond the scope of this book to discuss how the court system can be changed for the better. The concept of restorative justice, which views crime as being against a victim instead of against the state, has many advocates who have put forth proposals for constructive change.

646 The Greek word used in this context (ἐλέγχω) means "to express strong disapproval of someone's action, reprove, correct" (BDAG, 2000, p. 315).

647 Wallace, 1996, p. 689. Note: All the "if" statements in this passage are third-class conditional statements.

648 Coenen and Trites, 1978, vol. 3, p. 1043.

649 BDAG, 2000, p. 619.

650 Strathmann, 1967, p. 489.

651 Strathmann, 1967, p. 489.

652 I have italicized these words to indicate the portion of this verse that is quoted by Jesus in Matt. 18:16.

653 Elwell, 1988, vol. 2, "Witness," pp. 2154-55.
654 CD 9:17-23; 11QTemple 61:6-7; 64:8 (others cite it as 11QTemple 19-20, 61:6-7; 64:8)
655 *Works of Josephus*, 1987, *Life*, 256, *Antiquities* 4:219.
656 Mishnah: *Sanhedrin* 3:3.
657 Mishnah: *Sanhedrin* 3:4.
658 Mishnah: *Sanhedrin* 3:5.
659 Mishnah: *Sanhedrin* 5:1.
660 Mishnah: *Sanhedrin* 5:3.
661 Young, 1995, p. xxxiv.
662 Ross, n.d., sec. IV, para. 4.
663 Laney, 1985, p. 53. Laney is commenting on the Matthew 18 passage.
664 Keener, 1993, p. 94.
665 Keener, 1999, p. 454. See also, Laney, 1985, p. 53.
666 Turner, 2008, p. 446.
667 Because this position is common, I am choosing not to single out this denomination by name.
668 In Acts 15:39 the biblical record states that Paul and Barnabas "separated." In essence, it is like they "divorced." (See Matt. 19:6; 1 Cor. 7:10, 11, 15, where Jesus and Paul use this same Greek word found in Acts 15:39, except without the prepositional prefix, to refer to divorce between a husband and wife.) The exact Greek word found in Acts 15:39 (with the prepositional prefix) occurs only one other place in the New Testament, in Rev. 6:14. There it refers to the sky splitting apart. We can therefore justifiably conclude that the break in Paul and Barnabas's relationship was dramatic and sharp. And yet there is no hint that either of these godly men was in sin (see Acts 15:41).
669 Plummer, 1910, p. 253.
670 Wallace, 1996, p. 696.
671 Peacemaker Ministries, 2005, sec. Mediation, para. 2. Sande and Kober, 2005, p. 18.
672 Sande and Kober, 2005, pp. 18-19; Peacemaker Ministries, 2005, sec. Mediation, para. 6 and following.
673 Sande, 2004, pp. 187-88.
674 This word for "testimony" here is etymologically related to the word for "witness." It also has the word *pseudo*, meaning "false," in front of it: pseudo-marturia (ψευδομαρτυρία).
675 This word is exactly the same word as that for "witness" (see next footnote below), except that it has the word *pseudo*, for false, in front of it: pseudomartus (ψευδόμαρτυς).
676 In the Greek, martus, (μάρτυς).
677 Nestle, E., and McReynolds, 1997, c1982, Matt. 18:15. (ἐλέγχω).
678 MacDonald, 1999, sec. Above Reproach
679 Guthrie, 1990, p. 118.
680 BDAG, 2000, p. 619.
681 Coenen and Trites, 1978, p. 1043; BDAG, 2000, p. 619; Strathmann, 1967, p. 489.
682 Ross and McLaughlin, 1949, p. 366.

683 Chapin, 1915a, pp. 182-84.
684 Chapin, 1915b, pp. 1-2.
685 Chapin, 1915b, p. 3.
686 Bakwin, 1949, p. 516.
687 Quoted in Bakwin, 1941, p. 469
688 Skeels, 1939, p. 119.
689 Skeels, 1939, p. 124.
690 Skeels, 1939, p. 124.
691 Skeels, 1966, p. 21.
692 Skeels, 1966.
693 Karen, 1998, pp. 21-22.
694 Garbarino, 1999, p. 57.
695 Garbarino, 1999, p. 52.
696 Garbarino, 1999, pp. 138-39.
697 Garbarino, 1999, p. 167.
698 Garbarino, 1999, p. 83.
699 Houghton Mifflin Company, 2009, para. 3.
700 Houghton Mifflin Company, 2009, para. 1.
701 Wallerstein and Lewis, 2004.
702 Wallerstein and Lewis, 2004, p. 359.
703 Wallerstein and Lewis, 2004, p. 363.
704 Wallerstein and Lewis, 2004, p. 366.
705 Ornish, 1998, p. 30.
706 Ornish, 2005, p. 56. Dr. Ornish is not alone in his observations. See Hawkley and Cacioppo, 2007, pp. 187-91, Hawkley and Cacioppo, 2003, p. S98; Dr. James Lynch, 2000, p. 1; Baumeister and Leary, 1995, p. 497.
707 Martin, 2007, p. 197.
708 Martin, 2007, p. 197.
709 Dennis and Grudem, 2008, pp. 2073-74.
710 Craddock, 1990, p. 273, commenting on Luke 23:34.
711 See Bock, 1996a, p. 1849; Barton, 1997, p. 538; Plummer, 1903, pp. 531-32; Godet, 1889, vol. 2, p. 333. See also 1 Corinthians 2:8.
712 Barton, 1997, on Luke 23:34, p. 538.
713 See, for example, Luke 5:20-25.
714 Bock, 1996a, on Luke 23:34, p. 1850.
715 Dennis and Grudem, 2008, pp. 1831, 1832.
716 Carson, 1984, p. 169.
717 Keener, 1999, p. 216.
718 France, 2007, p. 250.
719 BDAG, 2000, p. 743, ὀφείλημα.
720 BDAG, 2000, p. 1104. See also Wallace, 1996, p. 675.
721 Keener, 1999, p. 216.
722 See Stage 10 for fuller comments on Luke 17.

Works Cited

I list here only the resources that were referenced in the writing of this book. This bibliography does not contain the complete record of all sources consulted.

Allen, W. (1989). *Crimes and Misdemeanors* [Motion picture]. USA: MGM.

Alter, S. (1999, May). *Apologising for Serious Wrongdoing: Social, Psychological and Legal Considerations* [Final Report for the Law Commission of Canada]. Retrieved May 20, 2009, from http://epe.lac-bac.gc.ca/100/200/301/lcc-cdc/apologising_serious_wrong-e/apology.html

Amandus, J. (1997). A Wounded Pastor's Rescue. In M. Shelley (Ed.), *Leading Your Church Through Conflict and Reconciliation*. Grand Rapids, MI: Bethany House Publishers.

America's Most Wanted. (2009, February 14). *Haleigh Ann Marie Cummings*. Retrieved March 29, 2009, from FOX Television: http://www.amw.com/missing_children/case.cfm?id=63252

American Academy of Child and Adolescent Psychiatry. (2008, June). *Facilitated Communication* [Policy Statement]. Retrieved June 18, 2009, from http://www.aacap.org/cs/root/policy_statements/facilitated_communication

American Arbitration Association, American Bar Association, and Association for Conflict Resolution. (2005, August). *Model Standards of Conduct for Mediators*. Retrieved February 14, 2009, from http://www.abanet.org/dispute/news/ModelStandardsofConductforMediatorsfinal05.pdf

American Humanist Association. (1973). *Humanist Manifesto II*. Retrieved January 27, 2009, from http://www.americanhumanist.org/about/manifesto2.php

American Psychological Association. (1994, August). *PA Policy Manual* [Facilitated Communication]. Retrieved June 18, 2009, from http://www.apa.org/about/division/cpmscientific.html#6

American Psychological Association. (2003, November 20). *Facilitated Communication: Sifting the Psychological Wheat*. Retrieved June 18, 2009, from http://www.psychologymatters.org/facilitated.html

Amnesty International. (2006, November). *South Africa: Briefing for the Committee Against Torture*. Retrieved March 7, 2009, from http://www2.ohchr.org/english/bodies/cat/docs/ngos/AI-SouthAfrica.pdf

Andrews, R. (Ed.). (1990). *The Concise Columbia Dictionary of Quotations*. Irvington, NY: Columbia University Press.

Annan, K. (1998, October 6). *Statement by the United Nations Secretary-General Before the Special Commemorative Meeting of the General Assembly Honouring 50 Years of Peacekeeping*. Retrieved February 10, 2009, from United Nations: http://www.un.org/Depts/dpko/dpko/50web/8.htm

Antar, S. E. (2005-2009a). *Protect Yourself against White Collar Crime*. Retrieved March 21, 2009, from http://www.whitecollarfraud.com/index.html

Antar, S. E. (2005-2009b). *Available for Fraud Lectures at No Cost*. Retrieved March 21, 2009, from http://www.whitecollarfraud.com/1786425.html

Arendt, H. (1958). *The Human Condition*. Chicago, IL: The University of Chicago Press.

Arendt, H. (1991, 1992). *Eichmann in Jerusalem*. New York, NY: Penguin Books USA, Inc. (Original work published 1963, 1964)

Associated Press. (1985, April 5). Truth Sets False-Rape Victim Free. *Orlando Sentinel*, p. A1.

Associated Press. (1985, April 12). "He's Innocent!... I Told the Truth" Despite Plea by Woman Who Recants Rape Tale, Judge Keeps Man Jailed [Fort Lauderdale]. *Sun Sentinel*, p. 1.A..

Associated Press. (2009, March 11). *HBO, Mormons Square Off Over Airing of Sacred Rite*. Retrieved March 11, 2009, from Yahoo! News: http://news.yahoo.com/s/ap/20090311/ap_on_en_tv/tv_mormon_church_hbo

Association for Conflict Resolution. (2005, Fall). Spirituality and the Heart of Conflict Resolution. *ACResolution, 5*(1).

Auerbach, Y. (2004). Y. Bar-Siman-Tov (Ed.), *From Conflict Resolution to Reconciliation*. New York City, NY: Oxford University Press.

Augsburger, D. W. (1992). *Conflict Mediation Across Cultures*. Louisville, KY: Westminster / John Knox Press.

Augustine. (AD 388, orig. date). P. Schaff (Ed.), *Nicene and Post-Nicene Fathers: Vol. 4. The Anti-Manichaean Writings, The Anti-Donatist Writings* [On the Morals of the Manichaeans]. Retrieved January 28, 2009, from http://www.ccel.org/ccel/schaff/npnf104.iv.v.vii.html

Augustine. (AD 405, orig. date). P. Schaff (Ed.), *The Writings Against the Manichaeans and Against the Donatists* [Concerning the Nature of Good, Chapter 34]. Retrieved January 28, 2009, from http://www.ccel.org/ccel/schaff/npnf104.iv.x.xxxvi.html

Augustine. (AD 426, orig. date). P. Schaff (Ed.), *The City of God*. Retrieved January 28, 2009, from Internet Sacred Text Archive: http://www.sacred-texts.com/chr/ecf/102/index.htm

Bakwin, H. (1941). Loneliness in Infants. *American Journal of Diseases of Children, 62*, 468-69.

Bakwin, H. (1949, July-December). Emotional Deprivation in Infants. *The Journal of Pediatrics, 35*, 512-21.

Baldoni, N. (1999, May / June). Kosovo: The Status of Human Brutality - Ethnic Slaughter and Human Rights Abuse. *The Humanist, 59*(3), 4-5.

Bandura, A., Underwood, B., and Fromson, M. E. (1975, December). Disinhibition of Aggression through Diffusion of Responsibility and Dehumanization of Victims. *Journal of Research in Personality, 9*, 253-2569.

Bar-Siman-Tov, Y. (2004). Y. Bar-Siman-Tov (Ed.), *From Conflict Resolution to Reconciliation*. New York City, NY: Oxford University Press.

Bar-Tal, D., and Bennink, G. H. (2004). Y. Bar-Siman-Tov (Ed.), *From Conflict Resolution to Reconciliation*. New York City, NY: Oxford University Press.

Barker, K. (Ed.). (2008). *The NIV Study Bible*. Grand Rapids, MI: Zondervan Publishing House.

Barton, B. B. (1997). *Life Application Bible Commentary: Luke.* Carol Stream, IL: Tyndale House Publishers, Inc.

Baumeister, R. F., and Leary, M. R. (1995). The Need to Belong: Desire for Interpersonal Attachments as a Fundamental Human Motivation. *Psychological Bulletin, 117*(3), 497-529.

BDAG. Arndt, W., Gingrich, F. W., Danker, F. W., Bauer, W. (2000). *A Greek-English Lexicon of the New Testament and other Early Christian Literature* (3rd ed.) [BDAG] Chicago, IL: University of Chicago Press.

Beaumont, L. R. (2005-2009). *Violence: Harm to Another.* Retrieved February 19, 2009, from http://www.emotionalcompetency.com/violence.htm

Beck, H., and Brown, C. (1976). Peace. In C. Brown (Ed.), *The New International Dictionary of New Testament Theology* (Vol. 2). Grand Rapids, MI: Zondervan Publishing House.

Becker, O. (1975). Covenant. In C. Brown (Ed.), *The New International Dictionary of New Testament Theology* (Vol. 1). Grand Rapids, MI: Zondervan Publishing House.

Benjamin, R. (2003). Managing the Natural Energy of Conflict. In D. Bowling and D. A. Hoffman (Eds.), *Bringing Peace into the Room* (pp. 79-134). San Francisco, CA: Jossey-Bass.

Benjamin, R. (2009, February). *The Joy of Impasse: The Neuroscience of "Insight" and Creative Problem Solving.* Retrieved March 9, 2009, from Mediate.com: http://www.mediate.com/articles/benjamin44.cfm

Berkhof, L. (1958). *Systematic Theology.* Carlisle, PA: The Banner of Truth Trust. (Original work published 1948)

Bernstein, R. J. (1983). *Beyond Objectivism: Relativism, Hermeneutics, and Praxis.* Philadelphia, PA: University of Pennsylvania Press.

Bock, D. L. (1996a). *Luke 9:51-24:53* [Baker Exegetical Commentary on the New Testament]. Grand Rapids, MI: Baker Books.

Bock, D. L. (1996b). *Luke: The NIV Application Bible Commentary.* Grand Rapids, MI: Zondervan Publishing House.

Bonhoeffer, D. (2001). *Discipleship* (Vol. 4) [The Cost of Discipleship]. Minneapolis, MN: Augsburg Fortress. (Original work published 1949)

Booth, C. W. (2004). *The Diotrephes Syndrome.* Retrieved May 15, 2009, from http://www.thefaithfulword.org/diotrephes.html

Botcharova, O. (2001). Implementation of Track Two Diplomacy. In S. J. Helmick and R. L. Peterson (Eds.), *Forgiveness and Reconciliation* (pp. 269-94). Philadelphia, PA: Templeton Foundation Press.

Boulding, E. (1988). *Building a Global Civic Culture.* Syracuse, NY: Syracuse University Press. (Original work published 1990)

Bourne, P. G. (1997). *Jimmy Carter.* New York City, NY: A Lisa Drew Book/Scribner.

Boutros-Ghali, B. (1996, April 11). *Secretary-General Inaugurates Ralph Bunche Center at Howard University* [Press Release]. Retrieved June 18, 2009, from http://www.un.org/News/Press/docs/1996/19960411.sgsm5953.html

Bowling, D., and Hoffman, D. A. (Eds.). (2003). *Bringing Peace Into the Room: How the Personal Qualities of the Mediator Impact the Process of Conflict Resolution.* San Francisco, CA: Jossey-Bass.

Brahm, E., and Burgess, H. (2003, November). *Shuttle Diplomacy.* Retrieved May 25,

Works Cited

2009, from Beyond Intractability Knowledge Base: http://www.beyondintractability.org/m/shuttle_diplomacy.jsp

Brauns, C. (2008). *Unpacking Forgiveness*. Wheaton, IL: Crossway Books.

Brenner, R. R. (1995). *The Faith and Doubt of Holocaust Survivors*. Northvale, NJ: Jason Aronson Inc. (Original work published 1980)

Brown, F., Driver, S. R., and Briggs, C. A. (1976). *Hebrew and English Lexicon of the Old Testament*. Oxford: Clarendon Press. (Original work published 1907)

Bruce, A. B. (n.d.). W. R. Nicoll (Ed.), *The Expositor's Greek Testament: Vol. 1. The Synoptic Gospels*. Grand Rapids: MI: Wm. B. Eerdmans Publishing Company.

Bruce, F. F. (1988). *Commentary on the Book of the Acts* (Rev. ed.) Grand Rapids, MI: Wm. B. Eerdmans Publishing Company.

Brueggemann, W. (2001). *Peace*. St. Louis, MO: Chalice Press.

Brueggemann, W. (2005). *Theology Of The Old Testament: Testimony, Dispute, Advocacy*. Minneapolis, MN: Fortress Press.

Brunner, E. (1934). *The Mediator: A Study of the Central Doctrine of the Christian Faith*. Philadelphia, PA: The Westminster Press.

Budiansky, S. (1995, January 30). How Lawyers Abuse the Law. *U.S. News and World Report, 116*(5), 50-56.

Bultmann, R. (1964). G. Kittel (Ed.), *Theological Dictionary of the New Testament: Vol. 1. aphiemi (Greek, for forgiveness)* (G. W. Bromiley, Trans.). Grand Rapids, MI: Wm. B. Eerdmans Publishing Company.

Burtchaell, J. T. (1989). *The Giving and Taking of Life*. Notre Dame, IN: University of Notre Dame Press.

Bush, R. A. (1999, June). *New Jersey Statewide Conference on ADR*. Retrieved March 13, 2009, from http://www.transformativemediation.org/Speeches/Speeches%20-%20Two%20Pictures%20of%20the%20Future.doc

Bush, R. A., and Folger, J. P. (1994). *The Promise of Mediation*. San Francisco, CA: Jossey-Bass Inc. Publishers.

Bush, R. A., and Folger, J. P. (2005). *The Promise of Mediation* (Rev. ed.) San Francisco, CA: Jossey-Bass.

Buswell, J. O. (1962). *A Systematic Theology of the Christian Religion*. Grand Rapids, MI: Zondervan Publishing House.

Butler, J. (1838). *The Whole Works of Joseph Butler* [Fifteen Sermons]. London, England: Thomas Tegg and Son. (Original work published 1726)

Calvin, J. (1845). *Institutes of the Christian Religion* (H. Beveridge, Trans.). Edinburgh, Scotland: Calvin Translation Society. (Original work published 1559)

Cambodian Genocide Program, Yale University. (2009). *The CGP, 1994-2008: Introduction*. Retrieved February 21, 2009, from http://www.yale.edu/cgp/index.html

Camelot (1967, 1990). Warner Home Video.

Carbonara, P. (2007, December 25). *Takes One to Know One* [Article from Fortune Magazine]. Retrieved June 1, 2009, from CNNMoney.com: http://money.cnn.com/2007/12/21/news/newsmakers/antar.fortune/index.htm?postversion=2007122509

Carpenter, C., Episcopal Bishop, Durick, J., Roman Catholic Auxiliary Bishop, Milton, R., Rabbi, Hardin, P., Methodist Bishop, Harmon, N., Methodist Bishop, Murray, G., Episcopal Bishop, et al. (1963, April 12). *Statement by Alabama*

Clergymen. Retrieved February 21, 2009, from http://www.stanford.edu/group/King//frequentdocs/clergy.pdf

Carpenter, E., and Grisanti, M. A. (1997). W. A. VanGemeren (Ed.), *New International Dictionary of Old Testament Theology and Exegesis.* Grand Rapids, MI: Zondervan Publishing House.

Carson, C. (Ed.). (2000). *The Papers of Martin Luther King, Jr.: Vol. 4. Symbol of the Movement (January 1957-December 1958)* ["Loving Your Enemies" Sermon Delivered at Dexter Avenue Baptist Church, Nov. 17, 1957]. Berkeley and Los Angeles, CA: University of California Press.

Carson, D. A. (1984). F. E. Gaebelein (Ed.), *The Expositor's Bible Commentary: Vol. 8. Matthew.* Grand Rapids: MI: The Zondervan Corporation.

Carson, D. A. (2000a). *The Difficult Doctrine of the Love of God.* Wheaton, IL: Crossway Books.

Carson, D. A. (2000b). Systematic Theology and Biblical Theology. In T. D. Alexander and B. S. Rosner (Eds.), *New Dictionary of Biblical Theology* (pp. 89-104). Leicester, England: InterVarsity Press.

CBS Interactive, Inc., and Ander. (2008, August 17). *War Against Women: The Use Of Rape As A Weapon In Congo's Civil War* [*60 Minutes* Television Program]. Retrieved January 31, 2009, from http://www.cbsnews.com/stories/2008/01/11/60minutes/main3701249.shtml

Center for Reformed Theology and Apologetics (Ed.). (1996-2006). *Council of Chalcedon (451 A.D).* Retrieved May 15, 2009, from http://www.reformed.org/documents/index.html?mainframe=chalcedon.html

Center on Wrongful Convictions. (2006). *The Rape that Wasn't - the first DNA exoneration in Illinois.* Retrieved June 9, 2009, from http://www.law.northwestern.edu/wrongfulconvictions/exonerations/ilDotsonSummary.html

Chafer, L. S. (1947-1948). *Systematic Theology.* Dallas, TX: Dallas Seminary Press.

Chafer, L. S. (1974). J. F. Walvoord (Ed.), *Major Bible Themes: 52 Vital Doctrines of the Scripture Simplified and Explained.* Grand Rapids, MI: Zondervan Publishing House.

Chapin, H. D. (1915a). A Plea for Accurate Statistics in Infants. *Transactions of the American Pediatric* Society, 14, 180-85.

Chapin, H. D. (1915b). Are Institutions for Infants Necessary? *The Journal of the American Medical Association,* 64(1), 1-3.

Chapman, A. R. (2001). Truth Commissions as Instruments of Forgiveness and Reconciliation. In S. J. Helmick and R. L. Petersen (Eds.), *Forgiveness and Reconciliation* (pp. 247-267). Philadelphia, PA: Templeton Foundation Press.

Chicago Sun-Times. (2003, January 10). Ryan pardons Gary Dotson, p. 6.

Christianity Today International. (2004). *Managing Church Conflict: The Source, Pastors Reactions, and Effects.* Carol Stream, IL: Christianity Today Intl.

Cialdini, R. B. (2009). *Influence: Science and Practice* (5th ed.) Boston, MA: Pearson Education.

Clinton, H. R. (2003). *Living History.* New York City, NY: Simon and Schuster.

Clinton, W. (1998a, January 26). *Transcript: Clinton Denial.* Retrieved October 11, 2008, from New York Times Online: http://www.nytimes.com/specials/starr/7grounds_11.html

Clinton, W. (1998b, August 17). *Transcript: Addressing the Nation.* Retrieved October

Works Cited

11, 2008, from Online *NewsHour*: http://www.pbs.org/newshour/lewinsky_ address/address.html

Clinton, W. (1998c, September 11). *Transcript: Clinton Speaks to Prayer Breakfast.* Retrieved October 11, 2008, from CNN Online: http://www.cnn.com/ALLPO-LITICS/stories/1998/09/11/transcripts/clinton.prayer.html

Clinton, W. J. (2004). *My Life.* New York: Alfred A. Knopf.

Cloke, K. (2001). *Mediating Dangerously.* San Francisco, CA: Jossey-Bass Publishers.

Coenen, L., and Trites, A. A. (1986). Witness. In *New International Dictionary of New Testament Theology* (Vol. 3). Grand Rapids, MI: Zondervan Publishing House.

Cohen, A. (1995). *Everyman's Talmud.* New York, NY: Schocken Books Inc. (Original work published 1949)

Cohen, H. (2003). *Negotiate This!* New York, NY: Warner Books, Inc.

Cohen, M. (2002, March 28). A Lot to Forgive. *Far Eastern Economic Review,* 16-18.

Colloff, P. (1998, August). Contrition. *Texas Monthly,* 26(8).

Colosi, T. (1999). R. J. Lewicki, D. M. Saunders, and J. Minto (Eds.), *Negotiation: Readings, Exercises, and Cases* (3rd ed., pp. 421-28) Boston, MA: Irwin McGraw-Hill.

Columbia Encyclopedia. (2001-2007, 6th ed.). *Ethnocentrism.* Retrieved February 17, 2009, from Columbia University Press (New York): http://www.bartleby.com/65/et/ethnocen.html

Constable, T. L. (1999-2009). *Expository Bible Study Notes* (chap.) Retrieved February 24, 2009, from http://www.soniclight.com/constable/notes

Cose, E. (2008, April 21). *The Lessons of Rwanda.* Retrieved March 2, 2009, from Newsweek: http://www.newsweek.com/id/131754

Costantino, C. A., and Merchant, C. S. (1996). *Designing Conflict Management Systems.* San Francisco, CA: Jossey-Bass Publishers.

Cotts, C., and Fortado, L. (2009, January 13). *Madoff's Freedom Ignites Rage of Fellow New Yorkers (Update 2).* Retrieved March 4, 2009, from http://www.bloomberg.com/apps/news?pid=20601103&sid=a1RWArnXmIFw

CPP, Inc. (2008). Workplace Conflict and How Businesses Can Harness It to Thrive. *Human Capital Report.* CPP, Inc., Mountain View, CA.

Craddock, F. B. (1990). *Luke* [Interpretation: A Bible Commentary for Teaching and Preaching Series]. Louisville, KY: Westminster John Knox Press.

Crowe, Jr., W. J. (1993). *The Line of Fire.* New York, New York: Simon and Schuster.

Deibler, E. C. (1985). Philemon. In J. Walvoord and R. B. Zuck (Eds.), *The Bible Knowledge Commentary* (Vol. 2). Wheaton, IL: Victor Books.

Demarest, G. W. (1984). *1,2 Thessalonians, 1,2 Timothy, and Titus: The Preacher's Commentary: Vol. 32. The Preacher's Commentary Series.* Nashville, TN: Thomas Nelson, Inc.

Dennis, L. T., and Grudem, W. (Eds.). (2008). *ESV Study Bible.* Wheaton, IL: Crossway Bibles.

Dever, M. (2008). God's Plan of Salvation. In *ESV Study Bible.* Wheaton, IL: Crossway Bibles.

Diggs, C. (1996). H. Zehr (Ed.), *Doing Life: Reflections of Men and Women Serving Life Sentences.* Intercourse, PA: Good Books.

Dore, R. P. (1959). *Land Reform in Japan.* London, England: Oxford Press.

Works Cited

Doyle, M., and Straus, D. (1976). *How to Make Meetings Work*. New York, NY: The Berkley Publishing Company.

Dudley, C. S. (2000). *Conflict: Synonym for Congregation* [Facts on Fighting: Data from the Fact 2000 Study]. Retrieved June 9, 2009, from Faith Communities Today: http://fact.hartsem.edu/research/fact2000/topical_article3.htm

Dudley, C., Zingery, T., and Breeden, D. (n.d.). *Insights into Congregational Conflict*. Retrieved February 14, 2009, from Hartford Institute for Religion Research: http://fact.hartsem.edu/products/Insights_Into_Congregationa_Conflict.pdf

Durant, W., and Durant, A. (1967). *The Story of Civilization: Part 10. Rousseau and Revolution*. New York, NY: Simon and Shuster.

Durant, W., and Durant, A. (1968). *The Lessons of History*. New York, NY: Simon and Schuster.

Durbin, R. J. (2008, December 1). *Letter to the President*. Retrieved April 8, 2009, from United States Senate: http://www.chicagotribune.com/media/acrobat/2008-12/43676198.pdf

Earl of Birkenhead (Ed.). (1936). *The Albatross Book of English Letters*. Hamburg: The Albatross.

Edwards, D. M. (1956). Mediation. In J. Orr (Ed.), *The International Standard Bible Encyclopedia* (Vol. 3). Grand Rapids, MI: Wm. B. Eerdmans Publishing Company.

Eisenhower, D. D. (1957, February 20). *Broadcast by President Eisenhower*. Retrieved November 11, 2008, from Israel Ministry of Foreign Affairs: http://www.mfa.gov. il/MFA/Foreign+Relations/Israels+Foreign+Relations+since+1947/1947-1974/24+Broadcast+by+President+Eisenhower-+20+February.htm

Ellison, H. L. (1986). Matthew. In F. F. Bruce (Ed.), *The International Bible Commentary* (rev ed.) Grand Rapids, MI: Marshall Pickering.

Elwell, W. A. (Ed.). (1984). *Evangelical Dictionary of Theology*. Grand Rapids, MI: Baker Book House.

Elwell, W. A. (Ed.). (1988). Propitiation. In *Baker Encyclopedia of the Bible*. Grand Rapids, MI: Baker Book House.

Elwell, W. A. (2001). Atonement, Extent of. In W. A. Elwell (Ed.), *Baker Encyclopedia of the Bible* (2nd ed., pp. 114-116) Grand Rapids, MI: Baker Book House.

Elwell, W. A., and Buckwalter, D. (Eds.). (1996, c1991). *Topical Analysis of the Bible : With the New International Version (electronic ed.)* [Baker Reference Library; Logos Library System]. Grand Rapids, MI: Baker Book House.

Enright, R. D. (1996). *Counseling and Values*, 40, 107-26.

Epstein, I. (Ed.). (1952). *The Babylonian Talmud*. Retrieved December 22, 2008, from http://www.come-and-hear.com/nedarim/nedarim_39.html#39b_11

Fensham, F. C. (1996). Crime and Punishment. In D. R. Wood and I. H. Marshall (Eds.), *New Bible Dictionary* (3rd ed.) Downers Grove, IL: InterVarsity Press.

Fisher, R., and Ury, W. (1991). B. Patton (Ed.), *Getting to Yes* (2nd ed.) New York City, NY: Penguin Books.

Fitzgerald, P. J. (2008, May 27). *Statement of U.S. Attorney Patrick J. Fitzgerald*. Retrieved April 8, 2009, from U.S. Department of Justice: http://www.usdoj. gov/usao/iln/pr/chicago/2008/pr0527_01.pdf

Foulkes, F. (1996). Peace. In D. R. Wood and I. H. Marshall (Eds.), *New Bible Dictionary* (3rd ed.) Downers Grove, IL: Inter-Varsity Press.

France, R. T. (1985). *The Gospel According to Matthew.* Grand Rapids, MI: Wm. B. Eerdmans Publishing Company.

France, R. T. (2007). *The Gospel of Matthew (New International Commentary on the New Testament).* Grand Rapids, MI: Wm. B. Eerdmans Publishing Company.

Frayling, N. (1999, August 1). *Forgive and Forget Will Not Work in Ireland* [Press Release, Caux, Switzerland]. Retrieved April 7, 2009, from http://www.peace. ca/forgiveforgetireland.htm

Freud, S. (1962). *Civilization and Its Discontents* (J. Strachey, Trans.). New York, NY: W. W. Norton and Company.

Furst, D. (1975). Confess. In C. Brown (Ed.), *The New International Dictionary of the New Testament* (Vol. 1, pp. 344-348). Grand Rapids, MI: Zondervan Publishing House.

Fusco, C., Pallasch, A. M., and McKinney, D. (2007, August 21). *George Ryan Loses Appeal, But Remains Free.* Retrieved April 8, 2009, from Chicago Sun-Times: http://www.suntimes.com/news/georgeryantrial/518837,ryan082107.article

Gadamer, H.-G. (1993). *Truth and Method* (2nd, Rev. ed., J. Weinsheimer and D. G. Marshall, Trans.) New York, NY: Continuum.

Garbarino, J. (1999). *Lost Boys.* New York: Anchor Books.

Gaskins, J. L. (1999). An Analysis of the Relationship Between Internal Church Conflict and Church Growth: With Selected Case Studies of Southern Baptist Churches in the Shelby Association. *Doctoral Dissertation.* Mid-America Baptist Theological Seminary, Cordova, TN.

Geisler, N. L. (2002-2005). *Systematic Theology* (4 volumes). Minneapolis, MN: Bethany House.

German Embassy, Washington D.C. (2005). *Background Papers: German Compensation for National Socialist Crimes.* Retrieved October 1, 2005, from http://www.germany-info.org/relaunch/info/archives/background/ns_crimes.html

Glaser, T. (1998-2005). *A Conversation on Peacemaking with Jimmy Carter (A Book Summary).* Retrieved April 11, 2009, from Conflict Research Consortium: http://www.colorado.edu/conflict/peace/example/acon7268.htm

Gobodo-Madikizela, P. (2002, Winter). *Journal of Humanistic Psychology,* 42(1), 7-32.

Godet, F. (1889). *A Commentary on the Gospel of St. Luke* (4th ed.) Edinburgh: T. and T. Clark.

Goetzmann, J. (1975). C. Brown (Ed.), *The New International Dictionary of New Testament Theology* (Vol. 1, pp. 357-359). Grand Rapids, MI: Zondervan Publishing House.

Goldstein, N. J., Martin, S. J., and Cialdini, R. B. (2008). *Yes: 50 Scientifically Proven Ways to be Persuasive.* New York, NY: Free Press.

Gotbaum, R. (2007, October 6). *Practice of Hospital Apologies is Gaining Ground.* Retrieved April 11, 2009, from National Public Radio: http://www.npr.org/templates/story/story.php?storyId=15073418

Gottman, J. M. (2001). *The Relationship Cure.* New York, NY: Crown Publishing Group.

Greenhouse, C. J. (1986). *Praying for Justice: Faith, Order, and Community in an American Town.* Ithaca, NY: Cornell University Press.

Gregory, T. M. (1976). Peace. In M. C. Tenney (Ed.), *Zondervan Pictorial Encyclopedia of the Bible* (Vol. 4). Grand Rapids, MI: Zondervan Publishing House.

Griffin, J. H. (1977). *Black Like Me.* New York, NY: Penguin Books. (Original work published 1960)

Griffin, S. (2004). P. R. Loeb (Ed.), *The Impossible Will Take a Little While: A Citizen's Guide to Hope in a Time of Fear.* Cambridge, MA: Basic Books.

Groopman, J. (1997). *The Measure of our Days.* New York City, NY: Penguin Books, Inc.

Grounds, V. (1975). Faith, The Christian. In C. F. Pfeiffer, H. F. Vos, and J. Rea (Eds.), *Wycliffe Bible Encyclopedia* (Vol. 1). Chicago, IL: Moody Press.

Grudem, W. (1994). *Systematic Theology.* Grand Rapids, MI: Zondervan Publishing House.

Grudem, W. (2008). D. Lane and W. Grudem (Eds.), *English Standard Version Study Bible.* Wheaton, IL: Crossway Bibles.

Guerin, E. (1977). T. Edwards (Ed.), *The New Dictionary of Thoughts* (rev. ed.) [Subject: Repentance] New York: Standard Book Company. (Original work published 1852)

Gunther, W. (1978). Sin. In C. Brown (Ed.), *The New International Dictionary of New Testament Theology* (Vol. 3, pp. 573-76). Grand Rapid, MI: Zondervan Publishing House.

Guthrie, D. (1981). *New Testament Theology.* Leicester, England: Inter-Varsity Press.

Guthrie, D. (1990). *The Pastoral Epistles* (2nd ed.) Grand Rapids, MI: Wm. B. Eerdmans Publishing Company.

Hadaway, C. K. (2006, December 11). *Facts on Growth.* Retrieved March 1, 2009, from Hartford Institute for Religion Research at Hartford Seminary: http://fact. hartsem.edu/CongGrowth.pdf

Hare, D. R. (1993). *Matthew (Interpretation, a Bible Commentary for Teaching and Preaching).* Louisville, KY: John Knox Press.

Harris, D. (2008, November 11). *Ted Haggard Speaks Out.* Retrieved February 10, 2009, from ABC News: http://abcnews.go.com/Video/playerIndex?id=6235998

Harris, D., Woo, W., and Caron, C. (2009, January 28). *Ted Haggard Speaks Out After Two-Year Silence.* Retrieved February 10, 2009, from ABC News: Nightline: http://abcnews.go.com/US/Story?id=6742630&page=3

Harris, L. R., Archer, G. L., and Waltke, B. K. (Eds.). (1980). *Theological Wordbook of the Old Testament* (Vol. 2). Chicago, IL: Moody Press.

Harrison, E. F. (1982). Holiness. In G. W. Bromiley (Ed.), *The International Standard Bible Encyclopedia* (rev. ed., Vol. 2, p. 725). Grand Rapids, MI: William B. Eerdmans Publishing Company.

Haugk, K. C. (1988). *Antagonists in the Church.* Minneapolis, MN: Augsburg Publishing House.

Haus, C. (2003, September). G. Burgess and H. Burgess (Eds.), *Reconciliation* [Beyond Intractability Knowledge Base]. Retrieved April 21, 2009, from http://www2. beyondintractability.org/m/reconciliation.jsp

Hawkley, L. C., and Cacioppo, J. T. (2003). Loneliness and Pathways to Disease. *Brain, Behavior, and Immunity, 17 (Supplement 1),* S98.

Hawkley, L. C., and Cacioppo, J. T. (2007). Aging and Loneliness. *Current Directions in Psychological Science,* 16(4), 187-91.

Hermann, T. (2004). Y. Bar-Siman-Tov (Ed.), *From Conflict Resolution to Reconciliation.* New York City, NY: Oxford University Press.

Hertz, T. (2007, September/October). *Forgiveness on American Idol* (4th ed., Vol. 66). Retrieved January 29, 2009, from Ignite Your Faith Magazine: http://www. christianitytoday.com/cl/2007/004/24.34.html

Hewitt, D. (Executive Producer). (1994, July 10). Nasty Girl [CBS Television Network]. *"60 Minutes" Transcript.*

Hicks, D. (2001). The Role of Identity Reconstruction in Promoting Reconciliation. In S. J. Helmick and R. L. Petersen (Eds.), *Forgiveness and Reconciliation* (pp. 129-49). Philadelphia, PA: Templeton Foundation Press.

History Place, The. (1999). *Genocide in the 20th Century.* Retrieved January 28, 2009, from http://www.historyplace.com/worldhistory/genocide/rwanda.htm

Hoare, s.P., L. J. (2001, September 17). *A Divine Dilemma.* Retrieved June 18, 2009, from http://www.theservants.org/priestlypeople/pp%204-99%20part1.html

Hoehner, H. W. (2001). Love. In W. A. Elwell (Ed.), *Evangelical Dictionary of Theology* (2nd ed., pp. 708-11) Grand Rapids, MI: Baker Book House.

Houghton Mifflin Company. (2009). *Biography: Roger Tory Peterson.* Retrieved March 11, 2009, from http://www.houghtonmifflinbooks.com/peterson/rtp/ biography.shtml

Houston, J. H. (1988). W. A. Elwell (Ed.), *Baker Encyclopedia of the Bible* (Vol. 1, pp. 810-12) [Forgiveness]. Grand Rapids, MI: Baker Book House.

Hunter-Gault, C. (2003, May 13). *The South Africa Miracle? How Alive? How Well?* [Copyright (c) 2005 by the President and Fellows of Harvard College] Retrieved February 16, 2008, from http://www.iop.harvard.edu/pdfs/transcripts/hunter-gault_05.13.03.pdf

Ignatieff, M. (1997, November 10). Digging Up the Dead. *The New Yorker.*

International Ombudsman Association. (2007). *IOA Standards of Practice.* Retrieved February 14, 2009, from http://www.ombudsassociation.org/standards/Stds_ Practice_1-07.pdf

Jacoby, S. (1983). *Wild Justice: The Evolution of Revenge.* New York, NY: Harper and Row, Publishers.

Janusz, L. (1992, Spring). The Wounded Healer. *Odyssey,* 101-8.

Jewett, P. K. (1976). M. C. Tenney (Ed.), *The Zondervan Pictorial Encyclopedia of the Bible: Vol. 4. Propitiation* (pp. 903-5). Grand Rapids, MI: Zondervan Publishing House.

JLS1950B. (2008, November 12). *Online Comments* [Exclusive: Ted Haggard Breaks His Silence]. Retrieved February 10, 2009, from *Good Morning America*: http://abcnews.go.com/GMA/comments?type=story&id=6235564

Kairos Document (1985) [signed by 158 signatories from over 20 South African denominations]. Retrieved March 27, 2009, from http://www.sahistory.org.za/pages/ library-resources/official%20docs/kairos-document.htm

Kaner, S. (1996). *Facilitator's Guide to Participatory Decision-Making.* Gabriola Island, British Columbia, Canada: New Society Publishers.

Kaner, S. (2007). *Facilitator's Guide to Participatory Decision-Making* (2nd ed.). San Francisco, CA: Jossey-Bass.

Kantzer, K. S. (2006, December 11). *The Road to Restoration: How Should the Church Treat Its Fallen Leaders?* [Article originally appeared in the Nov. 20, 1987 issue of Christianity Today.] Retrieved January 3, 2009, from Christianity Today (Web-Only): http://www.christianitytoday.com/ct/2006/decemberweb-only/150-14.0.html

Karen, R. (1998). *Becoming Attached: First Relationships and How They Shape Our Capacity to Love.* New York: Oxford University Press.

Kass, J. (2008, December 17). *Willises Want to Look into Ryan's Eyes, Heart.* Retrieved February 5, 2009, from Chicago Tribune: http://www.chicagotribune.com/news/columnists/chi-kass-17-dec17,0,3344706.column

Keener, C. S. (1993). *The IVP Bible Background Commentary: New Testament.* WI, Madison: InterVarsity Press.

Keener, C. S. (1999). *A Commentary on the Gospel of Matthew.* Grand Rapids, MI: Wm. B. Eerdmans Publishing Company.

Ki-Moon, B. (2008, August 29). *Speech in Turin Italy.* Retrieved February 24, 2009, from UNDP WATCH: http://undpwatch.blogspot.com/2008/09/exclusive-ban-ki-moons-speech-in.html. See also http://www.foxnews.com/story/0,2933,419481,00.html

King Encyclopedia. (n.d.). *Birmingham Campaign.* Retrieved February 21, 2009, from http://www.stanford.edu/group/King/about_king/encyclopedia/birmingham_campaign.htm

King, M. L. (1963, April 16). *Letter from a Birmingham Jail.* Retrieved February 17, 2009, from http://www.stanford.edu/group/King/frequentdocs/birmingham.pdf

King, M. L. (1965, March 25). *Our God is Marching On.* Retrieved June 24, 2009 from http://mlk-kpp01.stanford.edu/index.php/kingpapers/article/our_god_is_marching_on

Kohler, K. (1918). *Jewish Theology: Systematically and Historically Considered.* New York, NY: The Macmillan Company.

Korecki, N. (2008, November 26). *Lura Lynn: "His Conscience is as Clear as His Mind".* Retrieved April 8, 2009, from Chicago Sun-Times: http://www.suntimes.com/news/georgeryantrial/1300317,CST-NWS-prison26.article

Kreisler, H. (Interviewer). (1996, March 19). *A Life in Peace and War: Conversation with Sir Brian Urquhart.* Retrieved March 26, 2009, from Institute of International Studies, UC Berkeley: http://globetrotter.berkeley.edu/UN/Urquhart/urquhart5.html

Kriesberg, L. (1994, Spring). Conflict Resolution in Organizations of Goodwill. *PARC News, 81,* 7.

Kriesberg, L. (2007). *Constructive Conflicts* (3rd ed.) Lantham, MD: Rowman and Littlefield Publishers, Inc.

Krivis, J. (2006). *Improvisational Negotiation.* San Francisco, CA: Jossey-Bass.

Kurtz, H. (2004, June 17). *Bill Clinton's Very Personal Reflections.* Retrieved April 9, 2009, from *Washington Post*: http://www.washingtonpost.com/wp-dyn/articles/A47877-2004Jun16.html

La Guardia, A. (2003, December). Blessed are the Peacemakers (and Probably Norwegian). *New Statesman,* 18-20.

Laney, J. C. (1985). *A Guide to Church Discipline.* Minneapolis, MN: Bethany House Publishers.

Lazare, A. (1995, January). Go Ahead Say You're Sorry. *Psychology Today, 28*(1), 40ff.

Lazare, A. (2004). *On Apology.* Oxford, England: Oxford University Press.

Leas, S. (1979). *A Lay Person's Guide to Conflict Management.* Bethesda, MD: Alban Institute.

Lederach, J. P. (1997). *Building Peace*. Washington, DC: United States Institute of Peace.

Lederach, J. P. (1999). *The Journey Toward Reconciliation*. Scottsdale, PA: Herald Press.

Lederach, J. P. (2001). Five Qualities of Practice in Support of Reconciliation Process. In S. J. Helmick and R. L. Petersen (Eds.), (pp. 183-193). Philadelphia, PA: Templeton Foundation Press.

Lederach, J. P. (2005). *The Moral Imagination: The Art and Soul of Building Peace*. New York City, NY: Oxford University Press.

Lehrer, J. (2008, July 28). The Eureka Hunt: Why Do Good Ideas Come to Us When They Do? *The New Yorker*, 40-45.

Lewicki, R. J., and Tomlinson, E. C. (2003, December). *Trust and Trust Building*. Retrieved April 25, 2009, from http://www.beyondintractability.org/essay/trust_building/

Lewis, C. S. (1952). *Mere Christianity*. New York, NY: MacMillan Publishing Company, Inc.

Liefeld, W. I. (1988). Salvation. In G. W. Bromiley (Ed.), *The International Standard Bible Encyclopedia* (Rev. ed., Vol. 4, pp. 287-295). Grand Rapids, MI: William B. Eerdmans Publishing Company.

Lifton, R. J. (1986). *The Nazi Doctors*. New York, NY: Basic Book, Inc.

Lightner, R. P. (1995). *Handbook of Evangelical Theology*. Grand Rapids, MI: Kregel Publications.

Lindstrom, C. (2006, July 26). *RACI+S* [Version 1.0]. Retrieved April 25, 2009, from http://74.125.47.132/search?q=cache:F7-mPOzWmQUJ:www.ceptara.com/RACI_Model.pdf+raci+model&cd=4&hl=en&ct=clnk&gl=us&client=firefox-a

Livni, T. (2007, August 14). *Press conference with Japanese Foreign Minister Taro Aso* [Statements by Israeli FM Livni regarding Israeli Policy toward the Hamas and its Terrorism]. Retrieved May 27, 2009, from Israel Ministry of Foreign Affairs: http://www.mfa.gov.il/MFA/Templates/ArticleDynamicFix.aspx?NRMODE=Published&NRORIGINALURL=%2fMFA%2fAbout%2bthe%2bMinistry%2fForeign%2bMinister%2bLivni%2fSpeeches%2binterviews%2fStatements%2bby%2bIsraeli%2bFM%2bLivni%2bregarding%2bIsraeli%2bpolicy%2btoward%2bthe%2bHamas%2band%2bits%2bterrorism%2b11-Sep-20%2ehtm&NRNODEGUID=%7b9E2F26BD-1A99-452B-86BC-ACBC2C45C670%7d&NRCACHEHINT=Guest

Logos Hymnal. (1995). [Computer software] Oak Harbor, WA: Logos Research Systems.

Lomax, E. (1995). *The Railway Man: A POW's Searing Account of War, Brutality, and Forgiveness*. New York, NY: W. W. Norton and Company.

Longenecker, R. N. (1981). The Acts of the Apostles. In F. E. Gaebelein (Ed.), *Expositor's Bible Commentary* (Vol. 9). Grand Rapids, MI: Zondervan Publishing House.

Lord, R. P. (1991, October 9). Do I Have to Forgive? *Christian Century, 108*(28), 902-3.

Lorenzini, M. (2002-2009). *Conscience: Our Ally in Conversion*. Retrieved February 23, 2009, from Frontline Ministries: http://www.frontlinemin.org/ally.asp

Louw, J. P., and Nida, E. A. (1989). *Greek-English Lexicon of the New Testament* (2nd ed.) New York, NY: United Bible Societies.

Lowry, L. R., and Meyers, R. W. (1991). *Conflict Management and Counseling.* Waco: TX: Word, Inc.

Luther, M. (1949). *Project Wittenberg: Commentary on the Epistle to the Galatians* (T. Graebner, Trans.) [First written, 1535]. Retrieved January 23, 2009, from http://www.iclnet.org/pub/resources/text/wittenberg/luther/gal/web/gal3-10.html

Lynch, J. J. (2000). *A Cry Unheard: New Insights into the Medical Consequences of Loneliness.* Baltimore, MD: Bancroft Press.

MacArthur, J. (1945, September 2). *Japanese Sign Final Surrender.* Retrieved April 25, 2009, from http://www.youtube.com/watch?v=vcnH_kF1zXc

MacDonald, J. (1999, July 1). Five Moral Fences [Online at http://www.ctlibrary.com/le/1999/summer/9l3045.html]. *Leadership Journal, 20*(3).

Mantakana. (2008, August 14). *For All That and More, I Forgive You.* Retrieved April 8, 2009, from http://www.thoughts.com/mantakana/blog/for-all-that-and-more-i-forgive-you-134791/

Marshall, I. H. (1978). *The Epistles of John.* Grand Rapids, MI: Wm. B. Eerdmans Publishing Company.

Marshall, I. H. (1980). *The Acts of the Apostles.* Grand Rapids, MI: William B. Eerdmans Publishing Company.

Martin, S. (2007). *Born Standing Up: A Comic's Life.* New York, NY: Scribner.

Matera, F. J. (1996). Reconciliation. In P. J. Achtemeier (Ed.), *HarperCollins Bible Dictionary* (rev. ed.) San Francisco, CA: HarperCollins Publishers.

McDowell, J., and Stewart, D. (1980). *Answers to Tough Questions Skeptics Ask About the Christian Faith.* San Bernardino, CA: Here's Life Publishers.

McKeever, J. (2001, January 1). *Broken Pastor, Broken Church* [Leadership Journal, Winter 2001]. Retrieved February 26, 2009, from Christianity Today Library: http://www.ctlibrary.com/le/2001/winter/8.57.html

McLean, C. (2005, December 26). *Holy Terror.* Retrieved May 15, 2009, from Western Standard: http://www.westernstandard.ca/website/article.php?id=1333&start=0

Memmott, C. (2006, October 8). *For Grisham, A New Turn Into Non-Fiction* [*USA Today* Newspaper Article]. Retrieved February 8, 2008, from http://www.usatoday.com/life/books/news/2006-10-08-grisham_x.htm

Menkin, E. S. (1994, September 4). *Life After Death.* Retrieved April 23, 2009, from *San Jose Mercury News*: http://www.vorp.com/articles/lifeaft.html

Metcalf, B. D., and Metcalf, T. R. (2006). *A Concise History of Modern India* (2nd ed.) Cambridge, England: Cambridge University Press.

Michaud, C. (2009, February 7). *Sharpton Calls for Justice Outside Madoff's Home.* Retrieved March 4, 2009, from http://www.reuters.com/article/domesticNews/idUSTRE51623C20090207

Michel, O. (1967). G. Friedrich and G. W. Bromiley (Eds.), *Theological Dictionary of the New Testament* (Vol. 5, G. W. Bromiley, Trans.). Grand Rapids, MI: Wm. B. Eerdmans Publishing Company.

Miles, Jr., R. E. (1978, Sept.-Oct.). The Origin and Meaning of Miles' Law. *Public Administration Review, 38*(5), 399-403.

Milgram, S. (1974). *Obedience to Authority: An Experimental View.* New York: NY: Harper and Row.

Minow, M. (1998). *Between Vengeance and Forgiveness.* Boston, MA: Beacon Press.

Molhan, S. (1992, Spring). Mediation and Reconciliation. *Odyssey,* 108-10.

Monsma, P. H. (1976). Forgiveness. In M. C. Tenney (Ed.), *The Zondervan Pictorial Encyclopedia of the Bible* (Vol. 2, pp. 596-600). Grand Rapids, MI: Zondervan Publishing House.

Moo, D. J. (2000). *The Letter of James (Pillar New Testament Commentary).* Grand Rapids, MI: Wm. B. Eerdmans Publishing Company.

Moore, C. W. (2003). *The Mediation Process* (3rd ed.) San Francisco, CA: Jossey-Bass Publishers.

Morris, L. (1965a). *The Apostolic Preaching of the Cross* (3rd ed.) Grand Rapids, MI: Wm. B. Eerdmans Publishing Company.

Morris, L. (1965b). *The Cross in the New Testament.* Grand Rapids, MI: William B. Eerdmans Publishing Company.

Morris, L. (1988). Propitiation. In W. A. Elwell (Ed.), *Baker Encyclopedia of the Bible* (Vol. 2). Grand Rapids, MI: Baker Book House.

Morris, L. (1995). *The Gospel According to John.* Grand Rapids, MI: Wm. B. Eerdmans Publishing Company.

Morro, W. C., and Harrison, R. K. (1982). Forgiveness. In G. W. Bromiley (Ed.), *The International Standard Bible Encyclopedia* (Fully Rev. ed., Vol. 2, pp. 340-44). Grand Rapids, MI: William B. Eerdmans Publishing Company.

Moses, H. (Producer). (1983, February 6). The Devil is a Gentleman [CBS Television Network]. *60 Minutes Transcript.*

Moyers, B. (2008, January 25). Interview with John Grisham. In *Bill Moyers Journal.* PBS: On the Web: http://www.pbs.org/moyers/journal/01252008/watch4.html.

Murningham, J. K. (2002, February). *Journal of Management Education,* 26(1), 56-69.

Murray, K. A. (1998). *Hermeneutics (Herman Who?).* Retrieved April 25, 2009, from http://www.svcc.edu/academics/classes/murray/hum210/hermwho.htm

NASA's Career Management Office. (2002, February). Words of Wisdom. *Work / Life Navigator,* 26, 3-4.

National Public Radio. (2007, October 6). *Practice of Hospitals Apologies is Gaining Ground* [Segment: All Things Considered]. Retrieved April 11, 2009, from http://www.npr.org/templates/player/mediaPlayer.html?action=1&t=1&islist =false&id=15073418&m=15073402

Neil. (2001, November 20). *I Am Sorry.* Retrieved April 8, 2009, from http://www.forgivenessweb.com/apologies.htm

Nestle, E., and McReynolds, P. R. (1997, c1982). *Nestle Aland 26th Edition Greek New Testament With McReynolds English Interlinear.* Oak Harbor, WA: Logos Research Systems, Inc.

Net Bible (electronic edition) (1996-2003) [Biblical Studies Press]. Retrieved June 18, 2009, from http://www.bible.org/netbible/

New Living Translation (1996). Wheaton, IL: Tyndale House Publishers, Inc.

New York Times. (1985, April 12). Recanting of a Rape Charge Fails to Free Convict, p. A.1..

Newman, L. E. (1987, Fall). The Quality of Mercy: On the Duty to Forgive in the Judaic

Works Cited

Tradition. *The Journal of Religious Ethics*, 15, 155-72.

Newman, L. E. (1998). *Past Imperatives: Studies in the History and Theory of Jewish Ethics*. Albany, NY: State University of New York Press.

News4Jax.com. (2009, February 10). *Family, Friends Pray As Search For Missing 5-Year-Old Continues*. Retrieved February 16, 2009, from Jacksonville News Station WJXT: http://www.news4jax.com/news/18686639/detail.html#-

Nobel Foundation, The. (1950, 2007). *Ralph Bunche: Biography*. Retrieved March 23, 2009, from http://nobelprize.org/nobel_prizes/peace/laureates/1950/bunche-bio.html

North, J. (1998). The "Ideal" of Forgiveness: A Philosopher's Exploration. In R. D. Enright and J. North (Eds.), *Exploring Forgiveness* (pp. 15-34). Madison, WI: The University of Wisconsin Press.

O'Conner, M., and Bush, R. (2006, April 17). *Ryan Convicted in Corruption Trial*. Retrieved April 7, 2009, from ChicagoTribune.com: http://www.chicagotribune.com/news/custom/newsroom/chi-060417ryantrial,0,4525779.story?page=1&coll=chi-homepagepromo440-fea

Oepke, A. (1967). G. Kittel and G. W. Bromiley (Eds.), *Theological Dictionary of the New Testament* (Vol. 4, G. W. Bromiley, Trans.). Grand Rapids, MI: Wm. B. Eerdmans Publishing Company.

Oren, M. (2007, February 14). *Travis Smiley Show*. Retrieved April 2, 2009, from http://www.pbs.org/kcet/tavissmiley/archive/200702/20070214_oren.html

Ornish, D. (1998). *Love and Survival: The Scientific Basis for the Healing Power of Intimacy*. New York, NY: HarperCollins Publishers, Inc.

Ornish, D. (2005, October 3). Love Is Real Medicine. *Newsweek*, 56.

Palfreman, J. (1993, October 19). Prisoners of Silence [Transcript of Show #1202. See also http://www.pbs.org/wgbh/pages/frontline/programs/transcripts/1202.html]. In *Frontline*. PBS.

Palmer, M. (2002). *Quick Overview of the History of the Greek Language*. Retrieved March 11, 2009, from Greek Language and Linguistics: http://greek-language.com/historyofgreek

PBS. (2001a). *Ralph Bunche: An American Odyssey*. Retrieved March 23, 2009, from http://www.pbs.org/ralphbunche/peace_inter1.html

PBS. (2001b). *Ralph Bunche: An American Odyssey*. Retrieved March 23, 2009, from http://www.pbs.org/ralphbunche/peace_inter3.html

PBS / WGBH. (1999-2000). *American Experience: Reagan* [PBS Online]. Retrieved June 18, 2009, from Enhanced Transcript: http://www.pbs.org/wgbh/amex/reagan/filmmore/transcript/transcript2.html

PBS / WGBH. (2004-2006 (PBS), 1997-2004 (WGBH)). *American Experience: MacArthur* [PBS Online]. Retrieved April 21, 2009, from http://www.pbs.org/wgbh/amex/macarthur/filmmore/transcript/transcript3.html

Peacemaker Ministries. (2005). *Resolving Conflict Through Christian Conciliation*. Retrieved May 29, 2009, from http://www.peacemaker.net/site/c.aqKFLTOBIpH/b.931105/k.F95D/Resolving_Conflict_through_Christian_Conciliation.htm

Peli, P. H. (1984). *Soloveitchik on Repentance*. Ramsey, NY: Paulist Press.

Petersen, J. A. (1983). *The Myth of the Greener Grass*. Wheaton, IL: Tyndale.

Petersen, R. L. (2001). A Theology of Forgiveness. In S. J. Helmick and R. L. Petersen

(Eds.), *Forgiveness and Reconciliation* (pp. 3-25). Philadelphia, PA: Templeton Foundation Press.

Pettigrove, G. A. (2003). *Seeking Forgiveness: Studies in Moral and Political Philosophy.* University of California Riverside, Riverside, CA (UMI No. ATT 3100634).

Plantinga, Jr., C. (1995). *Not the Way It's Supposed to Be: A Breviary of Sin.* Grand Rapids, MI: Wm. B. Eerdmans Publishing Company.

Plummer, A. (1903). *Gospel According to St. Luke.* New York: Charles Scribner's Son.

Plummer, A. (1910). *An Exegetical Commentary on the Gospel According to St. Matthew.* New York: Charles Scribner's Sons.

Poincaré, H. (1908). *Mathematical Creation* [*Resonance Journal of Science Education* (February, 2000)]. Retrieved March 12, 2009, from Indian Academy of Sciences: http://www.ias.ac.in/resonance/Feb2000/pdf/Feb2000Reflections. pdf

Pope, A. (1977). T. Edwards (Ed.), *The New Dictionary of Thoughts* (rev. and enlarged). New York: Standard Book Company.

Portfolio Staff. (2009, February 26). *The Madoff Panel Transcript.* Retrieved March 4, 2009, from http://www.portfolio.com/executives/2009/02/26/Wiesel-and-Madoff-Transcript?page=5#page=5

Prager, D. (2004, March 30). *What Does "Judeo-Christian" Mean?* Retrieved May 28, 2009, from Jewish World Review: http://www.jewishworldreview.com/0304/prager_2004_03_30_04.php3

Prager, D., and Telushkin, J. (1983). *Why the Jews? The Reason for Antisemitism.* New York City, NY: Simon and Schuster.

Princeton University (Ed.). (2006). WordNet: "Judeo-Christian" (Version 3.0) [Computer software]. New Jersey: Princeton University. Retrieved May 21, 2009, from http://wordnet.princeton.edu/

Protzman, F. (1990, April 13). E. Germans Apologize for Nazis. *Austin American Statesman,* p. A 1.

Rawls, J. (2005). *A Theory of Justice: Original Edition.* Cambridge, MA: Harvard University Press. (Original work published 1971)

Rediger, G. L. (1997). *Clergy Killers: Guidance for Pastor and Congregations Under Attack.* Louisville, KY: Westminster John Know Press.

Reuters. (1990, April 13). Upheaval in the East: Excerpts From East Berlin Statement of Apology. *The New York Times,* p. A 7.

Rifkin, J. (1980). *Entropy: A New World View.* New York City, New York: Viking Press.

Ritzer, G. (2000). *Sociological Theory* (5th ed.) New York, NY: McGraw-Hill.

Robbennolt, J. K. (2003, December). Apologies and Legal Settlement: An Empirical Examination. *Michigan Law Review,* 102(3).

Robertson, A. T. (1997). *Word Pictures in the New Testament.* Oak Harbor, WA: Published in electronic form by Logos Research Systems. (Original work published 1930-1933)

Robinson, D. W. (1996). Sons (Children) of God. In D. R. Wood and I. H. Marshall (Eds.), *New Bible Dictionary* (3rd ed.) Downers Grove, IL: Inter-Varsity Press.

Robinson, M. (2007, November 6). *Ryan Says He Has a "Clear Conscience" Before Reporting to Prison.* Retrieved April 8, 2009, from *Chicago Sun-Times*: http://

Works Cited

www.suntimes.com/news/georgeryantrial/637068,110607ryana.article

Rosenzweig, F. (1971, 1970). *The Star of Redemption* (W. W. Hallo, Trans.). New York, NY: Holt, Rinehart, and Winston. (Original work published 1930)

Ross, A. (n.d.). *An Exposition of the Gospel of Matthew.* Retrieved March 4, 2009, from http://www.bible.org/page.php?page_id=3938

Ross, J. B., and McLaughlin, M. M. (Eds.). (1949). *The Portable Medieval Reader.* New York: The Viking Press.

Ross, M. H. (2004). Ritual and the Politics of Reconciliation. In Y. Bar-Siman-Tov (Ed.), *From Conflict Resolution to Reconciliation* (pp. 197-223). New York, NY: Oxford University Press.

Ryrie, C. C. (1999). *Basic Theology.* Chicago, IL: Moody Press.

Sack, K. (2008, May 19). *Doctors Say "I'm Sorry" Before "See You in Court."* Retrieved March 21, 2009, from *New York Times*: http://www.nytimes.com/2008/05/18/us/18apology.html?_r=3&hp=&adxnnl=1&oref=slogin&adxnnlx=1211116456-DMJLNmyLTi42Vbmqj3m7Xg

Sadat, A. (1977a, November 9). *Speech to the Inaugural Session of the People's Assembly.* Retrieved February 14, 2009, from http://sadat.umd.edu/archives/speeches%5CAAER%20Speech%20to%20Assembly11.9.77pdf.pdf

Sadat, A. (1977b, November 20). *President Anwar Sadat's Address.* Retrieved February 14, 2009, from http://www.jewishvirtuallibrary.org/jsource/Peace/sadat_speech.html

Safer, M. (Reporter). (1994, February 20). Less Than a Miracle [Transcript: Volume XXVI, Number 23]. In *60 Minutes.* CBS.

San Diego Union. (1985, April 12). Rape charge upheld despite claim, p. A.2..

Sande, K. (2004). *The Peacemaker: A Biblical Guide to Resolving Personal Conflict* (3rd ed.) Grand Rapids, MI: Baker Books.

Sande, K., and Kober, T. (2005). *Guiding People Through Conflict.* Billings, MT: Peacemaker Ministries.

Sawyer, D. (Reporter). (1992, January 23). Free From Silence [Transcript #229]. In Hsia, L. (Producer), *ABC News Primetime Live.* ABC News.

Schellenberg, R. C., and Parks-Savage, A. (2007, June). Reducing Levels of Elementary School Violence. *Professional School Counseling,* 10(5), 475-81.

Schimmel, S. (2002). *Wounds Not Healed by Time.* Oxford, England: Oxford University Press.

Schmadeke, S. (2008, December 11). *Ryan Apologizes to People of Illinois.* Retrieved April 8, 2009, from Chicago Breaking News Center: http://www.suntimes.com/news/georgeryantrial/1329077,george-ryan-apology-text-121208.article

Schroder, Gerhard. (2005, May 12). *Press Releases.* German Embassy, Washington, DC. Retrieved June 25, 2009, from http://search.globescope.com/relaunch/info/press/releases/pr_05_12_05.htm

Senft, L. P. (2007, Winter). *ACResolution,* 6(2), 18-21.

Shaw, M. (1996, March 29). *Conference on Mediation* [Geneva, Switzerland]. Retrieved March 25, 2009, from http://www.wipo.int/amc/en/events/conferences/1996/shaw.html

Shedd, W. G. T. (2003). A. W. Gomes (Ed.), *Dogmatic Theology* (3rd ed.) Phillipsburg, NJ: Presbyterian and Reformed Publishing. (Original work published 1888-1894)

Works Cited

Shelley, M. (1985). *Well-Intentioned Dragons.* Grand Rapids, MI: Bethany House.

Simon, R. I. (2008). *Bad Men Do What Good Men Dream.* Washington, DC: American Psychiatric Publishing, Inc.

Skeels, H. M. (1966). Adult Status of Children with Contrasting Early Life Experiences: A Follow-up Study [Serial No. 105]. *Monographs of the Society for Research in Child Development,* 31(3), 1-65.

Skeels, H. M., and Dye, H. B. (1939). A Study of the Effects of Differential Stimulation on Mentally Retarded Children. *Proceedings and Addresses of the American Association on Mental Deficiency,* 44, 114-36.

Smedes, L. B. (1984). *Forgive and Forget: Healing the Hurts We Don't Deserve.* New York, NY: Pocket Books.

Smedes, L. B. (1996). *The Art of Forgiving.* Nashville, TN: Morrings.

Solzhenitsyn, A. I. (1973, 1974). *The Gulag Archipelago* (Vol. 1, T. P. Whitney, Trans.). New York, NY: Harper and Row.

Sorry Works! Coalition. (2007). *About Us.* Retrieved March 21, 2009, from http://www.sorryworks.net/about.phtml

Southern Baptist Convention. (1995, June). *Resolution On Racial Reconciliation On The 150th Anniversary Of The Southern Baptist Convention.* Retrieved March 5, 2009, from http://www.sbc.net/resolutions/amResolution.asp?ID=899

Spokesman for the Secretary-General. (2003, June 2). *Daily Press Briefing.* Retrieved May 15, 2009, from http://www.un.org/News/briefings/docs/2003/db020603.doc.htm

Staub, E., and Pearlman, L. A. (2001). Healing, Reconciliation, and Forgiving after Genocide and Other Collective Violence. In R. S. Helmick and R. Petersen (Eds.), *Forgiveness and Reconciliation* (pp. 195-217). Radnor PA: Templeton Foundation Press.

Stedman, S. J., Rothchild, D., and Cousens, E. M. (Eds.). (2002). Introduction. In *Ending Civil War: The Implementation of Peace Agreements* (pp. 1-40). Boulder, CO: Lynne Rienner Publishers.

Stott, J. R. (1964). *Confess Your Sins: The Way of Reconciliation.* Waco, TX: Word Books.

Stott, J. R. (1986). *The Cross of Christ.* Downers Grove, IL: InterVarsity Press.

Stotts, J. L. (1973). *Shalom: The Search for a Peaceable City.* Nashville, TN: Abingdon Press.

Strathmann, H. (1967). Witness (G. Bromiley, Trans.). In G. Kittle (Ed.), *Theological Dictionary of the New Testament* (Vol. 4, pp. 474-514). Grand Rapids, MI: Wm. B. Eerdmans Publishing Company.

Strong, A. H. (1907). *Systematic Theology.* Old Tappan, NJ: Fleming H. Revell Company.

Sun-Times Staff. (2008, November 12). *Text of George Ryan's Apology.* Retrieved April 8, 2009, from *Chicago Sun-Times*: http://www.suntimes.com/news/georgeryantrial/1329077,george-ryan-apology-text-121208.article

Susskind, L. E. (2000, April). Confessions of a Public Dispute Mediator. *Negotiation Journal,* 16(2), 129-32.

Taft, L. (2000). Apology Subverted: The Commodification of Apology. *Yale Law Journal,* 109(5), 1135ff.

Tangney, J. P. (1998, August). Recent Advances in the Empirical Study of Shame and

Works Cited

Guilt. *The American Behavioral Scientist, 38*(8), 1132-1145.

Tangney, J. P., and Dearing, R. L. (2002). *Shame and Guilt.* New York, MY: The Guilford Press.

Tangney, J. P., Boone, A. L., and Dearing, R. (2005). Forgiving the Self: Conceptual Issues and Empirical Findings. In E. L. Worthington, Jr. (Ed.), *Handbook of Forgiveness* (pp. 143-158). New York City, NY: Taylor and Francis Group.

Tavuchis, N. (1991). *Mea Culpa: A Sociology of Apology and Reconciliation.* Stanford, CA: Stanford University Press.

Tenney, M. C. (1975). Gospel. In C. F. Pfeiffer, H. F. Vos, and J. Rea (Eds.), *Wycliffe Bible Encyclopedia* (Vol. 1). Chicago, IL: Moody Press.

Thiessen, H. C. (1949). *Introductory Lectures in Systematic Theology.* Grand Rapids, MI: Wm. B. Eerdmans Publishing Company.

Thiessen, H. C. (1979). V. D. Doerksen (Ed.), *Lectures in Systematic Theology.* Grand Rapids, MI: William B. Eerdmans Publishing Company.

Thomas, S. B. (1999, September). *Anatomy of an Apology.* Retrieved April 18, 2009, from   http://www.emory.edu/ACAD_EXCHANGE/1999/sept99/anatomy. html

Thomasson, D. (1998, September 14). Pleadings along the contrition trail. *The Washington Times,* p. A16.

Tinder, G. (1989, December). Can We Be Good Without God?. *The Atlantic Monthly,* 264(6), 68-85.

Tolle, E. (2005). *A New Earth.* New York, NY: Penguin Group.

Ton, J. (1976, March 26). The Socialist Quest of the New Man. *Christianity Today,* 6-9.

Truth and Reconciliation Commission. (1996, September 11). *Bisho Massacre - Day 3.* Retrieved April 23, 2009, from http://www.doj.gov.za/trc/hrvtrans/bisho1/ day3.htm

Truth and Reconciliation Commission. (1998-2003). *Truth and Reconciliation Commission of South Africa Report* [7 Volumes]. Retrieved May 27, 2009, from http://www.doj.gov.za/trc/report/

Turner, D. L. (2008). *Matthew (Baker Exegetical Commentary on the New Testament).* Grand Rapids, MI: Baker Academic.

Turner, T. (1991, January). Humanism's Fighting Chance. *The Humanist: Buffalo, 51*(1), 12-15, 34.

Tutu, D. (1998, November). *Nobel Peace Laureates Conference: Human Rights, Conflict, Reconciliation.* Retrieved February 14, 2009, from University of Virginia: http://www.virginia.edu/nobel/transcript/tutu.html

Tutu, D. (1999a). *No Future Without Forgiveness.* New York City, NY: DoubleDay.

Tutu, D. (1999b). Truth and Reconciliation Commission (Ed.), *Truth and Reconciliation Commission of South Africa Report: Vol. 1. Chairperson's Forward* (pp. 4-22). London, England: Macmillan Reference Limited. (Original work published 1998)

Tutu, D. (2004). *God Has a Dream: A Vision of Hope for Our Time.* New York: DoubleDay.

Twachtman-Cullen, D. (1997). *A Passion to Believe: Autism and the Facilitated Communication Phenomenon.* Boulder: CO: Westview Press.

Twain, M. (1899, September). *Concerning the Jews* [Originally published in Harper's Magazine, pp. 527-535]. Retrieved February 24, 2009, from http://www.

classicreader.com/book/3095/1/

U.S. News and World Report. (2003, February 16). *DNA's Twists Of History* [This story appears in the February 24, 2003 print edition.]. Retrieved January 18, 2008, from http://www.usnews.com/usnews/culture/articles/030224/24dna.b.htm

UN Paper. (2002, September 10). *Restoring Social Services / Identifying Priorities (Guatemala).* Paper presented at the Fifty-fifth Conference of the Rxiin Tnamet DPI/NGO/UN Health Association. Retrieved May 15, 2009, from United Nations: http://www.un.org/dpi/ngosection/annualconfs/55/toj.pdf

United Nations. (1945, June 26). *Charter of the United Nations.* Retrieved May 15, 2009, from http://www.un.org/aboutun/charter/

United States Department of Justice. (2004, January 14). *The Justice System.* Retrieved January 28, 2009, from http://www.ojp.usdoj.gov/bjs/justsys.htm

United States Department of Justice and Federal Bureau of Investigation. (2008, September). *2007 Crime Clock.* Retrieved January 28, 2009, from http://www.fbi.gov/ucr/cius2007/about/crime_clock.html

United States Department of State. (2008, February). *Background Note: South Africa* [Bureau of African Affairs]. Retrieved March 7, 2009, from http://www.state.gov/r/pa/ei/bgn/2898.htm

United States Institute of Peace. (2004). *Certificate Course in Conflict Analysis* [3.3 Genocide]. Retrieved January 28, 2009, from http://www.usip.org/training/online/analysis/3_3_2.php

http://texaspolitics.laits.utexas.edu/html/exec/governors/21.html

UPI. (1985, April 15). Judge "Sorry" Over Rape Case. *New York Times,* p. D. 13.

Urquhart, B. (1993). *Ralph Bunche: An American Life.* New York, NY: W. W. Norton and Company.

Ury, W. (1993). *Getting Past No* (rev. ed.) New York, NY: Bantam Books.

Value Based Management.net. (2009, March 23). *Raci Model (Rasci).* Retrieved April 25, 2009, from http://www.valuebasedmanagement.net/methods_raci.html

VanGemeren, W. A. (Ed.). (1997). *New International Dictionary of Old Testament Theology and Exegesis.* Grand Rapids, MI: Zondervan Publishing House.

Vine, W. E. (1996). F. F. Bruce (Ed.), *Vine's Expository Dictionary of Old and New Testament Words.* Oak Harbor, WA: Published in electronic form by Logos Research Systems. (Original work published 1981)

Volf, M. (1996). *Exclusion and Embrace.* Nashville, TN: Abingdon Press.

Volf, M. (2001). Forgiveness, Reconciliation, and Justice. In S. J. Helmick and R. L. Petersen (Eds.), *Forgiveness and Reconciliation* (pp. 27-49). Philadelphia, PA: Templeton Foundation Press.

Volf, M. (2005). *Free of Charge.* Grand Rapids, MI: Zondervan.

Volkan, V. (1997). *Bloodlines: From Ethnic Pride to Ethnic Terrorism.* New York, NY: Farrar, Straus, and Giroux.

von Rad, G. (1964). G. Kittel and G. W. Bromiley (Eds.), *Theological Dictionary of the New Testament* (Vol. 2, G. W. Bromiley, Trans.). Grand Rapids, MI: Wm. B. Eerdmans Publishing Company.

Vorlander, H. (1975). Forgiveness. In C. Brown (Vol. Ed.), *The New International Dictionary of New Testament Theology* (Vol. 1, pp. 697-703). Grand Rapids, MI: Zondervan Publishing House.

Vos, H. F. (1988). M. F. Unger, R. K. Harrison, and C. J. Barber (Eds.), *The New Unger's*

Bible Dictionary (rev. and updated ed.) Chicago, IL: Moody Press. (Original work published 1957)

Wallace, D. B. (1996). *Greek Grammar Beyond the Basics.* Grand Rapids, MI: Zondervan Publishing House.

Wallerstein, J., and Lewis, J. M. (2004). The Unexpected Legacy of Divorce: Report of a 25-Year Study. *Psychoanalytic Psychology,* 21(3), 353-70.

Walsh, J. (2003, August 19). *Letter from a Birmingham Jail.* Retrieved February 20, 2009, from http://dir.salon.com/story/opinion/freedom/2003/08/19/king/index.html

Waltke, B. K. (2005). *The Book of Proverbs: Chapters 15-31 (New International Commentary on the Old Testament).* Grand Rapids, MI: Wm. B. Eerdmans Publishing Company.

Warner, M. (1995, January 31). Why Gay Men are Having Risky Sex. *Village Voice,* 32-36.

Webb, C. C. (1985). *Forgive Me.* Old Tappan, NJ: Fleming H. Revell Company.

Webster, S. K. (1999, October 4). *Gordon Allport.* Retrieved May 26, 2009, from Westminster College: http://www.psych.westminster.edu/psy311/allport/ppframe.htm

Wenham, G. J. (1988). Civil Law and Justice. In W. A. Elwell (Ed.), *Baker Encyclopedia of the Bible* (Vol. 1, pp. 473-77). Grand Rapids, MI: Baker Book House.

White, L. L. (2001). *Hope in Process: A Qualitative Study of Victim Offender Mediation/ Dialogue in Texas.* Doctoral Dissertation, Texas A&M University. (UMI No. 3033898).

White, R. E. O. (1984). Reconciliation. In W. A. Elwell (Ed.), *Evangelical Dictionary of Theology* (pp. 917-18). Grand Rapids, MI: Baker Book House.

Wiesel, E. (1960). *Night.* New York, NY: Bantam Books.

Wiesenthal, S. (1997). *The Sunflower: On the Possibilities and Limits of Forgiveness* (revised and expanded). New York City, NY: Schocken Books.

Wikipedia, The Free Encyclopedia. (2008, May 13). *Civil Law (common law).* Retrieved September, 14, 2008, from http://en.wikipedia.org/wiki/Civil_law_(common_law)

Wikipedia, The Free Encyclopedia. (2009, April 3). *Shuttle Diplomacy.* Retrieved April 10, 2009, from http://en.wikipedia.org/wiki/Shuttle_diplomacy

William Barclay Estate, The. (2003). *The Letters to Timothy, Titus, and Philemon: The New Daily Study Bible.* Louisville, KY: Westminster John Know Press. (Original work published 1975)

Willis, J. (2006, September 5). *Letter to the Honorable Judge Pallmeyer* [Copy of signed letter]. Retrieved February 5, 2009, from *Milwaukee Journal Sentinel* Online: http://graphics.jsonline.com/graphics/news/img/sep06/willis090906.pdf

Willis, S. (2006, September 5). *Letter to the Honorable Judge Pallmeyer* [Copy of signed letter]. Retrieved February 5, 2009, from Milwaukee Journal Sentinel Online: http://graphics.jsonline.com/graphics/news/img/sep06/willis090906.pdf

Wills, G. (1990). *Under God: Religion and American Politics.* New York: NY: Simon and Schuster.

Wilmot, W. W., and Hocker, J. L. (2001). *Interpersonal Conflict* (6th ed.) New York, NY: McGraw-Hill Companies, Inc.

Wilmot, W. W., and Hocker, J. L. (2007). *Interpersonal Conflict* (7th ed.) New York, NY:

McGraw Hill Companies, Inc.

Witherington III, B. (1995). *Conflict and Community in Corinth: A Social-Rhetorical Commentary on 1 and 2 Corinthians.* Grand Rapids, MI: Wm. B. Eerdmans Publishing Company.

Witty, C. J. (2001). *Class Lecture Notes, Culture and Conflict, Week 2.* Unpublished manuscript, Nova Southeastern University.

Works of Josephus (New Updated Edition) (1987) (W. Whiston, Trans.). Peabody, MA: Hendrickson Publishers.

Worchel, S. (1999). *Written in Blood: Ethnic Identity and the Struggle for Human Harmony.* New York, NY: Worth Publishers.

Xinhua. (2006, April 1). *Hamas Leader Urges Int'l Community to Respect Palestinian People's Choice.* Retrieved July 15, 2008, from http://news.xinhuanet.com/english/2006-04/02/content_4373348.htm

Yardley, J. (2007, March 17). *John Howard Griffin Took Race All the Way to the Finish.* Retrieved May 15, 2009, from The *Washington Post:* http://www.washingtonpost.com/wp-dyn/content/article/2007/03/16/AR2007031602173.html

Yazzie, R., and Zion, J. W. (1996). Navajo Restorative Justice: The Law of Equality and Justice. In B. Galaway and J. Hudson (Eds.), *Restorative Justice: International Perspectives* (pp. 157-73). Monsey, NY: Criminal Justice Press.

Young, B. H. (1995). *Jesus the Jewish Theologian.* Peabody, MA: Hendrickson Publishers, Inc.

Youngblood, R. F. (1986). G. W. Bromiley (Ed.), *The International Standard Bible Encyclopedia: Vol. 3. Peace* (revised ed.) Grand Rapids, MI: William B. Eerdmans Publishing Company.

Zehr, H. (2005). *Changing Lenses* (3rd ed.) Scottsdale, PA: Herald Press.

Zerwick, M. (1981). M. Grosvenor (Ed.), *A Grammatical Analysis of the Greek New Testament* (M. Grosvenor, Trans.). Rome: Biblical Institute Press.

Subject Index

LaVergne, TN USA
26 March 2010
177344LV00005B/1/P